D0105904

INDUSTRIAL RELATIONS RESEARCH

ASSOCIATION SERIES

The Older Worker

AUTHORS

Monroe Berkowitz

Elizabeth L. Meier

Olivia S. Mitchell

Herbert S. Parnes

Philip L. Rones

Steven H. Sandell

Lois B. Shaw

Lester Trachtman

EDITORIAL BOARD

First edition

Library of Congress Catalog Card Number: 50-13564

ISBN 0-913447-41-2

PRICE $15.00

INDUSTRIAL RELATIONS RESEARCH ASSOCIATION SERIES
Proceedings of the Annual Meeting (Spring publication)
Proceedings of the Spring Meeting (Fall publication)
Annual Research Volume
Membership Directory (every third year)
IRRA Newsletter (published quarterly)

Inquiries and other communications regarding membership, meetings, publications, and general affairs of the Association, as well as orders for publications, copyright requests on publications prior to 1978, and notice of address change should be addressed to the IRRA publication office: Barbara D. Dennis, Editor; David R. Zimmerman, Secretary-Treasurer; Marion J. Leifer, Executive Assistant.

INDUSTRIAL RELATIONS RESEARCH ASSOCIATION
7226 Social Science Building, University of Wisconsin
Madison, WI 53706 U.S.A.   Telephone 608/262-2762

CONTENTS

PREFACE

It was the suggestion of our late colleague, Michael E. Borus, that the Industrial Relations Research Association sponsor as one of its annual research volumes a collection of papers exploring the present state of knowledge about the status, characteristics, and problems of older workers. With the approval of the IRRA Executive Board, Mike assumed the leadership role in suggesting the major contours of the volume and in recruiting the authors. It was his intention to write the introductory chapter and to coordinate the communication between the editors and each of the authors.

Although Mike's sudden death in June of 1987 required the other editors to assume the latter two functions, the structure of the volume nevertheless continues to reflect Mike's influence, and we believe that his name appropriately remains first among the list of editors. The book is respectfully and affectionately dedicated to the memory of Michael Borus, with the hope that it would have satisfied both his high professional standards and his dedication to policy relevant research.

We offer our thanks to the authors not only for their thoughtful papers, but for their faithful observance of deadlines. To Barbara Dennis we express our gratitude for the editorial work that only a professional editor can provide and that has distinguished her long service with the IRRA.

Herbert S. Parnes
Steven H. Sandell
Bert Seidman

CHAPTER 1

Introduction and Overview

HERBERT S. PARNES
The Ohio State University

STEVEN H. SANDELL
U.S. Department of Health and Human Services

The older author of this chapter began his formal study of labor economics and industrial relations exactly a half century ago, using as assigned texts Carroll Daugherty's *Labor Problems in American Industry* (1938) and the three-volume work of Millis and Montgomery (1938). He remembers vividly that each of these widely used texts accorded considerable attention to the problems of the "older worker," in part because of the disadvantages they were perceived to suffer in the labor market and in part because of the absence of alternatives to work as a means of assuring a livelihood (Daugherty, 1938, pp. 122–30; Millis and Montgomery, 1938, Vol. 2, Ch. 8).

The labor market disadvantages stemmed from failing health, skill obsolescence, discriminatory personnel practices of employers, and the fact that, because of the trend toward greater educational attainment, older workers were on average less well educated than their younger counterparts. The problem of "superannuation"— being "too old to work but too young to die" in the words of the trade union song—was a very serious one in the absence of public or private pension programs for the overwhelming majority of the work force.

Over the past half-century remarkable economic and institutional changes have considerably ameliorated the labor market problems of all workers, and older workers in particular. In addition to the increase in real per capita income attributable to undreamed of growth in the output of the economic system, greater equity in the labor market has been achieved through the enactment of a variety of legislative programs, especially during the 1930s and

1

the 1960s (Parnes, 1984), and the substantial expansion of the trade
union movement during the 1930s and the ensuing decades
(Freeman and Medoff, 1984). From the vantage point of the older
worker, the most significant of these changes have been the
inauguration in 1939 of the Social Security system and its
subsequent liberalization, the widespread development of private
pensions and their partial protection through the Employee
Retirement Income Security Act (ERISA) of 1974, and the
proscription of discrimination contained in the Age Discrimination
in Employment Act (ADEA) of 1967 and its amendments. Access to
retirement income has allowed some older persons facing labor
market difficulties to withdraw from the labor force. In addition,
the educational disadvantage of the elderly has become less
pronounced over time; the median number of school years
completed rose between 1959 and 1984 from 11.0 to 12.6 for all
persons 25 and older, but from 8.3 to 11.4 for those 65 and older
(Adler, 1987). Whether their health has improved is still a matter of
dispute (Berkowitz, Chapter 4 in this volume), but even if it has not,
the change in occupational structure has probably reduced the
extent of health-imposed barriers to employment (Social Security
Administration, 1986).

However, despite the fact that older persons have become less
and less likely to work and that those who do work have seen their
labor market position enhanced over the past half-century, interest
in and concern for the "older worker" problem continues unabated,
as the appearance of this volume testifies. Even excluding studies
relating to retirement, Social Security, and pensions, there have
been more than ten volumes published during the past five years
that have focused on the problems of older workers from the
standpoint of either the worker or the employer.[1] The Ninth Annual
Report of the National Commission on Employment Policy (NCEP,
1985) was devoted to an examination of *Older Workers: Prospects,
Problems and Policies.*

The continued interest in the employment problems of the
elderly has at least two explanations. First, despite the marked

[1] See, for example, Birren, Robinson, and Livingston (1986); Bureau of National
Affairs (1987); Burtless (1987); Copperman and Keast (1983); Doering, Rhodes, and
Schuster (1983); Gollub et al. (1985); Humple and Lyons (1983); Kieffer (1983);
Lester (1984); Lyon (1987); Mowsesian (1986); Parnes (1983); Sandell (1987); and
Shaw (1985).

improvements that have occurred over the past half-century, some of the earlier problems remain. It is true that workers 45 and over as a whole suffer no labor market disadvantage relative to other age groups; indeed, on average they enjoy both higher occupational status and higher earnings and also have lower unemployment rates (although their *duration* of unemployment tends to be longer). Nevertheless, a not inconsiderable minority—and especially members of minority groups, women, and those with health problems—are plagued by unstable employment, low wages, and menial jobs (NCEP, 1985, p. iii; Parnes, 1985, p. 210). Moreover, despite the ADEA, there is ample evidence that discrimination against older workers is still practiced (Sandell, Chapter 9 in this volume; NCEP, 1985, p. iii; Knowles, 1983).

Probably the more important reason for the current interest in older workers, however, are several demographic and labor force participation trends that will continue to extend the life expectancy of that group, make them far more numerous both absolutely and relatively in the future than they are now, and at the same time remove ever-increasing proportions of them from the labor force— a prospect that gives rise to dual fears of labor shortages and increased financial burdens that society may have to bear.

These prospects give rise to a series of important research questions and policy issues. Among the former are the following: Will the prospective change in the age structure of the population in fact create labor shortages in the absence of a reversal in the declining labor force participation of older workers? Will the increase in longevity be accompanied by improvements in health that, along with changes in the character of the world of work, will allow increased labor force participation of the elderly? With increased longevity, will older workers *wish* to spend more years in the labor force? What will be the costs to the Social Security system of providing comparable benefits (relative to earnings) to retirees in the future, assuming the continuation of demographic trends and trends in labor force participation? If it is desired to reverse the trend toward early retirement, what are the most effective means of doing so?

Answers to these questions are by no means easy, but the policy issues are even more difficult, because their resolution depends upon a choice among alternative values as well as on the answers to the kinds of "analytical" questions illustrated above. *Should* older workers be encouraged to remain in the labor force? If increased labor force participation is desired, should greater emphasis be placed on the carrot (opportunities or rewards) or the stick (penalties)? If increased opportunities for employment are to be provided, what kinds of instruments should be used to influence employers' personnel policies?

It would be foolish to pretend that the present volume provides definitive answers to either the analytical questions or the policy issues described above; the chapters in it, however, are designed to shed light on many of them. In the remainder of this introduction we (1) explore the demographic and retirement trends that give rise to the questions outlined above, (2) provide a preview of the remaining chapters, and (3) present a very brief synthesis of their principal themes.

Demographic Trends[2]

Just as individuals *inevitably* age, populations *may* do so, and that indeed is the prospect for the United States and most other industrialized countries of the world. That is, the age composition of the population is expected to change in such a way as to increase the proportion of older individuals. This aging will occur as a result both of an increase in life expectancy and of reductions that have occurred in fertility, but the latter is by all odds the more important factor. The paramount influence of birth rates on age composition is evident in the calculation that even if individuals lived forever, only one-tenth of a population with a gross reproduction rate[3] of 3.0 would be over 60 years of age, in contrast with four-tenths if the reproduction rate were 1.5 and nearly 100 percent if the rate were 1.0 (Coale, 1980).

Whatever the causes, an aging population can create problems for society as a whole, just as the aging of an individual creates personal problems and requires personal adjustments. The individual and social implications, of course, are intertwined; an aging population means that larger proportions of individuals are experiencing the personal problems associated with aging, and this

---

[2] This section draws upon Parnes (1983) and Sandell (1987).

[3] The gross reproduction rate is based on the average number of female children who would be born to a cohort of 1,000 women in their lifetime if they were to experience the age-specific birth rates that prevail in the given year and were to survive for the entire period. This number is expressed as a ratio to the original cohort of 1,000.

in itself may be part of the social problem. The problems of aging—of both the individual and society—obviously transcend the labor market, although this volume is rather narrowly confined to those that relate to labor market activity. It deals, in other words, with some of the human resource implications of aging.

Life Expectancy

As is well known, there has been a dramatic increase in life expectancy over the past half-century, although most of it is the result of reductions in mortality at younger ages rather than at the top of the age hierarchy. In 1940, a newborn child could, on average, expect to live to age 63; by 1980 this figure had reached 74, an 11-year increase. A man age 65 in 1940 could expect to attain age 77; by 1980 this had increased to almost 80. Although starting from a higher base, the life expectancy of a 65-year-old woman increased somewhat more over the same period—from age 79 to age 83. These trends, moreover, are expected to continue; according to Social Security Administration projections, by the year 2025 the life expectancy of a 65-year-old will be 83 in the case of men and 87 in the case of women (Sandell, 1987, p. 4).

The Effect of Changes in Fertility Rates

As has been noted, more important than increases in longevity in affecting age composition are variations in birth rates. More specifically, the high birth rates that prevailed during the two decades following World War II ("baby boom") and the equally dramatic decline that occurred thereafter ("baby bust") have important implications for recent and prospective trends in the population's age structure. As a specific example, the proportion of the population between the ages of 45 and 64, currently standing at about 19 percent, will rise to about 23 percent by the year 2000 as the result of the aging of the "baby boomers," but will then begin to fall as the "baby bust" generation enters that age range (NCEP, 1985, p. 7). The proportion of persons 65 and over, which had risen from 8 percent in 1950 to 11 percent in 1980, will rise to about 13 percent in 2010 and about 20 percent in 2030 when the full effect of the baby boom is felt.

Clark and Spengler (1980, p. 2) have calculated a number of ratios that capture anticipated demographic changes that are most significant from the standpoint of the labor market, some of which are reproduced in Table 1. From the standpoint of the labor market status of older workers, several aspects of these data are worthy of comment. The expected reduction in the ratio of young people (18–24) to those approaching retirement age (55–64) and the reduction in the ratio of "prime age" to "older" persons (20–39/40–64) may be expected to increase the labor market opportunities of older workers. Indeed, it is these trends that lead some, on the assumption of the maintenance of full employment, to expect labor shortages in the absence of increased labor force participation of the elderly (Morrison, 1983). It should also be noted from the behavior of the ratio of those 75 and over to those 65 and over that the expected increase in the proportion of those 65 and older will be greatest in the upper portion of that age range, among whom the likelihood of labor force participation is relatively slight.

TABLE 1

Projected Age Structure Ratios
Assuming Replacement-Level Fertility

Age Ratio	1976 (actual)	2025	2050
0–17/18–64	.51	.42	.42
65+/18–64	.18	.30	.30
18–24/18–64	.22	.16	.16
18–24/55–64	1.40	.78	.81
55–64/18–64	.16	.20	.20
20–39/40–64	1.16	.88	.88
75+/65+	.38	.39	.44

Source: Based on Clark and Spengler (1980), Table 2, p. 13.

From the perspective of economic burdens on society (which are only peripherally relevant to the chapters in the present volume), the increase in the ratio of persons 65 and over to those 18–64 signifies an increase in the *old age* dependency ratio. But this is to a considerable degree offset by a drop in the *child* dependency ratio (0–17/18–64), so that the *total* dependency ratio rises by only three percentage points by the middle of the 21st century. When projections of labor force participation rates are taken into account, the peak dependency ratio will actually be lower than that which prevailed between 1950 and 1970 (Sandell, 1987, pp. 4–5).[4]

It cannot be emphasized too strongly that all of the foregoing generalizations are based on assumptions about the future course of mortality and fertility rates. Short-term forecasts (i.e., up to 15 years) of the age structure of the population *of working age* can be made with a great deal of confidence, because all of the potential members of that group have already been born, and because dramatic changes in mortality rates over a 15-year period are unlikely. Experience clearly demonstrates, however, that when the forecast period goes beyond 15 years and when forecasts of age structure of the *total* population are made, the results are subject to considerably greater doubt because of uncertainty about what will happen to the fertility rate—and, as has been seen, this is the really crucial element in producing changes in age structure. Demographers' forecasts of the fertility rate have been notoriously unreliable; neither the postwar baby boom nor the ensuing bust had been predicted (Munnell, 1977, p. 102). This is, of course, not intended to suggest that demographic forecasts should not be made or that they deserve no attention, but rather to "stress the need for a healthy skepticism about some of the major premises underlying the debate on important policy issues" (Parnes, 1983, p. 7).[5]

Retirement Trends

In addition to trends in the age structure of the population, trends in retirement behavior also need to be examined in order to provide a backdrop for the issues that are discussed in the ensuing

---

[4] If the dependency ratio is defined as the number of nonworkers (those not doing paid work) per 100 workers, the apex of the ratio occurred in 1965, when there were 154 nonworkers for every 100 workers. Since then the ratio has declined steadily as women's labor force participation increased and birth rates fell. This downward trend is expected to continue during the next 20 years and then rise to peak at 115 nonworkers per 100 workers. This is substantially lower than the levels reached between 1950 and 1970, when there were more than 140 nonworkers supported by each 100 workers (Sandell, 1987, pp. 4–5).

[5] The demographic trends discussed in the text relate to the somewhat distant future and reflect primarily the movement of the baby boom generation into the retirement ages, a process that will not begin until the second decade of the 21st century. For the same reason, dramatic growth of the over-55 labor force will not occur until after the year 2000. Based upon projections of labor force participation rates, the relative importance of persons over age 55 in the labor force will actually decline through the rest of the 20th century. Furthermore, because most people over 65 are not in the labor force, the recent and projected future growth of the population 65 and older is not affecting the age composition of the *labor force* (Sandell, 1987, p. 6).

chapters. That the institution of retirement in its present dimensions is a relatively recent development is indicated by the fact that as late as 1948 the labor force participation of men 65 and over was almost 50 percent, in contrast to the current 16 percent rate. Even among men 55 to 64 the proportion in the labor force decreased over the same time period from about nine-tenths to two-thirds. Among women, to be sure, no comparable trend is discernible. The dramatic increase in women's labor force participation at all ages has tended to swamp whatever tendency there might have been toward earlier retirement, so that the participation rates of women 65 and over dropped only several percentage points (from 9 to 7) from 1948 to the present, while the proportion of those 55 to 64 who were in the labor force actually grew from under one-third to over two-fifths.

Juxtaposing the demographic and retirement trends, assuming that both continue, one is led to the conclusion that at the same time that the proportion of older persons in the population increases, the fraction of that group that continues to work will decline. This means that the actual old age dependency ratio will increase by a greater degree than demographic trends alone would suggest. Moreover, the potential labor shortages of the future are also greater than changes in age structure alone portend.

Whether the trend toward earlier retirement will continue is, of course, uncertain. In any case, as compared with the trend in fertility, the trend in retirement may be more readily amenable to manipulation through public and private policy variables, and this is a matter with which a number of the ensuing chapters are directly or indirectly concerned.

Remainder of the Volume: A Summary

Labor Market Characteristics of Older Workers (Chapter 2)

In the following chapter, Philip Rones presents a factual framework for the other chapters in the volume, drawing upon Bureau of Labor Statistics (BLS) data from the Current Population Survey (CPS). Emphasizing the point that the elderly (defined as those over age 55) are not a homogeneous group, Rones calls attention to the marked differences in labor market status and experience among them according to sex, race, educational attainment, and retirement status.

Using cohort analysis to document the marked trend toward earlier retirement among men in their sixties, he shows that the trend for women is less pronounced. If per capita hours worked are the measure, he reports that work activity of men 65 and over has dropped by half since 1967 as compared with a decline of less than a third for women. Moreover, the dramatic increase in labor force participation among women in their forties over the past 30 years will, he predicts, make their retirement behavior 20 years from now substantially different from that of the current generation of those in their sixties.

Prior to retirement, there is not much difference between older workers and their younger counterparts in occupational assignment, hours of work, or earnings, and they actually enjoy more stable employment. On the other hand, for the minority of persons who continue to work after conventional retirement, there are marked differences: they are much more likely to work part time, to be in occupations of lower socioeconomic status, and to have lower rates of pay.

Rones acknowledges that CPS data do not provide clear evidence as to the reasons for retirement and on the extent to which retirees want or can be induced to take jobs. He tends to believe, however, that labor market participation by this group would be greater if the disincentives that currently exist in both public and private pension systems were to disappear, and, more importantly, if more attractive opportunities for part-time work and phased retirement were to exist. What the future will bring in this regard is difficult to predict, he believes; the crucial factor is the extent to which a full employment economy prevails.

Older Women Workers (Chapter 3)

By emphasizing the substantial difference in the problems that older women face as compared with men of the same age, Lois Shaw elaborates the theme of heterogeneity introduced by Rones. Male-female differences stem from the women's previous commitment to family roles and their consequently less continuous attachment to the labor market. The special problems faced by women (e.g., the displaced homemaker) lead Shaw to adopt a somewhat lower age for inclusion in the "older worker" category— generally 40 years or older.

Heterogeneity abounds even within this group of women

workers. To begin with, the stereotype of the single exit and reentry to the labor market during child-rearing turns out to be contrary to fact; much more common is a pattern of repeated exits and reentries, adding up to lengthy periods out of the labor force. But these patterns vary considerably; in some cases they reflect increasing attachment and in others decreasing attachment to the labor market.

The work interruptions that most women workers experience have an adverse effect on their job opportunities and pay when they reenter the labor market, principally as the result of their not accumulating additional work experience and possibly because of skill deterioration. Middle-aged and older women are paid less than younger women by virtue of their lower educational attainment. However, the earnings differentials between women and men cannot be fully accounted for by these human capital factors; most studies have concluded that not more than half of the pay differential can be explained in those terms. The remainder is generally attributed to sex discrimination in the labor market and in society generally, although Shaw acknowledges that other factors might explain part or all of the residual. Women also face age discrimination, but this is generally hard to document, and most studies focus on men rather than women.

Pension coverage in their own right is less common for women than for men. Both participation and extent of vesting are lower among women than men, primarily because of differences between the sexes in occupational assignments, extent of part-time employment, and stability of labor force participation. Moreover, when women receive pensions, their benefits are lower than those of men because of their lower pay and shorter tenure.

Shaw expects future generations of older women workers to fare better than the current cohort because of their better education and greater work experience. However, she cautions that differences may be less pronounced than is popularly assumed. Despite high labor force participation rates, many young women even today continue to work only part time or part year. She calls for more research on whether "part-time employment is a viable means of keeping up current work skills or acquiring new ones," on the effects of job displacement on women workers, and on the equity of current pension arrangements from the standpoint of women.

Functioning Ability and Job Performance (Chapter 4)

Monroe Berkowitz opens an exploration of the evidence on the relation between age and job performance with an intriguing description of the difficulties in defining the terms that are commonly used in such discussions. That certain changes occur in individuals as they age is indisputable; whether these are changes in "health," whether changes in health imply changes in functional abilities, and whether changes in the latter necessarily imply changes in job performance are by no means clear.

There is incontrovertible evidence that at any point in time older persons are less "healthy" than younger persons irrespective of how health is measured (e.g., by self-evaluations, by extent of disability, by functional limitations). If, however, the question is whether the job performance of middle-aged and older workers suffers from these age-related health factors, the evidence is considerably less clear. There has been a multitude of studies, with mixed results, and many have suffered from methodological inadequacies. Berkowitz finds support for the generalization that "the older worker has assets or experience and reliability which may compensate for the deficits in physical functioning." If the criterion is absenteeism or accidents, the evidence shows that distinctions need to be made between frequency, on the one hand, and duration or severity on the other. Older workers tend to be absent less frequently, but for longer durations than younger workers; similarly, accident rates are lower for older workers, but severity is greater.

Quite aside from the moment-of-time relationship between age and various measures of health and job performance, what can be said about trends over time? More specifically, has the health of older workers tended to improve, and what is the outlook for the future? Although the evidence of improved mortality is clear, there is controversy about whether this has been accompanied by better health or whether greater longevity has actually produced larger proportions of infirm persons among the elderly. His careful review of the evidence on this issue leads Berkowitz to the "hesitant conclusion" that a trend toward declining health among persons aged 55-70 that was perceptible beginning in 1969 has more recently appeared to be reversing, but that inadequacies in the data make almost any conclusion on the matter somewhat dangerous.

On all of the issues he sees the need for additional research based upon better measures of health and better conceptual models than have hitherto been used. In the meantime, his policy prescription is for "intelligent placement which makes the most of the residual functioning capacity of those older workers who remain in the labor force."

The Decision to Retire (Chapter 5)

In reviewing the literature on the retirement decision, Herbert Parnes considers multivariate analyses of the correlates of retirement, reasons for retirement reported by retirees retrospectively or gleaned from their longitudinal records prior to retirement, and efforts to assess the influence of the Social Security program on the labor supply of the elderly. Rather severe methodological problems plague research on all these topics; moreover, there has been so much diversity in definition of retirement and specification of models that confident conclusions are frequently elusive.

The evidence *is* clear, however, that retirement is primarily a voluntary phenomenon. However undesirable they may have been from the standpoint of equity, mandatory retirement rules were responsible for a very small proportion (less than 5 percent) of retirements during the past two decades, and labor market adversity accounted for at most an additional 10 percent. Poor health has probably accounted for more withdrawals than both of the foregoing; nevertheless a majority of retirements appear to have been accounted for by none of these factors.

Parnes concludes that retirement decisions are complex, being influenced by a variety of factors, including current and prospective earnings, assets, prospective retirement income, health, and attitude toward work in general and one's specific job in particular. While it is not possible to assess in any precise way the relative importance of economic and noneconomic factors, it is clear that the explanatory power of specific factors depends on exactly what one is trying to explain. Poor health, for instance, is far more important in accounting for retirement prior to age 65 than at 65 or later.

The specific provisions of the Social Security Act have affected the number of retirees and the timing of their retirement, but probably by less than is popularly supposed. Changes in eligibility requirements and benefit levels are likely to affect retirement *income* more substantially than retirement *behavior*. Additional policy instruments that Parnes mentions for affecting retirement decisions are regulation of private pensions plans, intensifying efforts to eliminate age discrimination, improving work opportunities for older workers, and, in the longer run, improving both the health of individuals and the quality of their working lives.

For further research, he suggests increased attention to the retirement behavior of women, development of data banks with better measures of health and of the detailed characteristics of pension plans, and more complete specification of models. In the latter context he calls for greater intellectual interchange between economists and gerontologists, who appear to have created quite separate bodies of literature on the retirement decision.

Pensions and Older Workers (Chapter 6)

The phenomenal growth of pensions in the United States during and since the Second World War is well known, and the pension system that has been created is generally thought of exclusively in its role of providing financial security during retirement. Olivia Mitchell's review and analysis of the relevant literature indicate that in addition to generating retirement savings, pensions may have significant labor market consequences. Depending upon which of two alternative theoretical frameworks one regards to be more realistic, both the pensions themselves and government attempts to regulate them are likely to have quite different effects on job opportunities for the elderly.

In one view, pensions are "deferred wages." Since they are fully "owned" by workers, having been bought by accepting lower wages than otherwise would have been received, they thus should be paid with certainty and in full. From this perspective, such features as restrictive eligibility rules or any departure from immediate and full vesting are suspect. In contrast, the view of pensions as "implicit contracts" emphasizes that pensions are deliberate attempts to influence worker behavior (e.g., reduce turnover) in the interest of greater productivity, and that this function—which brings benefits to both employers and workers— necessarily involves uncertainties with respect to receipt of the "promised" pensions (e.g., leaving the firm before vesting rights are achieved).

To illustrate the differing implications of these theoretical orientations, Mitchell observes that in the pensions-as-deferred- wages view the requirement of continued accrual of pension benefits with employment beyond, say, age 65 is not only equitable but benign; in contrast, the "implicit contract" view emphasizes the increase in labor costs that this entails and suggests that it may lead to curtailed employment opportunities for older workers.

Admitting that the empirical evidence that she reviews permits only tentative conclusions, she nevertheless believes it points to the likelihood that some regulatory changes introduced to benefit older workers may actually have had perverse effects, including "disemployment among the older group. . . ." But because "these implications are only suggestive," she calls for "more careful theoretical and empirical analysis of the economic function of employer-sponsored pension plans."

Managing an Older Work Force (Chapter 7)

Drawing heavily on research sponsored by the American Association of Retired Persons (AARP), Elizabeth Meier considers means of increasing the interest of older workers in remaining economically active, examines training needs for such workers, and surveys the extent of alternatives to the standard 40-hour week as means of attracting them into or keeping them in the labor market.

Because job satisfaction may be presumed to motivate older workers to remain at work, methods of achieving it are suggested. These include the provision of training opportunities and career counseling, effective performance appraisal, opportunities for more challenging work and/or community relations activities, and means of acknowledging and rewarding the accomplishments of such workers.

The impact of a changing technology on training needs in both manufacturing and the service industries is analyzed, and examples of programs designed to meet these needs are described. In response to a general perception that older workers are less amenable to successful training than are younger workers, the author calls attention to a 1986 AARP-sponsored nationwide survey showing that large majorities of full-time workers age 40 and over had received training in the recent past and that even larger majorities expressed interest in receiving such training.

Phased retirement plans have been introduced by only very few employers in the United States, and the evidence suggests something less than great enthusiasm among workers for such plans unless they are accompanied by payment of partial pensions.

Flextime arrangements are also viewed as an inducement to delay retirement by only a minority of older workers. Part-time work appears to be more popular; large majorities of workers indicate that they would prefer to continue to work part time rather than to retire completely. Nevertheless, there is no evidence that older workers are seeking such employment in sufficient numbers to halt the trend toward earlier and complete retirement.

Organized Labor and the Retired Worker (Chapter 8)

Except for references to preretirement counseling programs, Lester Trachtman's chapter deals with programs that unions have established for their members subsequent to retirement. A number of motivations lie behind unions devoting resources to the establishment of retiree clubs: their interest in the potential political power of the "seniors," their sense of debt to those who have helped build the union, and their genuine social concern for the problems of the elderly. Yet these concerns compete for scarce resources with other more immediate objectives, with the result that relatively few unions have developed such programs.

Although many local unions and district organizations have regular programs, internationals rarely provide financial support. There are, however, notable exceptions: the United Auto Workers (UAW), the American Federation of State, County, and Municipal Employees (AFSCME), the Amalgamated Clothing and Textile Workers Union (ACTWU), and the International Ladies' Garment Workers' Union (ILGWU). The UAW was the first to adopt a formal structure for its retirees, having established a special department for retiree activities in 1957. In AFSCME, the presidents of all retiree chapters form a Retiree Council, whose president attends the meetings of the international's executive board. Both the ACTWU and the ILGWU have long made financial contributions to programs serving the "social, psychological, and recreational needs of their members."

Trachtman believes that union support for housing is a significant but often overlooked accomplishment in the interest of retired workers. Under the aegis of federal housing programs, unions have "sponsored or supported over 100 different projects across the country that have provided housing for seniors regardless of income."

Faced with more immediate problems and frequently with

declining financial resources, it is not surprising that many
international unions have not accorded priority to the development
of retiree programs. It may be, Trachtman believes, that the real
"ballgame" will be at the local level, particularly in activities of
central labor councils. Especially if such organizations were to
engage in volunteer services in response to community needs, "the
union, the retiree, and the community would benefit." Trachtman
believes that organized labor and the retirees need each other, but
that the initiative must come from the unions. Only time will tell, he
concludes, whether organized labor will meet the challenge of
serving these mutual interests.

Public Policies and Programs (Chapter 9)

Among the many government policies and programs that he
recognizes may affect the employment prospects of older workers,
Steven Sandell singles out for primary attention the Age
Discrimination in Employment Act (ADEA), government employment and training programs, and retirement policies of various
kinds. Before reviewing the evidence relating to these programs and
policies, however, he emphasizes the fact that public policy in these
spheres, as in most others, is shaped more by the "interaction of
pressures from interest groups than from dispassionate analysis of
social problems."

Although acknowledging the impossibility of measuring the
effectiveness of the ADEA by ascertaining empirically the extent of
discrimination, Sandell points out that EEOC and court cases make
it clear that age discrimination continues to exist. However, even if
it were to be completely eliminated, many of the employment
problems of older workers would not disappear, because they stem
from sources other than discrimination—for example, inadequate
education or training and poor health.

Public employment and training programs are a potentially
valuable tool for meeting some of the labor market problems of
older workers, but it is doubtful that the current Job Training
Partnership Act (JTPA) or its predecessor, the Comprehensive
Employment and Training Act (CETA), have fully lived up to that
potential. Among those eligible for the programs, participation is
considerably lower by older than by younger workers. Much of the
lower program participation can be explained by the lower
probability of older persons seeking work and thus being interested

in training. This in turn results, at least in part, from the perception of poor employment prospects among the older age group. Nonetheless, on the basis of comparisons of the employment and earnings records of those who do participate in the programs with eligible individuals who do not, it appears that CETA-type training programs have been helpful to those older workers who take advantage of them.

In his discussion of the effects of retirement policy upon labor market behavior of older workers, Sandell notes that the interaction among policies and programs frequently makes it inappropriate to consider the effects of one in isolation. One example is the removal of the age 70 "cap" by the 1986 amendments to ADEA, which, considered alone, may seem to be of little consequence for labor force participation in the light of past evidence on the effect of mandatory retirement rules. However, the fact that other legislation of the same year requires employers to continue to make pension contributions for post-retirement-age workers who continue to work for the firm creates a new set of incentives for older workers to remain employed, and may thus make results of past research on the effect of mandatory retirement irrelevant.

Economic realities must also be taken into account in interpreting the effects of government policies on older workers, Sandell urges. For example, the earnings test under Social Security and the "1000 hour rule" under the Employment Retirement Income Security Act may seem to stimulate part-time work by post-retirement-age workers, but because economic considerations dictate that part-time work generally has a lower rate of pay than full-time work for comparable jobs, many retirees will prefer complete retirement.

A Cautious Synthesis

The chapters in this volume are sufficiently disparate in subject matter and approach that any attempt to synthesize them is somewhat foolhardy, and also runs the risk of inappropriately attributing our own views to the other authors. Nevertheless, there appear to be a sufficient number of common threads running through the chapters, or at least unarticulated major premises underlying them, that we are emboldened to attempt to set them forth here without elaboration.

1. Any stereotype of the older worker is bound to be mis-

leading: there are profound differences among them in health, in physical and cognitive capabilities, in education, and in labor market status and experience. Creating categories by race, gender, and educational attainment reduces but by no means eliminates the heterogeneity.

2. Taken as a group, older workers fare at least as well, and perhaps better, than other age groups in the labor market; nevertheless significant minorities continue to suffer labor market disadvantages imposed by poor health, inadequate education and training, and labor market discrimination. Also, many older women face problems stemming from their discontinuous lifetime labor market participation.

3. With the prospect of increasing proportions of older persons in the population, and decreasing proportions of the group in the labor market, society has an interest in promoting increased work opportunities for older persons and in eliminating disincentives for continued employment.

4. The extent to which this can be done is not entirely clear. The authors are not completely agreed on the extent to which retirees leave their jobs reluctantly and on the proportions that are likely to be drawn back into the work force; Rones and Sandell, for instance, appear to accord labor market adversity a greater role in explaining "retirement" than does Parnes.

5. If greater labor force participation of the elderly is perceived to be socially necessary, incentives are to be preferred to penalties. Because older persons are not a homogeneous group, those who cannot work and those for whom there are no suitable job opportunities need to be provided for.

6. In considering appropriate public policies, their direct and indirect effects need to be considered, as well as the relationships that exist among them. As Mitchell shows, policies designed to be beneficial to older workers may have unintended adverse effects; as Sandell points out, the simultaneous introduction of two policies (e.g., amendments in 1986 to ADEA and ERISA) may have an effect that would not be predicted for either of them alone.

7. There remain ample opportunities for further research on the older worker. A number of questions whose answers are crucial to formulation of national policy decisions remain unanswerable on the basis of currently available evidence.

8. In any case, the authors agree that a primary objective of

social policy should be to preserve and broaden individual options. This implies intelligent placement policies by employers to maximize the utilization of the physical capabilities of older workers, the continued effort to eliminate age discrimination, and, perhaps above all, the maintenance of high levels of employment.

References

Adler, Michele, Data Book on the Elderly: A Statistical Portrait. Washington: U.S. Department of Health and Human Services, Office of the Assistant Secretary for Planning and Evaluation, 1987.
Birren, James E., Pauline K. Robinson, and Judy Livingston. Age, Health and Employment. Englewood Cliffs, NJ: Prentice-Hall, 1986.
Bureau of National Affairs, Inc. Older Americans in the Workforce: Challenges and Solutions. Washington: Bureau of National Affairs, 1987.
Burtless, Gary T. Work, Health, and Income Among the Elderly. Washington: The Brookings Institution, 1987.
Clark, Robert L., and Joseph J. Spengler. The Economics of Individual and Population Aging. Cambridge: Cambridge University Press, 1980.
Coale, Ansley J. "Increases in Expectation of Life and Population Growth." International Population Conference, Vienna, 1958. Vienna: Im Selbstverlag, 1959. Pp. 36–41. Cited in Robert L. Clark and Joseph J. Spengler, The Economics of Individual and Population Aging. Cambridge: Cambridge University Press, 1980. P. 14.
Copperman, Lois, and Frederick D. Keast. Adjusting to an Older Work Force. New York: Van Nostrand Reinhold, 1983.
Daugherty, Carroll R. Labor Problems in American Industry. Boston: Houghton Mifflin, 1938.
Doering, Mildred, Susan R. Rhodes, and Michael Schuster. The Aging Worker: Research and Recommendations. Beverly Hills, CA: Sage, 1983.
Freeman, Richard B., and James L. Medoff. What Do Unions Do? New York: Basic Books, 1984.
Gollub, James O., et al. Older Worker Employment Comes of Age: Practice and Potential. Washington: National Commission for Employment Policy, 1985.
Humple, Carol Seagrave, and Morgan Lyons. Managing the Older Work Force: Policies and Programs. New York: American Management Association, 1983.
Kieffer, Jarold A. Gaining the Dividends of Longer Life: New Roles for Older Workers. Boulder, CO: Westview Press, 1983.
Knowles, Daniel E. "Keeping Older Workers on the Job." In Policy Issues in Work and Retirement, ed. Herbert S. Parnes. Kalamazoo, MI: W. E. Upjohn Institute for Employment Research, 1983.
Lester, Brenda. A Practitioner's Guide for Training Older Workers. Washington: National Commission for Employment Policy, 1984.
Lyon, Phil. Nearing Retirement: A Study of Late Working Lives. Brookfield, VT: Gower, 1987.
Millis, Harry A., and Royal E. Montgomery. The Economics of Labor, Vol. 2, Labor's Risks and Social Insurance. New York: McGraw Hill, 1938.
Morrison, Malcolm H. "The Aging of the U.S. Population: Human Resource Implications." Monthly Labor Review 106 (May 1983), pp. 13–19.
Mowsesian, Richard. Golden Goals, Rusted Realities: Work and Aging in America. New York: New Horizon Press, distributed by Macmillan, 1986.
Munnell, Alicia H. The Future of Social Security. Washington: The Brookings Institution, 1977.
National Commission for Employment Policy. Older Workers: Prospects, Problems and Policies. Washington: U.S. Government Printing Office, 1985.

Parnes, Herbert S. "Introduction and Overview." In *Policy Issues in Work and Retirement*, ed. Herbert S. Parnes. Kalamazoo, MI: W.E. Upjohn Institute for Employment Research, 1983.
————. *Peoplepower*. Beverly Hills, CA: Sage, 1984.
————. "Conclusion." In Herbert S. Parnes et al., *Retirement Among American Men*. Lexington, MA: Lexington Books, 1985.
Sandell, Steven H. "Prospects for Older Workers: The Demographic and Economic Context." In *The Problem Isn't Age: Work and Older Americans*, ed. Steven H. Sandell. New York: Praeger, 1987.
Shaw, Lois B. *Older Women at Work*. Washington: Women's Research and Education Institute, 1985.
Social Security Administration. "Increasing the Social Security Retirement Age: Older Workers in Physically Demanding Occupations or Poor Health." *Social Security Bulletin* 49 (October 1986), pp. 5–23.

Chapter 2

Employment, Earnings, and Unemployment Characteristics of Older Workers

Philip L. Rones
Bureau of Labor Statistics,
U.S. Department of Labor

If this volume is to consider older workers from so many varied perspectives, it should start by identifying the characteristics of this group. The information presented in this chapter will not only summarize the employment experience of workers age 55 and over,[1] but will also identify the extent of displacement, discouragement, or unemployment among the members of this group who might wish to be employed.

My task may be somewhat easier than that of some of my colleagues. The chapters on the retirement decision and on employer-provided pensions, for example, attempt to sort through complex and often conflicting research on the effects of various economic and personal factors on work and retirement behavior. My job is less severely hampered by conflicting evidence; to a large extent, fact is fact—although, as we shall see, things are not quite that simple. If the national labor force survey shows that, on average in 1986, 14 million persons age 55 and over worked, within a narrow range of statistical error, that is quite likely so.

This chapter, then, will attempt to provide a factual framework from which the reader of the following chapters will benefit. Some of the shortcomings are intentional. There is no need to duplicate

---

[1] While age 55 is a somewhat arbitrary cutoff, younger ages were not included because the issues related to retirement, particularly, are rarely relevant prior to that age. The reader certainly will note that several different groups of age breaks are used in the analysis and tables. This is largely a function of data availability. Ideally, for most measures, at least the following age groups would be broken out: 55–59, 60–61, 62–64, and 65 and over. In some cases the 60–61 and 62–64 age groups have been combined.

the extensive material covered in later chapters by Shaw on the special problems of older women or by Parnes on the complex retirement decision, for example. An attempt has been made, however, to provide at least a cursory examination of a wide range of measures of employment and earnings of older persons, and of labor market problems experienced by this group.

The fact that the elderly are not a homogeneous group has become a cliché. The first step in avoiding the use of a universal definition of the older worker is to present data for men and women separately. Most older men have spent nearly all of their adult lives, prior to retirement, in the labor force. This has not been true of older women. Thirty years from now the same concepts of careers and retirement will most likely apply to the majority of women. However, for the current generation of older women, long-term, career-oriented labor market participation has been more the exception than the rule.

Also, the data on older workers reveal two other distinct groups of older workers, somewhat divided by age, but also by health and financial resources, among other factors. In one group are the persons still completely committed to their jobs or careers. These workers are typically employed year round, full time, and if they lose their jobs, they do not (and often cannot) consider leaving the labor force as a viable option. In the second group are a sizable number of persons who typically are older or in poorer health, whose employment activity is more marginal. Persons in this group may work part time or part year, work in lower paying jobs, and, if unemployed, may not undertake a job search or persevere in that search. Typically, this limited market attachment follows retirement from a long-term job. Of course, even such a dichotomy only improves slightly on the concept of the "universal" older worker, but it does highlight the diverse circumstances of such individuals.

This analysis will focus on persons age 55 and over for several reasons. Nonwork options are rarely availale to able-bodied men prior to age 55. Also, just as important, virtually all data sources use 55 as an age break, making such a choice convenient.

Most of the data in this analysis come from the Current Population Survey (CPS), a nationwide monthly survey of about 60,000 households, conducted for the Bureau of Labor Statistics by the Bureau of the Census.[2] Data from other sources are used to supplement CPS findings.

With some very minor exceptions, persons are classified in the CPS as *employed* if they worked at least one hour during a reference week as paid employees, or in their own business, profession, or firm (self-employed) or were temporarily absent from a job (vacation, ill health, etc.). Persons are *unemployed* if they did not work at all during the reference week, had actively looked for work sometime during the previous four weeks, and were currently available for work. Persons are *not in the labor force* if they neither worked nor looked for work. The *labor force* includes both the employed and unemployed.

Trends in Employment

The introductory chapter gives a historical assessment and projections of labor force participation rates for older workers. Chart 1 provides a perspective on trends in participation that is a bit different from the cross-sectional or time-series approaches usually used. It traces a particular generation of older persons (those 70–74 years old in 1986) back in time to track their labor force history. This group's history is compared to that of men and women 10 years older.

As the chart shows, only a decade has made a marked difference in work and retirement patterns. For both cohorts of men, it is fair to say that almost all were active in the job market during middle age. However, at what is generally considered normal retirement age, in one's sixties, the older group had a much smaller dropoff in work activity. The trend toward earlier retirement continues with later generations (not shown). For example, only 55 percent of men age 60–64 in 1986 were in the labor force compared to 64 percent of that age group 10 years earlier.

For women, drastic changes in participation are occurring at all but the older ages. For example, when the women now in their early seventies were in their forties, only about half worked at any point in time. In contrast, women now in their forties have participation rates of over 70 percent. Certainly, this greater career orientation will affect retirement patterns of these women 20 years from now. At the older ages, more recent cohorts of women around retirement

---

[2] For a detailed discussion of CPS concepts and methods, see the explanatory notes of any issue of the Bureau of Labor Statistics' monthly publication, *Employment and Earnings*.

CHART 1

Labor Force Participation Rates of Two Cohorts of Men and Women, Through Age
70-74

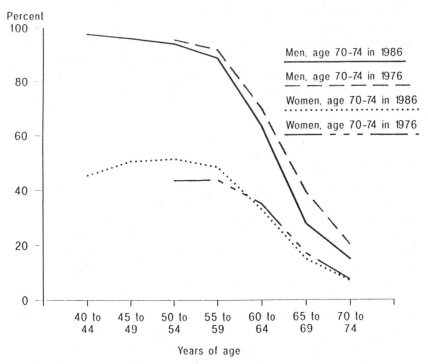

Men, age 70-74 in 1986

Men, age 70-74 in 1976

Women, age 70-74 in 1986

Women, age 70-74 in 1976

Years of age

age have had lower participation rates than their elders did, but not
dramatically so.

Measures of Current Work Activity

The most basic questions to be asked regarding work activity of
older persons are how many, how much, and what kind. Since the
monthly CPS labor force data are used most frequently, these data
will be examined first. Approximately 8.4 million men and 5.9
million women age 55 and over were employed in an average
month in 1986. This represents about one of every eight employed
persons.

Possibly the most useful measures of work activity of these 14
million workers captures the combined effects of employment and

hours. Table 1 shows per capita weekly hours for all persons in a particular population group, whether they worked or not, and average hours for those actually at work. For the per capita measure, the number of persons at work was multiplied by their average weekly hours and then divided by the number of persons in the relevant age group.

TABLE 1

Per Capita Weekly Hours of Work and Actual Hours,
by Sex and Age, 1968 and 1986 Annual Averages

	Per Capita Weekly Hours			Average Hours at Work		
Sex and Age	1968	1986	Percent Change 1968–86	1968	1986	Percent Change 1968–86
Men						
35–44 years	41.5	38.3	−7.7	45.7	44.7	−2.2
55–59 years	36.4	30.3	−16.7	44.3	43.0	−2.9
60–64 years	29.8	19.9	−33.2	42.7	40.8	−4.4
65 years and over	8.5	4.4	−48.2	34.7	31.2	−10.1
Women						
35–44 years	15.7	23.9	+52.2	35.5	36.8	+3.7
55–59 years	15.9	16.4	+3.1	36.9	35.9	−2.7
60–64 years	11.6	9.9	−14.7	35.6	33.7	−5.3
65 years and over	2.6	1.8	−30.8	30.6	26.8	−12.4

The per capita measure demonstrates that both employment rates and hours have played a significant part in the decline in older persons' work activity, although the employment effect generally dominates. The combined employment and hours effects are striking; since 1967, weekly per capita hours have been cut in half for men age 65 and over and by a third for women. The results for older women may be even more dramatic because they occurred during a period when the work activity for younger women (such as the 35–44 age group shown) grew by more than half. The decline in the average workweek has been sharpest in the oldest groups (a 10 percent decline for men age 65 and over and a 12 percent decline for women in that age group). This mostly reflects a change in the part-time/full-time mix among persons in that age group.

The March work-experience supplement to the CPS broadens the time horizon from a single week within each month to an entire calendar year. Each March, information is obtained from CPS respondents relating to their work activity during the previous calendar year. The advantage of these data for this analysis is that they isolate the importance of part-year work.

During 1985, the most recent year for which work experience data are available, 13.2 million people age 55 to 64 had some employment, as compared with 11.5 million who worked in an average week. The corresponding figures for persons age 65 and over were 41 million and 2.9 million. Thus, the work experience total for these two groups exceeded the monthly average employment by 15 percent for those age 55 to 64 and 47 percent for those age 65 and over. In contrast, for the central age group, 25 to 54, this excess was only 11 percent.

Until age 62, those men and women who continue to work are about as likely to work year round, full time as are younger workers (see Table 2). Apparently, little "phased retirement" occurs at these ages. However, for persons in the oldest age group shown, 65 and over, work schedules are skewed dramatically toward more limited activity.

Limited work activity may take two forms—part time and part year. Table 3 provides the major reason cited for part-year work in 1985. Among the youngest group of older men, labor market problems are particularly important, followed by poor health. Retirement becomes increasingly important as men get older and job market problems less so. This is consistent with the notion that persons with viable nonwork options remove themselves from poor job prospects by retiring.

Data in Table 2 dramatically demonstrate the decline in the full-schedule work commitment among the oldest groups of women and men. However, the table ignores the decline in work force participation, which has had much more of an impact on the extent of work activity than has the downward trend in work schedules.

Work After Retirement

The biggest weakness of the CPS regarding older workers is its very limited longitudinal capability. Patterns of job mobility, career switching, and post-retirement employment are more difficult to glean from the CPS than from longitudinal surveys. Beck (1985), using the National Longitudinal Survey of Mature Men (NLS), and Palmore et al. (1985), using the Longitudinal Retirement History Survey, among others, have shown that retirement is final for about

TABLE 2

Distribution of Work Schedules, by Sex and Age,
1967 and 1985

Sex and Age	Total	Year Round, Full Time[a]		Part Year, Full Time		Year Round, Part Time		Part Year, Part Time	
		1967	1985	1967	1985	1967	1985	1967	1985
Men									
35–44 years	100	85	80	13	15	1	2	1	3
55–59 years	100	81	79	15	15	1	3	3	3
60-61 years	100	79	77	15	15	2	4	4	4
62-64 years	100	72	65	19	20	5	7	6	8
65 years and over	100	41	33	20	17	16	22	23	28
Women									
35–44 years	100	49	56	24	17	10	12	17	15
55–59 years	100	55	58	19	14	12	14	13	14
60-61 years	100	53	55	20	16	12	12	15	17
62-64 years	100	50	43	20	17	15	18	15	21
65 years and over	100	29	22	19	14	21	30	31	34

Source: Bureau of Labor Statistics.
[a] Year round is at least 50 weeks; full time is 35 hours per week or more.

TABLE 3

Main Reason for Part-Year Work, by Sex and Age, 1985

Sex and Age	Total Employed Part Year (thousands)	Total	Percent Distribution				
			Unemployed, Layoff, No Work Available	Illness, Disability	Taking Care of Home	Retired	Other
Men							
55–59 years	779	100	49	19	1	17	13
60-64 years	751	100	31	12	1	45	10
65 years and over	1,148	100	9	11	3	69	8
Women							
55–59 years	934	100	28	11	35	8	18
60-64 years	857	100	19	11	24	28	18
65 years and over	774	100	11	14	23	40	13

Source: Bureau of Labor Statistics.

two-thirds of workers. The other third has post-retirement work experience, although generally of a marginal nature. CPS data confirm the permanence of retirement. Once an older worker is out of the labor force *for a full year*, the probability of working the next year is minuscule. Chart 2 shows that CPS reentry rates—the probability of a person being out of the labor force one month and back in the next—decline markedly with age. Monthly rates are only about 2 percent for men age 65 and over and less than 1 percent for women that age.[3] Reentry rates for their younger counterparts (55–59 and 60–64 years old) are, in comparison, quite high. (While not germane to this discussion, it is also interesting to note that reentry rates for older men have recently been lower than they were in the late-1960s and early 1970s, contributing to the decline in their participation rates.)

Beck (1986) points out that constraints to employment often relegate retired workers to jobs in the secondary labor force. Applying the Duncan Socioeconomic Index to NLS data, he found that 70 percent of retired workers moved down the status hierarchy in their post-retirement job, 10 percent stayed the same, and about 20 percent moved up. This is reflected in the occupational data, which differ markedly between the youngest and oldest older workers (discussed below). Despite evidence that older workers would often prefer to continue to work part time for their old employer after retirement (Sheppard and Mantovani, 1982), few such opportunities exist. Beck concludes (1986, p. 528), "Restrictions on the types of jobs available for older people will force most of these potential working-retirees to either accept different and usually less-rewarding jobs or to stay out of the labor force altogether." Post-retirement jobs typically involve a reduction in work schedule and, often, a decline in occupational status.[4] However, as Parnes and Less (1985) point out, many older persons who work are not retirees; rather they have continued in their full-

---

[3] These data are based on a comparison of the labor force status of persons in the six (out of eight) CPS rotation groups that can be matched over two consecutive months. These are generally referred to as "gross flows" data.

[4] Many studies have shown this connection between retirement and occupational status. Of particular interest is the Social Security Administration's New Beneficiaries Survey conducted in late 1982, which provides information on the characteristics of both the longest job and current job for Social Security recipients. See, for example, Iams (1986).

CHART 2

Monthly Rate of Labor Force Reentrance for Men and Women Age 55 and over,
1968–86 Annual Averages

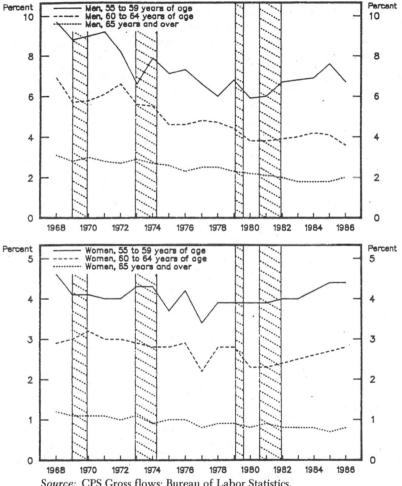

Source: CPS Gross flows; Bureau of Labor Statistics.
Note: See text for explanation.

time jobs. In fact, of older workers age 62 to 64, two-thirds of the
men and almost half of the women work full time, year round.

Job Mobility

As we have seen, one aspect of the transition from work to
retirement is the movement into and out of the labor force. Another

aspect relates to job or occupational switching. The dramatic trend toward earlier retirement has probably increased the interest in the subject of "second careers," which generally refers to a switch in occupations late in one's worklife. How common is such a practice? Two ways of assessing this are through information on job tenure—the period of time a person has been with the same employer—and occupational mobility—the extent of occupational change over a fixed period of time. The most current available data were collected by the CPS in January 1983. Table 4 shows the proportion of workers in each of several age/sex groups who had changed employers during the prior three years.

TABLE 4

Percent of Workers with Current Employer
Three Years or Less, by Sex and Age, January 1983

	Men		Women	
Age	1 Year or Less	3 Years or Less	1 Year or Less	3 Years or Less
35–44 years	16.7	31.7	24.2	45.4
45–54 years	11.2	21.0	15.5	31.0
55–59 years	9.6	17.7	10.5	22.5
60–64 years	7.7	15.4	11.3	23.2
65–69 years	10.5	23.1	9.6	21.1
70 years and over	9.5	18.0	11.6	21.1

Source: Bureau of Labor Statistics.

For both men and women, switching employers is considerably less common during the later work years than it is earlier. Men age 55 and over are about half as likely as are 35-44-year-olds to switch employers. However, the cumulative effect of all employer-switching after age 55 may have been much greater than the figures show. That is, while only 10 percent of male workers in each age group switched employers per year, the probability of switching at any time between 55 and retirement was much higher. One institutional impediment to job switching is that pension benefits are often lost in the transition, providing a large financial disincentive to change, particularly for those with only a limited number of years to recoup such losses through higher wages or benefits.

Tenure data for older women are quite similar to those of older men, only they mean something somewhat different. For men, a job switch generally entails going directly from one employer to another, possibly with an intervening period of unemployment. For women, however, a short tenure is more likely to indicate labor force reentry rather than a job switch.

Collected along with the tenure data in January 1983 was information on occupational mobility. Mobility rates, shown below, reflect the probability of persons employed in January of 1982 and 1983 having worked in different occupations those two months.

Occupational Mobility Rates, January 1982-83

	Men	Women
35–45 years	6.7%	7.8%
45–54 years	4.8	4.9
55–64 years	3.1	3.8
65 years and over	1.9	1.4

As these data show, the older the workers, the less likely they are to switch occupations. This certainly is not consistent with the notion of massive career switching. Since the CPS does not measure occupational mobility over a longer period of time, say five or ten years, it is difficult to translate the annual rates of occupational shift into longer-term rates. For example, it would be helpful to know how many persons switch occupations at any time after age 55, and whether such switches are largely voluntary or the result of job loss.

In summary, the tenure and occupational mobility data demonstrate that job switching, whether to a new occupation or not, tends to decline dramatically with age. Full-time workers tend to have much lower levels of occupational mobility than part-time workers.[5] This, of course, represents the occupational switching common between pre- and post-retirement jobs. Job switching and second careers are interesting topics because of the increase in both early retirement and life expectancy. Many people retire while still having decades of potentially productive years ahead of them. However, for most, retirement from a long-term job results in a permanent separation from the labor force. Many others retire but

---

[5] From unpublished CPS tabulations which examine the job tenure and occupational mobility of part- and full-time workers.

obtain new jobs in their same occupation, where their human capital will provide the best returns. Only a limited number of persons find new occupations; generally, these represent a step down the occupation/earnings ladder.

Occupation

As with most other measures of employment and unemployment of older persons, their occupational distribution tends to stray from that of central-age workers the older they get. Table 5 provides a convenient way of examining occupational data by age. It provides an index of age-group representation in each occupation. An index figure of 1.00 means that an age group constitutes the same proportion of men in a specific occupation as in all occupations combined. For example, men age 55–59 make up 7.2 percent of all men in professional specialties and 6.6 percent of all employed men. Thus, the index for professional specialty occupations is 7.2/6.6 = 1.09; this age group is overrepresented in the professional specialty occupations by 9 percent.

With a few exceptions, most notably technicians, men and women age 55 to 59 are not dramatically over- or underrepresented in any of the occupational categories. Men in this age group have

TABLE 5

Index of Age-Group Representation in Major Occupations,
by Sex and Age, 1986 Annual Average

	Men			Women		
Occupation	55–59 Years	60–64 Years	65 Years and Over	55–59 Years	60–64 Years	65 Years and Over
Executive, administrative, and managerial	1.26	1.25	1.14	1.03	1.03	.79
Professional specialty	1.09	1.05	1.07	.90	.76	.71
Technical and related support	.79	.59	.34	.51	.47	.38
Sales occupations	1.05	1.14	1.38	.93	.97	1.21
Administrative support, including clerical	.97	.93	.97	1.02	1.03	.83
Service occupations	.85	.95	1.24	1.03	1.16	1.56
Precision production, craft, and repair	.98	.86	.55	1.24	1.11	1.04
Operators, fabricators, and laborers	.85	.80	.52	1.22	1.16	.75
Farming, forestry, and fishing	1.08	1.55	3.38	1.46	1.39	2.58

Source: Bureau of Labor Statistics.

Note: See text for description of index.

their highest index among managers and administrators, an occupation generally not open to the very young, and are underrepresented in services, in which the very young and very old predominate, and the less-skilled, blue-collar jobs, from which poor health often leads to early withdrawal (Burtless, 1987).

Age 60–64 represents a transition between the pre- and post-retirement occupational distribution. Labor force activity drops off dramatically at age 62. Still, between ages 62 and 64, two-thirds of the employed men and over two-fifths of the employed women are still working full time, year round. The occupational indexes for men in the 65 and older category show a peculiar pattern. At the extremes, farming has triple its "fair share" of men in this group while technical occupations have only one-third. With the exception of farming, all of the physically demanding jobs have lost much of their employment share while the typical post-retirement fields— sales and services—jump dramatically. This unique occupational distribution reflects several factors:

- *Health.* As mentioned, persons in physically demanding jobs tend to leave those jobs (and often the labor force) early. Their health actually is, on average, worse than that of persons in other jobs, and also certain physical infirmities might allow a person to continue to work in a sedentary job but not in a physically demanding one.
- *Occupational retention.* Certain occupations tend to hold onto their workers. Professional jobs, for instance, often provide relatively high earnings and high levels of psychic reward, and they require relatively little physical effort. At the extreme, retention rates are probably highest among self-employed professionals (doctors, lawyers, etc.), who not only benefit from the factors just cited, but whose self-employment affords a high degree of flexibility in work schedules.
- *Second career and part-time employment.* Sales and service occupations are the most common stop-off points for persons in transition from a full-time career to full retirement. Many such jobs offer flexible schedules, particularly the part-time hours often not available in many other types of work. Also, the tasks are generally not strenuous. However, such employment often represents an occupational and earnings downgrade for

persons, as they lose both the value of their occupation-specific and firm-specific human capital in the transition.

- *Cohort effects.* This group of older workers had less education than did workers in younger generations. Also, they began their careers during a period when the industry and occupational composition of the labor force was far different than it is today. It is to be expected, then, that the jobs they hold late in their careers are quite different from those of younger, better educated workers.

I have limited the discussion of older women in the occupational context since Shaw's chapter on older women gives the issues related to their occupational employment considerable attention.

Education, Work, and Earnings

Education appears to be a key to understanding employment patterns among the elderly. One's level of education is the major influence on the type of job held throughout one's life, which, in turn, affects one's health, earnings, and the probability of staying in the labor force. At ages 60–64, for example, college-educated men and women are roughly twice as likely to be in the job market as are their least-educated counterparts. Likewise, more educated persons, when working, are far more likely to do so on a full-time, year-round basis. The relationship between education and extent of work effort is shown in Table 6. Among men age 65 and over, for example, those with less than a high school education made up 51 percent of the population in 1986, but only 29 percent of those working full time, year round. At the other extreme, college graduates made up only 12 percent of the 65 and over population, but have more than double that proportion of full-time, year-round workers. Older women followed very much the same pattern.

The relationship between education and earnings also appears to be strong. Indeed, education is generally the single best predictor of earnings. As just shown, education strongly influences the amount of work activity. As a result, the earnings of less educated persons are depressed by both their lower wage rates and their limited work activity. Examining the earnings of full-time, year-round workers eliminates the effect of a less than full work schedule.

TABLE 6

Percent Distribution of the Older Population, Workers, and
Nonworkers, by Educational Attainment, Age, and Sex, 1985

Sex and Educational Attainment	Age 55–64				Age 65 and Over			
	Population	Employed Year Round, Full Time	Other Employed	Non-workers	Population	Employed Year Round, Full Time	Other Employed	Non-workers
Men								
Total	100.0	100.0	100.0	100.0	100.0	100.0	100.0	100.0
Less than 8 years	20.8	14.6	22.9	32.2	37.2	16.7	28.8	40.6
1–3 years high school	14.5	12.2	17.4	17.1	15.8	10.9	13.0	16.7
4 years high school	33.5	35.0	33.2	30.0	26.4	35.4	29.4	25.0
1–3 years college	11.8	12.7	11.3	10.2	9.1	10.3	13.6	8.2
4 years or more college	19.4	25.6	15.2	9.8	11.5	26.6	15.2	9.5
Women								
Total	100.0	100.0	100.0	100.0	100.0	100.0	100.0	100.0
Less than 8 years	17.2	9.9	15.2	21.6	34.1	19.7	23.4	35.4
1–3 years high school	16.6	13.1	16.2	18.6	17.0	8.8	16.3	17.2
4 years high school	44.8	47.9	44.5	43.4	30.7	41.2	34.3	30.1
1–3 years college	11.5	14.5	13.5	9.2	10.3	15.2	14.4	9.8
4 years or more college	9.9	14.6	10.6	7.2	8.0	15.2	11.6	7.5

Source: Bureau of Labor Statistics.

Table 7 provides earnings of older workers by educational attainment. It should be noted that the earnings gap between more and less educated workers increases with age. For example, 25–34-year-old men with four years of college outearned men that age with four years of high school by only about a third in 1984; this ratio rises steadily until the gap peaks at a 65 percent differential for 55–59-year-olds. This is because, among the younger group, the high school graduates benefit from their greater work experience. That advantage disappears quickly, however.

TABLE 7

Mean Earnings of Year-Round, Full-Time Workers
by Level of Education, Sex, and Age, 1984

	Men			Women		
Educational Attainment	55–59 Years	60–64 Years	65 Years and Over	55–59 Years	60–64 Years	65 Years and Over
8 years or less	$17,970	$18,274	$11,882	$10,945	$10,848	a
1–3 years high school	22,642	20,421	18,380	12,495	10,848	a
4 years high school	25,246	24,046	24,643	14,693	14,978	$12,394
1–3 years college	30,282	29,303	26,793	16,257	17,126	a
4 years college	41,548	38,939	39,231	20,870	a	a
5 years or more college	45,757	47,617	39,395	29,527	30,242	a

Source: U.S. Bureau of the Census, "Money Income of Households, Families, and Persons in the United States: 1984," Series P-60, No. 151, April 1986, pp. 134–35.

[a] Median not shown when employment base is less than 75,000.

In summary, older workers' earnings are lower than those of younger workers largely because they work less. For those who continue to work full schedule, career-peak earnings are generally maintained until at least age 65, when the age group aggregates fall. This dropoff may reflect career switching, which generally entails earnings loss. Educational levels of older workers are improving with each cohort; while the relatively low average level of education for workers currently age 55 and over still serves to depress the group's average earnings, this influence is smaller than it was 10 years ago and will be even less important in the future. In terms of intra- rather than intergroup comparisons, education is clearly the key element in earnings differences. More than most other measures, the education/earnings data emphasize the vast gap between the haves and have nots, and this gap is widest for workers in their late fifties and early sixties.

Racial Differences in Employment

Blacks of all ages exhibit labor force patterns that are quite different from their white counterparts. These differences run the full range of labor force measures—participation, occupation, unemployment and earnings, among others. As Table 8 shows, the incidence of early labor force withdrawal is considerably higher for blacks than for whites.

TABLE 8

Labor Force Participation Rates by Sex, Race, and Age,
1986 Annual Averages

	Men		Women	
Age	White	Black	White	Black
55–59 years	79.8	70.8	51.0	52.9
60–64 years	55.7	45.9	33.1	33.3
65–69 years	25.3	21.0	14.3	13.9
70 years and over	10.7	7.2	4.1	4.6

Source: Bureau of Labor Statistics.

According to Sheppard (1977), using the National Longitudinal Survey of Mature Men, the early labor force withdrawal of black men is most likely to result from the combined effects of poor health and poor socioeconomic conditions. Black men who were self-identified as healthy and were employed when the NLS panel was first interviewed in 1966 were considerably more likely than whites to be either dead or out of the labor force for health reasons seven years later. Also, the probability of early withdrawal tends to increase the lower a person's job falls on occupational/skill or earnings scales. Blacks not only tend to be concentrated toward the bottom of such ratings, but also tend to have higher early-withdrawal rates than whites even when occupation (for example) is held constant. Again, much of this discrepancy is the result of blacks' relatively poor health.

Parsons (1980) adds that the rapid growth in the Social Security disability program during the 1960s and 1970s contributed heavily to the decline in black men's labor force participation during that period. Not only, as Sheppard pointed out, are blacks more likely to be in a position to take advantage of such a program expansion because of their relatively bad health, but their poorer job market

options (particularly their lower earnings) and the progressive
benefit structure of Social Security make the disability alternative
more attractive to blacks than to whites.

Like lower earnings, unemployment of the individual in the local
labor market also has a significant impact on early labor force
withdrawal. Apparently, unemployment affects not only the
incidence of retirement, but also the probability of a deterioration
in health status. Sheppard (1977, p. 187) presents the interplay of
health, unemployment, and race in a simple, yet revealing way. For
men in the labor force in 1966 who were between 52 and 64 as of
1973, early withdrawal rates were as follows:

	Early Withdrawal Rates as of 1973	
Race and Health Status in 1966	Employed in 1966	Unemployed in 1966
Healthy whites	19.1	29.5
Healthy blacks	22.5	37.5
Unhealthy whites	29.5	40.0
Unhealthy blacks	39.2	63.2

In all cases, withdrawal rates for blacks exceed the comparable
rates for whites (Sheppard included death as early withdrawal).
Kingson (1979), in his analysis of early retirement, also focuses on
the issue of early withdrawal (due to unemployment or sporadic
work history) which might arise from both the individual's and the
region's labor market experience. Obviously, such influence is felt
disproportionately by blacks.

Occupation and Race

As is the case for all ages, the occupational affiliation for older
blacks is quite different from that for whites. Table 9 shows an
occupational distribution for white and black men and women in
two age groups in 1986. The difference in racial patterns is striking.
At the extreme, older black men and women are both almost three
times as likely as whites to work in the service occupations. White
men have disproportionately high representation in professional
and sales jobs while black men are highly concentrated in the blue-
collar operators, fabricators, and laborers jobs. It is worth noting
that many of these racial differences in occupational employment

TABLE 9

Occupational Distribution of Older Workers,
by Race, Sex, and Age, 1986 Annual Averages

Occupation	White Males		Black Males		White Females		Black Females	
	Age 55–64	Age 65 and Over	Age 55–64	Age 65 and Over	Age 55–64	Age 65 and Over	Age 55–64	Age 65 and Over
Total	100.0%	100.0%	100.0%	100.0%	100.0%	100.0%	100.0%	100.0%
Executive, administrative, managerial	17.5	15.5	6.3	6.3	10.4	7.9	5.1	3.9
Professional specialty	12.9	13.1	6.5	3.6	11.8	10.9	12.2	3.9
Technicians and related support	2.2	1.0	0.8	1.8	1.5	1.2	2.5	2.9
Sales occupations	13.1	16.7	3.7	3.6	13.5	17.1	3.4	3.9
Administrative support, inc. clerical	5.4	5.5	5.9	5.4	31.7	26.7	14.3	8.8
Service occupations	7.3	10.7	19.3	26.8	16.3	24.0	48.6	68.6
Precision production, craft, repair	19.3	11.2	17.2	9.8	2.8	2.6	2.5	1.0
Operators, fabricators, laborers	16.1	10.2	34.7	25.0	10.3	6.5	10.7	6.9
Farming, forestry, fishing	6.1	16.2	5.7	16.1	1.7	3.1	0.4	1.0

exist even among workers in their twenties and thirties. These employment patterns among the young suggest that the dramatic occupational differences between older white and black workers are likely to persist for many decades.

Race and Earnings

The ratio of white to black earnings for older workers is not much different from that for younger workers. As the following data for median weekly earnings for full-time wage and salary workers in 1986 show, the racial differences in wages are more pronounced for men than for women.

Sex and Age	Median Weekly Earnings		Ratio
	White	Black	White/Black
Men			
25–54 years	$476	$350	1.36
55 years and over	492	342	1.44
Women			
25–54 years	314	280	1.12
55 years and over	300	253	1.19

Because older blacks tend to spend more time than their white counterparts unemployed or out of the labor force, a comparison of *annual* earnings would show even more of a racial spread than do the weekly data.

In summary, racial differences in labor force performance of older workers reflect patterns that have persisted throughout workers' lifetimes. And, as data for younger workers suggest, large discrepancies between the job status of blacks and whites will most likely continue through the foreseeable future. Older blacks tend to be in relatively poor health, and, at least for men, work less, work in lower status occupations, and earn considerably less than their white counterparts.

Unemployment and Other Labor Market Problems

A general overview of the employment status of older Americans has been presented; it is just as important to look at those who do not work but may wish to. Among the key measures of labor market problems are unemployment, discouragement, and displacement.

Unemployment

Unemployment is generally viewed as an important measure of labor market hardship. As measured in the CPS, it is something quite specific—unemployed persons did not work at all during the reference week, had actively looked for work at some point during the previous four weeks, and were available for work. (Persons on layoff from a job to which they expect to be recalled are the exception to the job search requirement.)

Thus, most simply, the unemployed are jobseekers. Some have lost their jobs, but others have quit theirs, or have entered job search after being out of the labor force. Not included in the category are persons who are out of the labor force or marginally employed.

Older workers generally have the lowest rates of unemployment of any group; certainly their rates are well below average. However, since the national average is inflated by the markedly high jobless rates for youth, it is probably better to compare the jobless rates of the elderly to the rates of those persons of central working age (25–54 years). Chart 3 shows unemployment rates for men and women age 55–64 and 65 and over compared to those age 25–54.

Prior to the late 1960s, the jobless rate for older men tended to be *higher* than those for the 25–54-year-olds. Since then, not only has the situation been reversed, but the gap between the older and younger groups has continued to grow. This gap tends to widen in recessions and narrow in recoveries. Some possible reasons for the recent differences in the rate of joblessness between older and younger men include:

- The frequency and severity of recessions between 1973 and 1982 certainly worked to the disadvantage of younger men, whose jobless rates are more sensitive to the business cycle.
- Improvements in pension income have probably made retirement a more viable alternative to unemployment for many older potential jobseekers. Social Security experienced several large benefit increases in the early 1970s and was subsequently indexed to the Consumer Price Index to protect against erosion from inflation. Coverage of employees by private pensions has also increased and legislation has improved vesting regulations. Thus, some persons who may have had to find a job in the past are now better able to retire (or stay retired).

- Rates of labor force reentry for older men are generally down from the late 1960s and early 1970s. Thus, there has not been any strong upward pressure on older workers' jobless rates from persons entering a job search from outside the labor force.
- There appears to be a considerable increase in the use of early retirement inducements as a means of reducing labor costs. This method used to be closely associated with recessions, but the increased competitive pressures of the 1980s has made this a fairly common occurrence, even in healthy industries in times of general economic expansion. Older persons may, thus, avoid layoff by retiring, an option not available to younger workers.

The reader will note that the above points are dominated by the issue of labor force withdrawal. This option, not feasible for many middle-aged workers (particularly men), complicates unemployment comparisons between age groups in two ways. First, the *incidence* of unemployment among older persons is limited by labor force withdrawal. For example, a 40-year-old job loser is much more likely to show up in the CPS as unemployed than is a 62-year-old, who may choose to retire. Second, labor force withdrawal after an unsuccessful job search also tends to lower the duration of unemployment—that is, a large proportion of the unemployment spells of older persons end in labor force withdrawal rather than employment (Rones, 1983). This, of course, serves to lower unemployment *rates* as well.

Are Older Jobseekers Marginal Jobseekers?

It is tempting to portray the older jobseeker as a more marginal labor force participant. Like teenagers, they may not need a job, but, under the right conditions, a job would be nice. This scenario certainly is consistent with the observed conclusions of their unemployment spells—a relatively high proportion leave the labor force rather than gain employment. While the "seriousness" of job search or how much someone wants or needs a job is difficult to measure, some related data on job search and the reasons for unemployment can shed some light on the issue.

The data presented below tend to support the contention that the older the jobseeker, the more marginal the job search. However, the stereotype of the older person as not needing a job—that is, can either take it or leave it—is in many cases invalid. It must first be

CHART 3

Unemployment Rates for Men and Women in Selected Age Groups, 1965–86

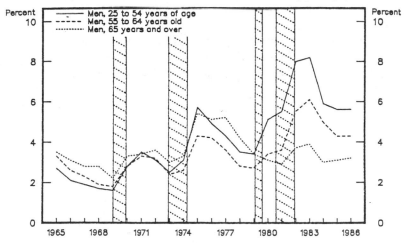

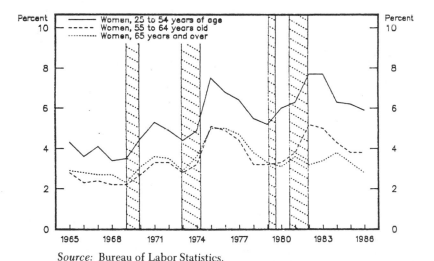

Source: Bureau of Labor Statistics.

recognized that the presumption of an uninspired job search is generally based on the assumption of alternative sources of income—teenagers have their parents and older persons have their pensions. Certainly, the higher the nonwage income, the less pressing the need for employment. But, for many workers,

retirement income is not available prior to age 62 (age of Social
Security eligibility). Thus, before this age, an older jobseeker may
be no more able to finance extended unemployment than would a
younger worker.

The majority of older jobseekers, particularly those under 62,
are persons who begin looking for work immediately after losing a
job; they are not coming out of retirement to look for work. As
Table 10 shows, in 1986 three-fourths of the unemployed men ages
55–59 were job losers—persons who were either on layoff or were
permanently separated from their jobs. Other surveys provide
evidence that older persons looking for work tend to be those who,
financially, cannot afford to retire (Rones, 1983, p. 12, fn. 27).

TABLE 10

Percent Distribution of Reasons for Unemployment and Type of Job Sought
for Persons age 55 and Over, by Sex, 1986 Annual Average

Reason for Unemployment and Type of Job Sought	Men			Women		
	55–59 Years	60–64 Years	65 Years and Over	55–59 Years	60–64 Years	65 Years and Over
Reason for unemployment						
Total	100	100	100	100	100	100
Job losers	76	65	43	63	55	50
Job leavers	6	8	7	8	8	3
Labor force entrants	18	26	50	29	36	47
Type of job sought						
Total	100	100	100	100	100	100
Full time	93	81	46	79	59	38
Part time	7	19	54	21	41	62

Source: Bureau of Labor Statistics.

These persons are not looking for marginal employment. Almost
all of the men and more than four out of five women ages 55–59
were looking for full-time jobs. And, as data from a 1976 CPS
supplement show, they are usually looking for permanent rather
than temporary employment.[6] In general, then, there is little
evidence to distinguish the level of labor force commitment of
unemployed persons in their upper fifties and early sixties from that
of prime-age workers. These are largely people who lost their jobs
and need (or want) full-time work.

---

[6] See Rosenfeld (1977). See also Rones (1983, p. 8).

On the other hand, the unemployed in the 65 and older age group display more of the characteristics of marginal jobseekers. They are far more likely to be seeking part-time work than are younger workers, they are often labor force reentrants, and according to CPS data collected in 1976, the job search effort of men in this age group is less intensive—men 65 and older spent roughly half the amount of time in job search as did their 25-54-year-old counterparts. Finally, they are less likely than younger persons to persevere in their job search, although it is certainly not clear to what extent their aborted job search is job-market related.

Discouragement

A second widely used measure of hardship is that of labor market discouragement, the only CPS measure of job market failure for those outside the labor force. Technically, discouraged workers are persons outside the labor force who say they want a job and that the reason they are not looking is that they think they could not find one. There is no presumption that any recent job search had taken place. In fact, some discouraged workers have not looked for work for many years and have no plans to do so (Rones, 1983, p. 9). Despite the marginal labor market attachment of some older discouraged workers, for several reasons the measure is still important for analyzing this group. First, it does not necessarily take a recent, active job search to conclude that the prospects of successful job search are not bright. In certain circumstances, a reasonable person might presume job prospects to be bleak without actually testing the waters. Second, if persons indicate that they are available for work and want a job, one must give some credence to that response. While job interest may be "soft," it may also be so for some of the unemployed who may have made only cursory job search efforts. And third, among the older age groups, particularly the 65 and over group, those outside the labor force make up the vast majority of their population, and labor market discouragement thus is one of the few available measures of their potential labor supply.

Table 11 presents the official unemployment rate for older and central-age workers alongside a modified jobless rate that includes discouraged workers in both the numerator and denominator. This is not to suggest that they should be combined, but rather demonstrates the effect on the jobless measure if they were. The

TABLE 11
Official Unemployment Rate and Rate Including Discouraged Workers, by Sex and Age, 1968–1986 Annual Averages

Selected Years	Men						Women					
	Age 25–54		Age 55–64		Age 65 and Over		Age 25–54		Age 55–64		Age 65 and Over	
	u[a]	u+d[b]	u	u+d	u	u+d	u	u+d	u	u+d	u	u+d
1968	1.7	1.8	1.9	2.3	2.8	6.6	3.4	4.5	2.2	4.2	2.7	8.6
1973	1.5	2.7	2.4	2.8	3.0	6.0	4.4	5.5	2.8	4.0	2.9	5.6
1978	3.5	3.7	2.8	3.3	4.2	7.2	5.5	6.5	3.2	4.6	3.8	9.3
1983	8.2	8.8	6.1	7.2	3.9	7.8	7.7	9.3	5.0	7.0	3.4	8.0
1986	5.6	6.6	4.3	5.2	3.2	5.9	5.9	6.9	3.8	5.1	2.8	8.3
Average,[c] 1968–1986	4.4	4.7	3.6	4.1	3.6	6.7	5.7	6.9	3.7	5.3	3.5	8.2

Source: Bureau of Labor Statistics.

[a] u is the official unemployment rate calculated by dividing the total unemployed by the civilian labor force.

[b] u+d counts all discouraged workers as unemployed; it divides the unemployed + discouraged workers by the civilian labor force + discouraged workers.

[c] Unweighted averages.

addition of discouraged workers has virtually no effect on central-age men and a small but significant effect for women in that age group. For the 65 and older group, however, the new "jobless rate" is quite high—more than double the original rate in the case of women.

Obviously, this is more a population phenomenon than a job market one. For women age 65 and over, for example, the not-in-labor-force group is 15 times as populous as the labor force group, and thus even a small portion of the former has a large impact when added to the latter. However, in comparison to the population of this group, discouraged workers are a minuscule portion—only half of 1 percent of persons age 65 and older and out of the labor force. At the other extreme, only about 6 percent of central-age men are out of the labor force, a very small pool from which discouraged workers may come. Workers this age—particularly men, but certainly many women also—do not have the "luxury" of labor force withdrawal, since alternative sources of income, at least for the long run, are rarely available.

In conclusion, one needs to be very careful when analyzing the fact that older workers tend to be "overrepresented" among the discouraged workers. Such a finding is to be expected when the potential pool of discouraged workers is all those outside the labor force, a group that accounts for the majority of the older population. The real problem of discouragement may go beyond the official measure. For many retirees, the types of job offers available to older workers are at such odds with what it would take to get them back in the work force that they may not even consider employment as a legitimate option. These people may certainly respond to the Census Bureau interviewer that they "do not want a job now," meaning that they do not want a job under the prevailing conditions of employment.

Displacement and the Older Worker

During the 1980s, employment in several key manufacturing industries has been hurt by both cyclical and structural problems. The extensive job losses in these industries—steel, autos, machinery, and textiles, among others—heightened interest in measuring permanent job displacement. Supplements to the CPS were conducted in January 1984 and 1986 to help quantify this problem. The January 1986 supplement found that 950,000 workers age 55 and older lost or left jobs at which they had three or more years of tenure because of plant closings or moves, slack work, or abolishment of their positions or shifts during the prior five-year period. These older workers comprised almost one-fifth of the 5.1 million displaced workers identified in the supplement. As of the survey date, displaced older workers were less likely to be reemployed and far more likely to be out of the labor force entirely than their younger counterparts. Those 55–64 years old were about as likely as all displaced workers to be officially classified as unemployed, but those 65 years or older were very much less likely to be.

Older workers, quite naturally, are a larger portion of those with three or more years of tenure than they are of the total employed; therefore, "displacement rate" comparisons based on employment share may tend to overstate the rate at which older workers are displaced relative to workers in other age groups. It is clear, however, that despite the protection from layoff that seniority might provide, the incidence of displacement among older workers is close enough to that of the rest of the work force that it cannot be ignored as a policy concern.

An important reason that displacement among older workers occurs so frequently is that more than half of all displacements are the result of plant closings, situations in which seniority affords little or no job protection. In fact, nearly two-thirds of displacements among older workers resulted from plant closings, and about 45 percent occurred among employees with 15 or more years of continuous job tenure.

Even among the reemployed, the impact of displacement is often severe for older workers. Among the reemployed, Podgursky and Swain (1986), using January 1984 data for displacement, found that persons with long tenure on the lost job often had the most substantial earnings losses. Among long-time employees, earnings losses were greatest for men in blue-collar jobs. High tenure, of course, characterizes the displaced older worker.

Other factors associated with job loss do not reveal many differences between older displaced workers and the total. As was the case for all displaced workers, just under two-thirds of older workers who lost jobs received unemployment insurance benefits. On the other hand, older workers more frequently reported long-term (27 weeks or more) receipt of unemployment benefits and were less likely to move to another city or county in search of a new job.

No national survey provides a complete count of job loss; the CPS, for example, limits the count of job losers to those who are not working and actively looking for a job. However, the National Longitudinal Survey of Mature Men has been used by Parnes et al. (1981) to document the extent of job loss among long-service male workers between 1966 and 1975. While somewhat dated, these data and the authors' analysis still are useful in the unemployment discussion. Among men who were 55–69 in 1976, one in 14 had lost a job in which they had been employed at least four years in the previous 10 years. This represented about a half million such men in the population.

Similar to the CPS displaced-worker data, the NLS data show that permanent layoff happened to men in all occupational groups and irrespective of educational background and tenure on the job. Shapiro and Sandell (1983), also using NLS data, analyzed all job losses rather than just those from long-term service, and in that context it was clear that a disproportionate share of job loss occurred among workers with short tenure. Both the Parnes and the Shapiro and Sandell studies showed that many of the reemployed experienced a decline in both occupational status and earnings. Parnes found no evidence that such an adverse impact softened with time, at least over the decade examined. As would be expected, the worse the general economic environment, the poorer the reemployment outlook for displaced workers and the longer the duration of unemployment. Shapiro and Sandell (1984) also found that high national unemployment rates had a profound effect on the likelihood of an older worker leaving the labor force following job loss.

Summarizing the extent of labor market problems of older workers is quite difficult, but some general observations are offered below:

- While a useful measure, unemployment may understate the extent of job market problems of older workers relative to younger ones because relatively more of the former than of the latter avoid a job search by withdrawing from the labor force—that is, they retire.

- Older jobseekers prior to age 62 are very similar to their younger counterparts. They rarely can (or want to) retire, and they look for full-time jobs. Those age 62 and beyond, particularly those age 65 and over, tend to exhibit the characteristics of the marginal jobseeker— they often look for part-time or temporary jobs, they have a less intensive job search, and they often give up following an unsuccessful job search.
- Only a tiny portion of those out of the labor force are technically "discouraged." This may not mean that retired workers would not have wanted a job, but rather that they did not want the types of jobs available to them. Once the retirement decision is made, for most it appears to be permanent.
- Permanent displacement from jobs is as much of a problem for older workers as for others, in some respects more so. Much of this permanent job loss is the result of plant closings and other actions from which seniority affords little or no protection.
- Older job losers typically face occupational and earnings downgrades, not unlike those faced by voluntary retirees who wish to find post-retirement jobs. Displacement late in ones career often precipitates premature labor force exit, particularly when the national jobless rate is high.

Summary and Conclusions

The many measures that have been used to describe the labor market experience of older workers clearly demonstrate that one can no more easily stereotype the older worker than one can stereotype all workers. Labor market performance of older workers differs markedly by sex, race, and educational attainment. Also, within each of these subsets of the population there are distinct differences between those who have retired and those who have not.

Prior to retirement, there is little to distinguish older workers' labor market experience from that of their middle-aged counterparts. Those pre-retired workers in their late fifties and early sixties tend to work the same schedules as younger workers, work in roughly the same occupations, and earn about the same amount. The older person's employment, in many ways, is more stable. Average tenure with the current employer is at its peak, employer switching is less common than at younger ages, and unemployment is less common. When they find themselves unemployed, these workers generally look to full-time, permanent employment, search just as intensively as younger workers, and persevere in their job search—that is, they look until they find work. Often, however, job loss late in a person's career means accepting a lower paying job, often in a different occupation from the lost job. Health, earnings, occupation, and, of course, the availability of retirement income are among the factors that determine how long someone continues to work before retirement.

On the other hand, retirement, or the option to retire, dramatically changes the older worker's job market behavior. About a third of all older persons work after receiving a pension. Few retire for an extended period and then return to work; most post-retirement employment occurs immediately after pension receipt. Such work is usually part time or part year, and often involves an occupational switch, generally toward jobs such as sales or services that are not physically demanding and allow for flexible schedules. Whether in the same or a different occupation from their pre-retirement job, pay rates are typically lower after retirement. Also, post-retirement jobseekers, on average, do not demonstrate the same level of commitment to their job search as do the pre-retirement unemployed.

There are some aspects of older workers' employment experience that we do not understand particularly well, especially the related issues of voluntary/involuntary labor force withdrawal and potential work interest among the retired elderly. Regarding the reasons for a person choosing to stop working (or not to look for work), it may be quite a lot to expect a survey respondent to be able to weigh the relative importance of health, income, job satisfaction, unemployment, etc., in the work/retirement decision. While most retirees who are out of the labor force report to CPS interviewers that they do not want a job, many analysts, including myself, feel that this is to some extent a reflection of the current mismatch between the types of jobs, pay, and work schedules available to older jobseekers and their desires in these areas.

Equally important in limiting work activity among the elderly has been the financial disincentives to work which, historically, have been built into Social Security and many private pension systems. That is changing, however, as both Social Security and private pension regulations are being altered to eliminate many of the disincentives for continued work.

This institutional change and the job market reality are often at odds. While laws are being passed to allow or encourage work beyond normal retirement age, many employers are providing financial incentives for their workers to retire earlier and earlier. And to further complicate the matter, while these cost-cutting buyouts and layoffs are occurring, some employers in fast-growing retail and service firms are, for the first time, actively recruiting older workers in response to shortages of young people entering the job market.

For most retirees, however, the present job market offers little incentive to leave retirement. Many workers nearing retirement say that they would like to continue part time in their old job after retirement age. Workers clearly know that they are more valuable to a long-time employer than they would be to a new employer, particularly in a new occupation. At present, the phased-retirement option is rarely available.

Will this change in the future? Many analysts are of the opinion that the not too distant future holds serious labor shortages, which would greatly expand the need for older workers and improve the quality of available jobs. But a similar argument was used regarding teenage unemployment, i.e., when their labor force numbers declined significantly, competition among jobseekers was expected to ease and jobless rates to decline. However, the group's population and labor force have been declining for most of a decade now without a dramatic effect on unemployment.

Public and private policy are at odds. Laws are being changed to allow, encourage, and even push older persons to work longer while many employers are looking to find ways to induce them to retire earlier. With that in mind, the future status of older workers cannot be assessed with any degree of certainty. Which forces will dominate—a labor surplus or a labor shortage, high or low unemployment? We understand changing demographics quite well. However, we cannot easily predict long-term economic growth, which is undoubtedly the key to future employment opportunities for older workers.

References

Beck, Scott H. "Determinants of Labor Force Activity Among Retired Men." *Research on Aging* 7 (1985), pp. 251-80.
_____. "Mobility from Preretirement to Postretirement Job." *The Sociological Quarterly* 4 (1986), pp. 515-31.
Burtless, Gary. "Occupational Effects on the Health and Work Capacity of Older Men." In *Work, Health, and Income Among the Elderly*, ed. Gary Burtless. Washington: The Brookings Institution, 1987.
Iams, Howard M. "Employment of Retired-Worker Women." *Social Security Bulletin* 49 (March 1986), pp. 5-13.
Kingson, Eric R. "Men Who Leave Work Before Age 62: A Study of Advantaged and Disadvantaged Very Early Labor Force Withdrawal." Ph.D. dissertation, Brandeis University, Heller School for Advanced Studies in Social Welfare, 1979.
Palmore, Erdman, B. Burchett, G. Fillenbaum, L. George, and L. Wallman. *Retirement: Causes and Consequences*. New York: Springer Publishing Co., 1985.
Parnes, Herbert S., Mary G. Gagen, and Randall H. King. "Job Loss Among Long-Service Workers." In *Work and Retirement: A Longitudinal Study*, ed. Herbert S. Parnes. Cambridge: MA: The MIT Press, 1981.
Parnes, Herbert S., and Lawrence J. Less. "Shunning Retirement: The Experience of Full-Time Workers." In *Retirement Among American Men*, ed. Herbert S. Parnes. Lexington, MA: Lexington Books, 1985.
Parsons, Donald O. "Racial Trends in Male Labor Force Participation." *American Economic Review* 70 (December 1980), pp. 911-20.
Podgursky, Michael, and Paul Swain. "Job Displacement and Earnings Loss: Evidence from the Displaced Worker Survey." Unpublished paper, Department of Economics, University of Massachusetts, April 1, 1986.
Rones, Philip L. "The Labor Market Problems of Older Workers." *Monthly Labor Review* 106 (May 1983), pp. 3-12.
Rosenfeld, Carl. "Job Search of the Unemployed, May 1976." *Monthly Labor Review* 100 (November 1977), pp. 39-42.
Shapiro, David, and Steven H. Sandell. *Age Discrimination and Labor Market Problems of Displaced Older Male Workers*. Research Report Series, RR-83-10. Washington: National Commission for Employment Policy, 1983.
_____, "Economic Conditions, Job Loss, and Induced Retirement." Paper presented at the 37th Annual Meeting, Industrial Relations Research Association, Dallas, December 1984.
Sheppard, Harold L. "Factors Associated with Early Withdrawal from the Labor Force." In *Men in the Pre-retirement Years*, ed. Seymour L. Wolfbein. Philadelphia: Temple University, School of Business Administration, 1977.
Sheppard, Harold L., and R. Mantovani. *Part-time Employment After Retirement*. Washington: The National Council on Aging, 1982.

Chapter 3

Special Problems of Older Women Workers

Lois B. Shaw°
U.S. General Accounting Office

The problems faced by older women workers differ substantially from those faced by men. Many of the employment problems of older women stem from their previous commitment to family roles. Most older women have spent many years either entirely out of the labor market or working only part time or intermittently. Older women who are recent labor market reentrants are, of course, at entirely different stages of their work careers than are older men. Even those who have worked part time or intermittently for years may require a reorientation of their work lives and in some cases additional training if they need to become completely self-supporting. As traditional family caregivers, older women are also vulnerable to further work interruptions if their husbands, parents, or adult children become ill and require care.

Problems that affect older workers of both sexes may have a different impact on women and men because of differences in their work experience. Even though age discrimination affects both sexes, the kinds of discrimination they encounter may be different. Because they are more likely to be entering the labor market, women may be more likely to encounter age discrimination at the point of hiring, whereas age-related involuntary terminations may be more important for men. Similarly, layoffs from long-term jobs will affect fewer women than men and may affect women differently when they do occur. Sex stereotyping of jobs and reluctance of employers to hire people for jobs unconventional for their sex may constrain the job choices of both women and men. However, since higher paying jobs tend to be stereotypically male,

---

° Opinions expressed in this chapter are those of the author and do not represent the views of the General Accounting Office.

any such sex discrimination weighs more heavily on women's job opportunities than on men's.

Because the problems of reentering the labor force and advancing beyond entry-level jobs will be a major focus of this chapter, the age range of the "older" workers described may be somewhat broader than that of other chapters in this volume. For example, displaced homemaker programs often use 35 or 40 years as a lower age limit. Most of the research reviewed here will focus on women who are 40 years old or over, but relevant research findings that include somewhat younger women will be mentioned as well.

The women who are the subject of this research have entered the labor market during a period of rapid increase in women's labor force participation and rapid change in norms concerning women's roles. At the upper end of the age range, women who are now age 65 reached age 18 as the Depression of the 1930s was ending. In 1941, as they were reaching adulthood, a survey of city school systems found that about 60 percent had policies of not hiring married women as teachers, and many more would hire them only if they had dependents to support or met other special criteria. During the 1930s, legislation barring married women from employment had been introduced in the legislatures of 26 states, though only one state actually passed such legislation (Oppenheimer, 1970). The contrast for women who are now 40 years old could hardly be greater. These women reached age 18 in 1965, just after the passage of legislation and executive orders making discrimination on the basis of sex illegal. Among the oldest women we are considering, probably few except the poor had themselves had mothers who worked outside the home, whereas for the youngest, working mothers had become a familiar phenomenon.[1] We should keep in mind, therefore, that as the background of women entering middle age changes, the problems of the older woman worker will change—a topic I will consider at greater length in my concluding remarks.

Problems of Labor Market Reentry

Labor market reentry has been a subject of interest to both the research community and to policymakers. The mature women's

---

[1] Further discussion of the changes in the social climate at the time different cohorts of women reached different life-cycle stages may be found in Shaw and O'Brien (1983), Jusenius and Parnes (1976), and Chafe (1972).

cohort of the National Longitudinal Surveys of Labor Market Experience (NLS) was initiated with the idea of collecting data to study the problems women encounter when they reenter the labor force after staying at home to rear children (Parnes, 1975). This data set is the source of the most extensive work history information for older women in the United States. The surveys were begun in 1967 with a representative sample of about 5,000 women who were then age 30–44. These women have been reinterviewed at one- or two-year intervals through 1987, and considerable research has been completed using these data through 1982 when the women were age 45–59. The availability of longitudinal data and the use of increasingly sophisticated research methodology have enabled researchers to begin to answer questions about women's work patterns, about the effects of work interruptions on women's earnings, and about the kinds of employment problems middle-aged women encounter.

Women's Varied Work Patterns

The stereotypic view of the reentrant depicts her as a woman who returns to the labor market after many years at home. Reentry is pictured as a one-time event. A woman leaves the labor force to raise children, stays at home until her children are in school or have left home or until she loses her husband. Then she returns to work and continues to be employed until retirement.

Research using work history data and labor force flow data reveals that these stereotypes are inaccurate. Analyses using the NLS show that few women with children have followed the single reentry pattern. Among women age 45–59 in 1982, about 40 percent of white women and 60 percent of black women first returned to work before their first child reached age six (Mott and Shaw, 1986). However, the great majority of these women had additional absences from the labor force, and even women who stayed out much longer often had further work interruptions. Overall only 20 percent of these women had worked fairly continuously from the time they first returned to work until the date of the 1982 interview. A similar result was obtained from life table models of working lives using data from the Current Population Survey. Researchers at the Bureau of Labor Statistics (BLS) estimated that as of 1977 the average 25-year-old woman will enter the labor force 2.7 times during her remaining life (Smith, 1982).

If repeated entries and exits are common, how many women experience long spells out of the labor market? In the NLS slightly more than 40 percent of middle-aged women with children had remained at home for as long as 10 years before returning to work, and about one quarter stayed at home for 15 years or more. The median length of work interruption before first returning to work was about seven years (Dex and Shaw, 1986). Although long interruptions were not uncommon for today's middle-aged woman, most women evidently followed a pattern of several shorter spells out of the labor force. However, these repeated spells, in many cases, added up to a total number of years out of the labor market that was quite large. In 1976 women in the NLS, who were in their forties and early fifties had, on average, spent a total of about 15 years at home and about 11 years at work since leaving school (Shaw, 1979).

The great diversity of work patterns among middle-aged women is striking. In a study of the work patterns of NLS women who were age 45–59 in 1982, Shaw (1986a) found that about one quarter of the sample demonstrated increasing work attachment over the previous 15 years. These women could be considered labor market reentrants who had not worked or, more frequently, had worked intermittently in the first years of the interviews, but had become steadily employed by the last five years of the period. Irregular work patterns with no clear trend toward permanent attachment were about as common as increasing attachment. About 20 percent had worked continuously throughout the 15 years, and about 5 percent appeared to have retired after a lengthy period of employment. The other quarter of the sample had not worked at all or had very minimal work records.

Displaced Homemakers: Myths and Realities

One reason for concern about labor market reentry has been that increasing divorce rates have caused many women to find that they must become self-supporting. The displaced homemaker movement was organized in the early 1970s primarily by middle-class women who had experienced a midlife divorce after many years of marriage.[2] As the term implies, the displaced homemaker was

___

[2] Shields (1981) provides an interesting account of the displaced homemaker movement by one of its organizers.

pictured as a woman displaced from her primary job of home-making and forced to become the primary earner because of divorce, separation, widowhood, or disability of her husband. Having no recent work experience, she had difficulty finding employment. She would not qualify for unemployment compensation because she had no recent work experience, would not qualify for welfare because her children were grown, and would not qualify for Social Security benefits because she was too young. In short, as this description implies, the displaced homemaker was viewed as the stereotypic reentrant.[3]

Legislation to provide job counselling and training for displaced homemakers was a major goal of the movement. Partly as a result of their efforts, federal displaced homemaker legislation was enacted in 1976 in amendments to the Vocational Education Act and in 1978 amendments to the Comprehensive Employment and Training Act (CETA). Funding for programs fell when CETA was replaced by the Job Training Partnership Act (JTPA), but the Carl D. Perkins Vocational Education Act of 1984 provided increased funding. By 1984, 24 states had enacted legislation supporting or providing funds for displaced homemaker programs (U.S. Congress, 1985).

Determining the number of women who might be classified as displaced homemakers is not a simple matter. Legislative definitions of the population eligible for services have varied, and privately sponsored programs have also catered to different groups. Understandably, government-sponsored programs have usually had income cutoffs so that only low-income women are served. Some programs have age limits, on the grounds that other programs such as the Work Incentive Program (WIN) serve younger welfare recipients with children, but many programs serve all ages.

The requirement that women must have spent a "substantial" number of years out of the labor force has been incorporated in some of the displaced homemaker legislation.[4] This requirement, if defined restrictively to mean that a woman cannot have worked at

---

[3] The reentry stereotype predates the displaced-homemaker movement. Middle-aged married women first began reentering the labor force in large numbers during World War II (Shaw and O'Brien, 1983). The idea of a second career after childbearing was widely discussed during the 1950s by social scientists such as Myrdal and Klein (1956).

[4] The 1978 amendments to CETA used this language, and some state legislation also incorporated it. However, the Perkins Vocational Education Act does not mention either time spent out of the labor market or age (U.S. Congress, 1985).

all during a period of five, 10, or 15 years, excludes many women who have supplemented family income with part-time or low-paid employment, but would have difficulty in becoming completely self-supporting. In a study of women eligible for the CETA displaced homemaker program, Shaw (1979) found that women who would have been eligible except that they had not been out of the labor force for at least five years were similar to the eligible population in education, wages, and poverty status. Two-thirds of the excluded group were black.

Researchers at the Urban Institute have estimated that about 2.2 million women could be classified as displaced homemakers in 1983 under a definition they developed (O'Brien and Nightengale, 1985; also reported in U.S. Congress, 1985). This definition included women age 35–64 who were widowed, separated, divorced, or had husbands who were disabled or long-term unemployed. A small number of single AFDC mothers were also included. Women in these categories were counted as displaced homemakers if they had employment-related problems, including current unemployment and having been unemployed or out of the labor force for at least 26 weeks in the previous year, working part time when a full-time job was desired, receiving pay below the minimum wage, or dropping out of the labor force because of discouragement. Spending a given number of years out of the labor force was not a requirement. Women whose youngest child was age 17–19 and who were receiving a substantial proportion of income from child support, AFDC, or Social Security dependent benefits were also included. The 2.2 million women meeting this definition represented about 6 percent of all women age 35–64. Among divorced, separated, and widowed women at these ages, about 17 percent could be considered displaced homemakers, while only 2 percent of married women were included.

These estimates, though the best available using a national data base, illustrate the difficulties of definition.[5] Because of limited funds, government-sponsored displaced-homemaker programs will probably continue to define the displaced-homemaker population so as to include only those in greatest need. However, using the minimum wage as the cutoff for considering that a woman has an

---

[5] Other estimates of the number of displaced homemakers and comparisons of the assumptions used in making them may be found in Vanski, Nightengale, and O'Brien (1983).

employment problem excludes many women who are in need of further training if they are to become fully self-supporting on a long-term basis. A full-time minimum wage job at present represents a yearly income of slightly under $7,000, which is above the poverty line for one person, but not for a person with one or more dependents. Even for a woman living alone $7,000 does not represent economic security. At this level many jobs do not carry health insurance and few provide pensions. Women who cannot obtain better jobs than these are living near poverty and are at risk of becoming poor if they encounter health problems or if they must rely on Social Security for most of their income when they retire. Obtaining a job at the minimum wage surely should not be taken to mean that an older person's employment problems are at an end. If a more realistic definition of "having an employment problem" were adopted, the estimated numbers of displaced homemakers would be considerably higher than those quoted above.

Even if we accept a particular definition of the number of women who could be classified as displaced homemakers in a particular year, virtually nothing is known about the dynamic aspects of the problem. One estimate placed the yearly flow into displaced homemaker status at 200 to 300 thousand.[6] This estimate is probably too low; if accurate it would suggest that many women remain displaced homemakers over an extended period.

Studies of the characteristics of displaced homemakers have found that about half have not completed high school (Vanski, Nightengale, and O'Brien, 1983; Shaw, 1979). Over 40 percent cite a service occupation as their current or most recent employment. Most had worked at some time in the previous five years, but the majority had less than 10 years of total work experience (Shaw, 1979). Any broadening of the definition of the displaced-homemaker population would probably bring women with more education or work experience into the group. Some privately funded programs do, in fact, serve women who are better prepared than those eligible for government programs.

Effects of Work Interruptions on Earnings and Job Opportunities

The major problem for reentrants is that the jobs they can obtain

---

[6] This estimate, which used 1976 CPS data, was made by Emily Andrews and is reported in Vanski, Nightengale, and O'Brien (1983).

are low paid.[7] According to human capital theory, the major determinants of wages are education, vocational training, and work experience, which provides on-the-job training.[8] An interruption in work experience can be expected to have an adverse effect on reentry pay for two reasons. First, any time spent out of the labor market will lessen the amount of work experience a person will have acquired by a given age. Second, job-related skills that are not utilized will depreciate (become rusty or in some cases obsolete).

Empirical research examining the effects of work interruptions on women's wages has consistently shown that the amount of women's previous work experience affects their wages. Support for the skill depreciation hypothesis is less clear. That work interruptions would cause skill depreciation appears plausible for persons holding high-skill jobs, but most middle-aged women who have been the subject of research on work interruptions had left jobs that required little specialized training. The predominant view appears to be that some deterioration in earnings capacity does occur during a work interruption, whether due to skill depreciation, loss of current information about job opportunities, or employers' preferences for hiring people with recent references.[9] Any or all of these factors might make it necessary for a labor market reentrant to take a job below her potential earnings capacity.

Mincer and Ofek (1982) observed a short period of rapid wage growth following reentry, which they attribute to "skill repair." Corcoran, Duncan, and Ponza (1983) point out that the wage growth might be due either to skill repair or to a trial period in which the reentrant's skills are assessed, either by the employer or by the reentrant herself, and a better job match secured. One study

---

[7] A study of the displaced-homemaker population in 1975 found that having pay below the minimum wage or having to accept part-time employment when full-time work was desired were more common problems than unemployment or dropping out of the labor force because of inability to find work (Vanski, Nightengale, and O'Brien, 1983).

[8] One of the first statements of human capital theory may be found in Becker (1964). Blaug (1976) provides a review of human capital research and a discussion of some of the problems with this approach.

[9] Large wage losses per year of work interruption were found by Mincer and Ofek (1982) and Mincer and Polachek (1978, 1974). Smaller losses, commonly 3–4 percent per year if measured near the point of reentry and as low as 1 percent or less after a few years of employment, have been found by Corcoran, Duncan, and Ponza (1983), Ferber and Birnbaum (1981), Corcoran and Duncan (1979), and Sandell and Shapiro (1978). A study of middle-aged reentrants found that three quarters had previously worked at occupations requiring less than a year to learn (Shaw, 1982); for these kinds of jobs skill depreciation is unlikely to have much long-term importance.

found that rapid wage growth was observed only for reentrants who changed employers in the first years after reentry (Shaw, 1984). This finding appears more congruent with an initial job mismatch than with skill repair as the cause of rapid wage growth. Of course, a period of rapid wage growth does not imply that work interruptions are not costly since any time out of the labor force will mean less work experience than would otherwise have been achieved.

Other information on how absences from the work force might affect the jobs reentrants obtain is more impressionistic. Directors of displaced-homemaker centers stress the need to build confidence through counselling and peer support groups, to offer practice in preparing for job interviews, and to provide information about the local job market and job search agencies. However, the fact that some centers offer refresher courses for women seeking clerical and nursing employment suggests that some women who formerly held jobs requiring specialized skills do find it useful to update their training (U.S. Congress, 1985).

Barriers to Better Jobs

From the perspective of an older woman worker without much recent work experience or with experience only in low-paid jobs, the outlook for obtaining well-paid employment is not promising. In 1986 the median earnings of all women workers who worked full time for the entire year were about $16,000 compared with nearly $26,000 for men.[10] Nearly one quarter of all year-round, full-time women workers earned less than $11,000. Median earnings for retail sales and service workers were about $10,000, for operatives $12,500, and for clerical workers $15,500. Since these occupations provide nearly 60 percent of employment of full-time women workers and a much higher percent for those without college or other specialized training, becoming self-supporting at a level approaching a middle-class standard of living presents a formidable problem for an older woman without much recent work experience or training.

Although their needs may be less pressing, other middle-aged women besides displaced homemakers are concerned with

---

[10] These figures are based on unpublished data from the March 1987 Current Population Survey, furnished by the Bureau of Labor Statistics.

acquiring new skills and obtaining better jobs. For many couples, financing their children's college education or preparing for financial security in old age may depend on wives' employment. In many black families especially, wives' earnings have been crucial for raising family income above the poverty line or achieving a middle-class standard of living. In addition, whatever the level of need of individual women and their families, we have widespread social consensus that barriers of age, sex, or race should not prevent people from moving into positions for which they are qualified.

The Need for Further Education and Training

The educational level of middle-aged women is well below that of younger women. In 1984 nearly 30 percent of women age 45–64 had not completed high school, compared with less than 15 percent of women age 22–34; only one quarter of the older women had completed at least one year of college compared with over 40 percent of the younger women (U.S. Bureau of the Census, 1986, Table 9). Older women were also less likely than older men to have completed at least one year of college.

The problem of upgrading the skills of disadvantaged older women is a difficult one. Most federally funded programs for disadvantaged workers have focused on youth or on workers displaced from long-term jobs. Although older women have participated in a variety of government-funded employment and training programs, displaced-homemaker programs provide the only ones specifically geared to the needs of middle-aged and older women.

No systematic research has been undertaken to evaluate displaced-homemaker programs. Studies of other training programs for disadvantaged workers have found that job training increases the earnings of women with little labor market experience (Bassi, 1983; Congressional Budget Office and National Commission for Employment Policy, 1982). However, the programs studied appear to have been less successful in training women for more than entry-level jobs (Harlan, 1985). Research is needed on what aspects of displaced-homemaker programs are most successful and on what kinds of job training provide the best prospects for helping older women to obtain better jobs.

In a survey of experienced directors of displaced-homemaker programs, a major problem identified was that many women find it impossible to work at a full-time job, manage a household, and participate in training even on a part-time basis. Many displaced homemakers need financial assistance to cover basic living expenses if they are to enroll in training programs, but funds for this purpose are very limited (U.S. Congress, 1985). Other problems mentioned include the need for some women to obtain basic literacy and mathematical skills before they can benefit from regular job training and the need for more encouragement for women to enter programs that offer training for nontraditional occupations that are better paid than the traditional jobs that older women tend to choose.[11]

Middle-aged women report considerable participation in job-related training. A study using the NLS found that between 1977 and 1981 about 16 percent of employed women reported participation in some kind of noncollege occupational training program that was not provided by their employers. About one quarter reported having participated in formal on-the-job training, but much of this training was of short duration, averaging 8 to 12 weeks (Shaw, 1983b). This study showed wage gains for women who had participated in on-the-job training or in some kinds of occupational training. However, occupational categories were too broadly defined to be very useful as a guide for job counselling. Appelbaum (1981) found that training leading to a professional certificate, but not clerical training, increased the wages of women with interrupted work careers.

Many older women have also obtained additional formal education in recent years. A study using the NLS found that about 4 percent of middle-aged women who had graduated from high school but not gone on to college had obtained their high school diplomas at age 35 or later; nearly 10 percent of black women with high school diplomas had obtained them at these ages (Morgan, 1986). A much larger percentage had attended college: 22 percent of women who were age 45–59 in 1982 had attended college at some time in the previous 15 years. However, among those who had attended college, only 15 percent had obtained a degree. In some cases, women may have been attending for recreational reasons or for limited objectives. For example, women whose most recent

---

[11] One study found that women in CETA training programs had a high probability of receiving training for traditional female jobs even if they expressed a preference for being trained for a traditionally male job (Waite and Berryman, 1984).

occupation was teaching or nursing were among those most likely to attend, and these women were probably renewing education or nursing credentials without necessarily wanting another degree. However, some women may have encountered difficulties, either financial or personal, that made continued attendance difficult.

In the past, educational institutions have not catered to the needs of part-time and older students. Returning women students, who are often employed and must attend part time, have faced such problems as lack of financial aid for part-time students, inflexibility in the scheduling of courses, and limited access to services such as counselling and job placement, which may not be available during evening hours.[12] The older woman may also have to deal with her own lack of confidence, uncertainty about career directions, sense of isolation, or opposition from family members.

Although many universities did open centers for the continuing education of women in the 1960s and 1970s, these were years when enrollment of traditional college-age students was soaring, and the needs of part-time and older students were often not adequately met. As the number of traditional students declines, colleges appear to be paying increasing attention to the needs of older returning students. Legislation passed in 1986 that will allow financial aid for part-time students may also make continuing college attendance possible for more middle-aged women who are seeking to upgrade their skills.

Sex Discrimination and the Kinds of Jobs Women Hold

The human capital research previously described has been the basis for attempting to show whether sex discrimination exists. Earnings differentials between women and men cannot be explained by differences in education and work experience alone. Commonly, not more than half of the differential can be explained by these human capital differences; some part of the remaining differential is usually attributed to sex discrimination.[13] However, it is possible that unmeasured productivity differences account for part or all of the unexplained earnings differences. Other

---

[12] See Tittle and Denker (1980) and Astin (1976) for overviews of some of the institutional barriers faced by older women students.

[13] Excellent reviews of theoretical and empirical research on sex discrimination may be found in Blau and Ferber (1986), Madden (1985), O'Neill (1985), and Cain (1984).

differences that have been shown to contribute to wage differentials include occupational differences (Treiman and Hartmann, 1981) and differences in college major and the kinds of rewards sought on the job (Daymont and Andrisani, 1984).

Some researchers believe that because of the heavier burden of household work they perform, women choose jobs that do not require as much effort or work involvement as men's jobs. Support for the view that women may seek less demanding jobs comes from a study of authority on the job, which is shown to be negatively correlated with responsibility for household tasks (D'Amico, 1986). Women's occupational segregation is also thought by some to be a result of the greater ease of combining stereotypically female jobs with family roles.[14] For example, female-dominated jobs may be chosen because they offer more opportunities for part-time employment than do male-dominated jobs (O'Neill, 1985).

Women's occupational choices may also be influenced by their perceptions of sex discrimination. Women may often be reluctant to enter male-dominated occupations; they may take the scarcity of women in an occupation to be a sign that women will encounter barriers to acceptance and advancement. A growing literature on the problems women encounter in male-dominated occupations attests to the relevance of this factor.[15]

Studies of company employment practices provide a different approach to investigating sex discrimination. The use of employee referrals when recruiting new workers, informal networks within companies from which "outsiders" such as women and minorities are excluded, and preferences for homogeneous work groups, which are believed to be more harmonious and productive, are some of the company practices found to limit opportunities for women and minorities (Roos and Reskin, 1984). Different promotion ladders for women and men and nearly complete segregation by job title were found in a study of 400 establishments in California (Bielby and Baron, 1984).

---

[14] Polachek (1981, 1979) has been a major proponent of this view, which he bases on the belief that skills depreciate more slowly in female-dominated occupations. However, other researchers such as England (1984, 1982) and Abowd and Killingsworth (1983) have not found evidence for differences in skill depreciation between male- and female-dominated occupations.

[15] See, for example, Kanter (1977) for women in management and Walshok (1981) for blue-collar workers. Also see discussions in Bergmann (1986) and Reskin and Hartmann (1986).

Women who are now past age 45 have undoubtedly encountered much more overt sex discrimination than is now legally
possible. Especially at the stage of making initial vocational choices,
preparing for nontraditional jobs was not encouraged by schools or
by what the woman herself might observe in the labor market. For
example, only after the antidiscrimination legislation of the 1960s
did it become illegal for employers to specify the desired sex of
applicants in job advertisements in newspapers. Many women who
are now in their fifties and sixties probably expected to remain full-
time housewives as their mothers had. Those who did expect to
work were well past the age of making initial vocational
commitments before a wider range of occupations began to appear
to be reasonable choices. Women in their forties have benefited
more from equal opportunity legislation, but most of these women
had also completed their educations before the legislation became
effective. Although older women have made some advances into
managerial jobs in recent years, younger women have accounted
for most of the increases in employment in the male-dominated
professional and managerial positions (Shaw, 1986a; Beller, 1984).

Whether many older women who have undertaken additional
education or training would have gone into nontraditional fields if
more training programs and supportive counselling had been
available is an open question. With relatively short remaining work
lives, older women may be unwilling to risk spending time on
training for an occupation in which they might find barriers to entry
or an inhospitable work environment.

If older women are, for the most part, already committed to
traditionally female occupations, raising wages in these occupations
becomes important for improving their earnings. In the 1970s
unions such as the American Federation of State, County, and
Municipal Employees brought suits charging that job evaluation
schemes were systematically biased in their ratings of typical
female jobs. Since that time, a number of states have undertaken
studies of state employee evaluation schemes and a few have
implemented pay increases for low-paid, predominantly female
jobs (Aaron and Lougy, 1986).

In the meantime, controversies have proliferated over the merits
of mandating equal pay for jobs judged by evaluation methods to
be of comparable worth. Proponents of comparable worth believe
that sex-biased evaluations are an important reason for women's

lower pay, while opponents believe that supply and demand in labor markets produce wages that accurately measure productivity.[16] One concern is that raising pay in female-dominated jobs might lead to increased unemployment among women. A study of the effect of raising minimum wage standards for women's occupations in Australia found rather small employment effects. However, the wage increases occurred at a time of rapid growth in industries that traditionally employ women (Gregory and Duncan, 1981). Some research suggests that the overall impact of pay equity schemes on the male-female earnings gap would be small because only wage differentials within companies or governmental units would be affected. Wage differentials between industries and between different companies within the same industry would remain.[17] However, some women working for companies or state governments that implemented pay equity would undoubtedly benefit. As more implementation occurs, additional research on the impact of comparable worth on wages and employment will be possible.

Age Discrimination

Public opinion polls show widespread agreement that older workers face age discrimination. Even employers agree with this perception, though they are usually unwilling to admit that they themselves practice it (McConnell, 1983). However, the extent of age discrimination and its importance for older women workers is not known. Research in this area is difficult and the little that exists is more likely to consider men than women. One problem is that if systematic differences in pay are found between older and younger workers with similar characteristics, it is hard to determine whether these differences are due to unmeasured differences in productivity or to discrimination. Another is that older workers who can find only poorly paid employment may drop out of the labor force entirely, so that comparisons between older and younger workers may not adequately reflect the disadvantages that older people face.

---

[16] In addition to Aaron and Lougy, see Remick (1984), Gold (1983), and Livernash (1980) for further discussion of the arguments on both sides.

[17] Johnson and Solon (1984) estimate that even if pay equity schemes were widely mandated, no more than 10 percent of the male-female earnings gap would be eliminated.

A few studies have attempted to determine whether wages decline with age after controlling for other worker characteristics, but most of this research pertains to older men. In one study of men and unmarried women, the earnings of older men but not women were found to decline with age (Hanoch and Honig, 1983). However, a study of earnings and promotion in a large company found that, after controlling for level of the first job and other worker characteristics, the age when both men and women first joined the company had a negative effect on their advancement (Rosenbaum, 1984).

Another line of research has attempted to document age discrimination by asking employers to answer questions on whether hypothetical job candidates would be hired or considered for promotion.[18] Again most of these studies have been confined to men. One study, which asked personnel specialists to rate secretaries, found no age-related differences in recommendations for promotion or salary increase (Schwab and Heneman, 1978). On the other hand, employers were less willing to hire 55-year-old than 25-year-old hypothetical applicants and also preferred men to women for semiskilled jobs even though the descriptions of competence were identical (Haefner, 1977). Although research of this kind is often suggestive of discrimination, the limited kinds of occupations involved and small sample sizes make generalization impossible.

Another approach to studying age discrimination is through examination of complaints and lawsuits filed under the Age Discrimination in Employment Act (ADEA). In a study of age discrimination charges filed in 1981, the complaint rate of women was slightly lower than that of men (McConnell, 1983). In a study of actual lawsuits under ADEA, Schuster and Miller (1984) found that women were more likely to be involved in cases concerning hiring, promotion, or wages and fringe benefits, whereas men were more frequently involved in cases of termination and early retirement. Women were found to be more likely to win their suits than men. The authors speculated that this result may have been due to women having the additional protection of legislation against sex discrimination, to courts being more responsive to the kinds of claims brought by women, or to companies being less prepared to

---

[18] See Doering, Rhodes, and Schuster (1983) for a review of this literature.

defend cases at the clerical level where the majority of female plaintiffs are employed.

If some employers have informal upper age limits on hiring for certain positions or if they have perceptions of appropriate ages for reaching certain job levels, any such hiring or promotion policies based on age would be particularly detrimental for older women who have not been continuously employed. Especially for hiring, this kind of discrimination may be difficult for individuals to detect because most people have little information about other job applicants and their qualifications. There may also be age-related barriers to receiving training. One study found that some offices of the Employment Service were less likely to provide job counselling or suggest training for women age 45 and over than for younger women (Pursell and Torrence, 1980).

Family Obligations That Interfere with Steady Employment

After first reentering the labor market following childbearing, many women have additional work interruptions, often associated with having additional children or with the needs of their families. However, by the time they reach middle age, fewer women have work interruptions associated with family obligations. A study of women age 40–54 in 1977 found that about 20 percent of women workers said they had left their last jobs for family-related reasons (Shaw, 1983a). One family circumstance leading to work interruptions at this age was moving to a different locality—often in response to the husband's job opportunities. Sandell (1977) found that migration led to lower earnings for married women, at least in the short run.

Another cause of work interruption may be a husband's health problem. Although in some cases the effect of husbands' health problems may be in the opposite direction, causing women to assume more responsibility for the family's support, some research suggests that the predominant effect is to cause women to leave the labor force or reduce their hours of work to provide care (Haurin, 1986; Gitter, Shaw, and Gagen, 1986). In 1982 about 4 percent of white married women and 9 percent of black married women age 45–59 said that the ill health of a family member limited their work (Gitter, Shaw, and Gagen, 1986). Although some of the family members with health problems were children and a few were parents, husbands constituted the largest single category.

In recent years with the rising cost of nursing home care and the increasing size of the population over age 75, the group at greatest risk of needing this care, the idea of providing more incentives for home-based care has become popular. The implications for the probable caregivers—most commonly older women—have frequently not been considered. A recent study of the caregivers of noninstitutionalized disabled elderly people found that about three quarters of the primary caregivers were women. Wives and daughters were the major caregivers among women, but husbands also provided a substantial amount of care (Stone, Cafferta, and Sangl, 1988). Women not only provided the major portion of care, but were also more likely to have caregiving responsibilities while still middle-aged. Daughters, especially, were more likely to be employed and to report conflicts between work and caregiving than were either wives or husbands, most of whom were age 65 or older. However, about 12 percent of both spouses and daughters reported having to quit a job to provide care. For some middle-aged women, caregiving for the elderly could come at the expense of being able to provide for their own economic security in old age.

Other Causes of Work Interruptions

Some causes of work interruptions and early retirement are probably not substantially different for women and men. Both sexes encounter health problems that limit their ability to work, and some older workers of both sexes experience displacement from long-term jobs. These topics have been discussed in other chapters of this volume. Here I will mention briefly research pertaining specifically to women workers and suggest ways in which these problems could be somewhat different for women and men.

Health appears to be an important cause of labor market withdrawal for older women (Gitter, Shaw, and Gagen, 1986; Chirikos and Nestel, 1985, 1983; Hanoch and Honig, 1983; Shaw, 1983a). However, the measures of health used in these studies are self-reported. They are thus subject to the same controversies that have surrounded research on men's health as a factor in labor force withdrawal (see Parnes, Chapter 5 in this volume). Because fewer women than men work at jobs that are physically demanding, it might be expected that women would be less likely than men to have health problems that limit their ability to work. One analysis found that among recently retired workers 47 percent of men, but only 29 percent of women, had last worked at jobs with medium or heavy strength requirements (U.S. Department of Health and Human Services, 1986). However, these figures were not adjusted to reflect differences in average strength between women and men.

Most of the research on job loss among long-term workers has focused on men, who are more likely than women to be long-tenured and to be employed in the declining manufacturing industries that have received the most attention. Women job-losers have also generally lost jobs that paid much lower wages than those of male job-losers. A recently completed study of older women job-losers with two or more years of job tenure showed reemployment at lower wages among women who lost better-paid jobs, whereas lower-paid workers showed little wage loss but a much higher probability of remaining unemployed or leaving the labor force (Gagen, 1987). Additional research on this subject should provide insight into the problems of the growing number of women who are long-service workers.

Women and Retirement

The factors that affect age of retirement are discussed in another chapter of this volume. Here we focus on the relationship between employment at older ages and economic security after retirement. Although most women will be eligible for Social Security benefits either on their own work records or as dependents or survivors, women who do not have other sources of retirement income have a much higher risk of becoming poor in old age than those who have pensions or those who continue to work beyond the usual retirement age. In 1984 the most vulnerable elderly women, those living alone, had an overall poverty rate of 25 percent. However, among those who were either employed or had a pension other than Social Security, only 5 percent were poor (U.S. Bureau of the Census, 1986, Table 11). The importance of pensions as a supplement to Social Security points up the importance of older women being able to move into jobs that provide pensions. The importance of continued employment beyond the usual retirement age raises questions about the kinds of work available to women workers in their sixties and seventies and the continued ability to work at advanced ages.

Problems of Pension Coverage and Entitlement

In 1984, 31 percent of nonmarried women ages 65–69 had

pension income other than Social Security either from their own jobs or in the form of survivor benefits from their husbands' pensions. Among married couples in this age range, 54 percent were receiving pension income (U.S. Department of Health and Human Services, 1985). As women who are now middle-aged move into retirement, these percentages may increase. Nearly one half of nonmarried women age 45–59 in the 1982 NLS expected to have pension income either from their own work or from survivor benefits from their husbands' pensions (Shaw, 1986b). Although these expectations may not be completely realized, the greater work attachment of this generation of women, together with recent changes in pension law, will probably lead to somewhat increased pension receipt when they retire.[19] However, some influences may be working in the opposite direction; pension coverage appears to have stabilized for working women and declined slightly for working men between 1979 and 1983 (Beller, 1986).

The most recent source of national data on pension coverage is the 1983 Current Population Survey (CPS) pension supplement. Andrews (1985), using this data set to estimate rates of coverage for all wage and salary workers, found that slightly over half of employed women were covered by pension plans; coverage was defined as working for an employer with a pension plan. However, because some employees are not included in their employers' pension plans, actual plan participation is a more relevant measure.[20] Beller (1986), using the same data to measure actual participation rates in private industry plans only, found that about 41 percent of full-time women workers were participating in a pension plan, but when part-time workers were considered as well, only about one-third of all women workers participated. However, participation is known to be much higher in the public sector. Snyder (1986), using data from the Social Security Administration's 1982 New Beneficiary Survey (NBS), found that 39 percent of women working in the private sector had participated in a pension

---

[19] For example, the likelihood of receiving survivor benefits from their husbands' pensions may be enhanced by the Retirement Equity Act of 1984, which requires that pension plans offering life annuities must provide survivor benefits unless the spouse waives her (or his) right to the benefit.

[20] This use of the terms "coverage" and "participation" appears to be widespread, though by no means universal, among pension analysts. However, common usage probably understands coverage to mean that a person is participating in a pension plan. Hence, use of the term "coverage" without explicit definition can be misleading.

on their longest job compared with 82 percent of women whose longest job was in the public sector.

In these studies men's coverage or participation exceeded that of women by 7 to 10 percentage points.[21] If only workers who are already vested (i.e., entitled to receive benefits or lump-sum distributions) are considered, the disparity is even larger.In Beller's study, 44 percent of women participants and 55 percent of male participants were vested. These figures include workers of all ages. Among women age 45–64, Beller found that about half of women full-time workers in private industry were participants. Vesting was also higher than among younger workers.

The major reasons that women's coverage, participation, and vesting are lower than men's involve their shorter average job tenure and the greater extent of their part-time employment. The kind of jobs they hold is another important factor. Pension coverage is high in durable goods manufacturing, communications, and utilities—industries that employ relatively few women—and low in retail trade and many service industries where women predominate (Andrews, 1985; Snyder, 1986). Other factors favoring pension coverage include firm size and unionization. Here again, women are less likely than men to work in firms with more than 500 employees, to be covered by a union contract, or to work in industries where coverage is high. In addition, high-wage workers are much more likely to be covered than are low-wage workers (Andrews, 1985).

Although Andrews found no significant difference in coverage between men and women after controlling for the factors discussed above, women and low-wage workers were less likely than men to report actually participating in a pension plan. One reason for this lower participation may be that in some pension plans workers' participation depends on their making contributions; low-wage workers of both sexes may feel unable to contribute, and women may not want to contribute if their husbands have pensions. A second reason may be that under the Employee Retirement Income Security Act (ERISA), employers could exclude up to 30 percent of their employees from pension plans even if they met minimum age and service requirements. No systematic information is available on the characteristics of workers who were excluded, but some

---

[21] Since both the CPS and the NBS depend on self-reporting of pension status, it may not always be clear to respondents whether the question refers to coverage or participation as defined above.

researchers believe that women may have been disproportionately affected. The Tax Reform Act of 1986 makes participation rules more stringent, but still allows some workers to be excluded (Congressional Budget Office, 1987). Additional data and research are needed on excluded workers and effects of the new legislation.

Among participants in pension plans, women are less likely than men to become vested largely because of their shorter job tenure. In the past most private pension plans have required 10 years of service before vesting. About 30 percent of newly retired women in the NBS had worked less than 10 years on the longest job they had ever held, as compared with less than 8 percent of men (Snyder, 1986). As part of the 1986 tax reform legislation, most private pension plans will be required in the future to reduce their vesting requirements to five years. This legislation should increase pension receipt among women, but the benefit amounts will probably be quite small in most cases.

A final reason for women's low rate of pension receipt is again related to low wages and short job tenure. Women are more likely than men to receive a lump-sum distribution in lieu of a monthly pension benefit. Over 20 percent of recently retired women, compared with 10 percent of men, covered by a private pension on their longest job received a lump-sum distribution (Snyder, 1986). Under ERISA lump-sum distributions are allowable for defined contribution plans, which are the most common type among small employers, but are allowed under defined benefit plans only if the value of the benefit is below quite low limits.[22]

Although women's pension receipt may continue to increase in the near future as women with more work experience reach retirement age, the long-run outlook for increasing pension coverage and receipt among women is not clear. The shift in employment out of manufacturing into services will affect men's pension coverage more than women's; a continuing decline in unionization would also affect men most. However, any trend toward greater concentration of employment in small firms would adversely affect women's pension coverage as well as men's. Whether increased tenure on jobs that do have pensions will offset such industrial shifts is not clear. Any decline in pension coverage

---

[22] The Retirement Equity Act of 1984 allows cashouts of pension benefits that have a present value of less than $3,500.

among men will also have an adverse effect on the probability of an elderly couple's having a pension and on widows receiving survivor benefits. If fewer men have pensions in the future, the importance of women's gaining pensions on the basis of their own employment will increase.

When women do have pensions, their benefits are considerably smaller than men's. A comparison based on the 1983 CPS found that women's benefits were, on average, about half those of men (McCarthy, 1986). However, when replacement rates per year of employment were calculated, the median replacement rate for women was 82 percent of that of men, and women's mean replacement rate was actually slightly larger than men's. (McCarthy did not attempt to explain this difference.) In any event, this analysis suggests that the difference between women's and men's benefits is largely explained by differences in wages and job tenure, the two major elements usually determining pension amounts.

Although pension plans cannot incorporate rules that discriminate against women directly, rules that give proportionately smaller pensions to low-wage or short-service workers will have a larger impact on women than on men. One rule that makes pensions relatively smaller for short-tenure workers than for long-tenure workers calls for larger benefit accruals as tenure increases. A second provision that has had an adverse impact on low-wage workers has been the integration of pensions with Social Security benefits. In pension plans with this feature, pensions are reduced by various formulas based on the size of the employee's Social Security benefit or the employer's contribution to the Social Security account of the employee; in the past these rules sometimes caused the pension to be eliminated entirely.[23] The Tax Reform Act of 1986 limited reductions that will be allowable under integration formulas.

A final problem for short-tenure workers is that many pension plans are based on salary in the last few years of employment. Under this kind of pension formula, a person who changes employers several times over the course of a career will have smaller pension benefits than a person who remains with one employer even if vested rights have accrued in all pensions and the

---

[23] For a discussion of the different kinds of rules under which private pension plans may be integrated with Social Security benefits, see U.S. General Accounting Office (1986) and Bell and Hall (1984).

total work experience and salary history of the two are the same. This is the case because salaries on earlier jobs are likely to be lower than the salary on the last job, and earlier job salaries are not indexed for inflation. Therefore pensions from the earlier jobs will have low current-dollar values when the person retires.[24] Even women with fairly extensive work experience may have small pension benefits if they have changed employers to accommodate their husbands' careers or upon returning to the labor force following other interruptions.

Working Beyond Normal Retirement Age

As discussed by Rones in Chapter 2, the work activity of both women and men decreases rapidly after age 60, and once retired, the majority do not return to work. However, there are a number of differences between women and men who continue to work at these older ages. Although both sexes show increasing employment in sales and service occupations, the largest single employment category for women remains administrative support occupations (primarily clerical work). As the figures on occupational distributions suggest, men are overrepresented in professional and managerial jobs at older ages (see Chapter 2, Table 5). Probably many continue to be employed as independent professionals or as high-ranking executives. However, older women are underrepresented in professional and managerial occupations. Few older women hold the kinds of jobs in these categories that older men hold. Most women professionals are teachers or nurses—jobs that are not so easy to continue at older ages. Perhaps in part because of this different job mix, men who continue to work at older ages are more likely than women to work at year-round, full-time jobs.

An interesting perspective on work after retirement can be gained by comparing women and men who continue to work after beginning to receive Social Security benefits. Although labor force participation rates of men are considerably higher than those of women at age 62 and above, if we look only at those who were drawing Social Security benefits as retired workers, women and men were equally likely to continue working; close to 20 percent were employed about a year after first receiving benefits (Holden,

[24] See Congressional Budget Office (1987) for examples of the effects of pension rules on workers who have work and salary experiences that are identical except for the number of employers.

1987; Iams, 1986). Furthermore, if only those who were working shortly before beginning to receive benefits are compared, women were more likely than men to continue working.[25]

There are probably several reasons why women with recent work experience were more likely than men to continue working after receiving Social Security benefits. The most important predictors of continued employment for women were marital status and receipt of another pension in addition to Social Security (Iams, 1986). Over 40 percent of unmarried women and 20 percent of married women without pensions were employed, compared with under 10 percent of both married and unmarried women with pensions. The amount of income other than earnings was also an extremely important predictor of employment, especially for unmarried women. Nearly half of unmarried women with other income of less than $500 per month were employed. These findings suggest that the higher employment rates of female retired workers compared with their male counterparts reflect their lower economic status. Women are less likely to have other pensions, and their Social Security benefits are lower, on average. In addition, because women earn less, they are more likely to be able to continue working, at least part time, without exceeding the Social Security earnings test, currently $6,120 per year before age 65.

Women were more likely to continue working if they had previously worked in sales or service occupations or were self-employed. Private household workers had the highest rate of continued employment, probably reflecting lack of a pension, low income, and the availability of part-time work in private households. Snyder (1987) found that women were more likely than men to remain in the same occupation if they continued to work after retirement. Thus the downward occupational mobility seen in the post-retirement jobs of men is less common for women, partly because many of those who continue to work were already in low-status, low-paying jobs.

Health limitations also influence post-retirement employment of both women and men (Iams, 1986). Especially among unmarried women with limited economic resources, health problems appear to be limiting the possibility of supplementing retirement income,

---

[25] For looking at retirement behavior, this kind of comparison is more meaningful than comparison of participation rates because persons with similar pre-retirement work attachments are being compared.

even in the early years of retirement. As these women age, fewer
will be able to work. A few may still become eligible for pensions
through their continued employment, but many others may be
counted among the elderly poor when they are no longer able to
work.

Summary and Conclusions

The special problems that confront older women workers today
are to a considerable extent due to their prior work patterns, which
for most women were characterized by work interruptions while
raising children. Traditional social norms, widely practiced sex
discrimination, and poor economic circumstances when they were
young also influenced vocational and educational choices and
precluded some kinds of careers for today's older women.
Increasing divorce rates meant that women who had not planned
for extensive work careers were forced to become self-supporting.

How will the problems of older women workers change in the
years ahead when women with very different work backgrounds
reach their middle and older years? To answer this question we
must first consider how much change has actually occurred. One
factor that should improve the employment prospects of future
generations is that older women in the future will be much better
educated than their counterparts today. Few will have less than a
high school education and many will be college graduates.

As to changes in work experience, we sometimes tend to believe
that few women will have had work interruptions, but this view
confuses high labor force participation rates with steady
employment. For example, in 1984 slightly over 60 percent of
women whose youngest child was under age 6 had worked during
the previous year, but only 27 percent had worked full time for at
least 40 weeks, and almost 40 percent had not worked at all (U.S.
Bureau of the Census, 1986). Similarly, 72 percent of women whose
youngest child was age 6–17 had worked for at least part of the
year, but only 42 percent had worked full time for 40 weeks or
more, and 28 percent had not been employed at any time.
Especially in the years when they have preschool children, most
women do not now engage in continuous full-time employment.

When they reach middle age, the next generation of women will
undoubtedly have more work experience than older women today.
However, a great diversity of work patterns can be expected.

Changing patterns can be monitored with data from the younger NLS samples. In one such study of women who were age 24–34 in 1978 (and are now age 33–43), Mott and Shapiro (1982) found that in the approximately seven years after the birth of their first child, only 12 percent of women had worked at least six months in all years and 30 percent had not worked as much as six months in any year. Among women who are still younger than these, the percentage of continuously employed women will surely increase and the percentage with long work interruptions will decrease, but as shown in the CPS figures cited above, many women will continue to experience work interruptions, and intermittent work patterns will continue to be common. The displaced homemaker who has difficulty becoming self-supporting will become less common but is not likely to completely disappear. The trend toward later childbearing could mean that older women in the future have more family responsibilities than older women today; we do not know what effect this trend will have on work patterns and employment problems.[26]

An important consideration is the quality of work experience acquired by women who work intermittently or part time. Do the kinds of jobs they hold provide work experience that would help a woman to become self-supporting, or are they mainly low-skilled jobs that are only viewed as a means of supplementing family income? An important question for further research is whether part-time employment is a viable means of keeping up current work skills or acquiring new ones. Research on older women has tended to show either no earnings growth associated with part-time employment (Corcoran, Duncan, and Ponza, 1983) or considerably slower earnings growth than for full-time employment (Shaw, 1984; Jones and Long, 1979). However, it is possible that the nature of part-time work is changing, and that in the future women who have invested in lengthy training will seek opportunities to continue to work at their usual occupations on less than a full-time basis in order to maintain their skills.[27]

---

[26] However, it is possible that the trend toward smaller families may offset the trend toward later childbearing, so that the average age of women at the birth of their last child will not increase.

[27] Kahne (1985) argues that new policies on part-time employment would benefit women and older workers as well as employers. She envisions an increase in part-time jobs that provide for career progression and prorated fringe benefits. She cites the Federal Employees Part-Time Career Act and describes numerous private industry plans as examples of the kind of part-time employment that might become common in the future.

In an economy undergoing industrial transformation, more research is needed on the effects of job displacement for women workers. Textiles, shoes, and electronics, industries that employ many women, are all under intense pressure from foreign competition. A much reduced demand for clerical workers has been predicted, but has so far not materialized.[28] Additional research on what kinds of training are most beneficial for older women could improve programs for both women displaced from long-term jobs and for displaced homemakers.

Research on pensions and retirement will undoubtedly continue to receive much attention as the population ages. More of the research on this subject should focus on the problems of women, who make up 60 percent of the elderly population. Our private pension system receives considerable subsidies from favorable tax treatment. Increasing concern has been expressed as to whether well-paid, long-tenured workers are being subsidized at the expense of lower-paid workers and those who have changed jobs (Congressional Budget Office, 1987). Because of women's employment patterns, this is an important issue for women workers. Research on the effects of the many changes in pension laws recently enacted and currently proposed should consider effects on women as well as men. Finally, the kinds of jobs women hold and their ability to continue working well into their sixties will become an increasingly important area to monitor as the normal age of retirement is increased to 67 under Social Security.

References

Aaron, Henry J., and Cameran M. Lougy. *The Comparable Worth Controversy.* Washington: The Brookings Institution, 1986.
Abowd, John, and Mark P. Killingsworth. "Sex Discrimination, Atrophy, and the Male-Female Wage Differential." *Industrial Relations* 22 (Fall 1983), pp. 387–402.
Andrews, Emily S. *The Changing Profile of Pensions in America.* Washington: Employee Benefits Research Institute, 1985.
Appelbaum, Eileen. *Back to Work: Determinants of Women's Successful Reentry.* Boston: Auburn House, 1981.
Astin, Helen S. *Some Action of Her Own: The Adult Woman and Higher Education.* Lexington, MA: D.C. Heath, 1976.
Bassi, Laurie J. "The Effects of CETA on Postprogram Earnings of Participants." *Journal of Human Resources* 18 (Fall 1983), pp. 539–56.

---

[28] An estimate by Leontief shows full office automation reducing the percentage of the labor force employed in clerical jobs from 18 to 12 percent (*Scientific American*, September 1984, p. 82). The major impact would fall on women, who are the majority of clerical workers.

Becker, Gary S. *Human Capital.* New York: National Bureau of Economic Research, 1964.

Bell, Donald, and Diane Hall. "How Social Security Payments Affect Private Pensions." *Monthly Labor Review* 107 (May 1984), pp. 15-20.

Beller, Andrea H. "Trends in Occupational Segregation by Sex and Race, 1960-1981." In *Sex Segregation in the Workplace: Trends, Explanations, Remedies,* ed. Barbara F. Reskin. Washington: National Academy Press, 1984.

Beller, Daniel J. "Coverage and Vesting in Private Pension Plans, 1972-1983." In *The Handbook of Pension Statistics,* eds. Richard A. Ippolito and Walter W. Kolodrubetz. Chicago: Commerce Clearing House, 1986. Pp. 53-118.

Bergmann, Barbara R. *The Economic Emergence of Women.* New York: Basic Books, 1986.

Bielby, William J., and James N. Baron. "A Woman's Place Is With Other Women: Sex Segregation Within Organizations." In *Sex Segregation in the Workplace: Trends, Explanations, Remedies,* ed. Barbara F. Reskin. Washington: National Academy Press, 1984.

Blau, Francine D., and Marianne A. Ferber. *The Economics of Women, Men, and Work.* Englewood Cliffs, NJ: Prentice-Hall, 1986.

Blaug, Mark. "The Empirical Status of Human Capital Theory: A Slightly Jaundiced Survey." *Journal of Economic Literature* 14 (September 1976), pp. 827-55.

Cain, Glen G. "The Economic Analysis of Labor Market Discrimination: A Survey." Special Report No. 37. Madison: Institute for Research on Poverty, University of Wisconsin, 1984.

Chafe, William H. *The American Woman.* New York: Oxford University Press, 1972.

Chirikos, Thomas N., and Gilbert Nestel. "Economic Consequences of Poor Health in Mature Women." In *Unplanned Careers: The Working Lives of Middle-Aged Women,* ed. Lois B. Shaw. Lexington, MA: D.C. Heath, 1983.

_____. "Further Evidence on Economic Effects of Poor Health." *Review of Economics and Statistics* 67 (February 1985), pp. 61-69.

Congressional Budget Office. *Tax Policy for Pensions and Other Retirement Saving.* Washington: U.S. Government Printing Office, 1987.

Congressional Budget Office and National Commission for Employment Policy. *CETA Training Programs: Do They Work for Adults?* Washington: Congressional Budget Office, 1982.

Corcoran, Mary E., and Greg J. Duncan. "Work History, Labor Force Attachment, and Earnings Differences Between Races and Sexes." *Journal of Human Resources* 14 (Winter 1979), pp. 3-20.

Corcoran, Mary E., Greg J. Duncan, and Michael Ponza. "A Longitudinal Analysis of White Women's Wages." *Journal of Human Resources* 18 (Fall 1983), pp. 497-520.

D'Amico, Ronald. "Authority in the Workplace: Differences Among Mature Women." In *Midlife Women at Work: A Fifteen-Year Perspective,* ed. Lois B. Shaw. Lexington, MA: D.C. Heath, 1986.

Daymont, Thomas N., and Paul J. Andrisani. "Job Preferences, College Major, and the Gender Gap in Earnings." *Journal of Human Resources* 19 (Summer 1984), pp. 408-28.

Dex, Shirley, and Lois B. Shaw. *British and American Women at Work: Do Equal Opportunities Policies Matter?* London: Macmillan, Ltd., 1986.

Doering, Mildred, Susan R. Rhodes, and Michael Schuster. *The Aging Worker.* Beverly Hills, CA: Sage, 1983.

England, Paula. "Wage Appreciation and Depreciation: A Test of Neoclassical Economic Explanations of Occupational Sex Segregation." *Social Forces* 62 (March 1984), pp. 726-49.

_____. "The Failure of Human Capital Theory to Explain Occupational Sex Segregation." *Journal of Human Resources* 17 (Summer 1982), pp. 358-70.

Ferber, Marianne A., and Bonnie G. Birnbaum. "Labor Force Participation Patterns and Earnings of Clerical Workers." *Journal of Human Resources* 16 (Summer 1981), pp. 416-25.

Gagen, Mary G. "Job Displacement of Established Women Workers: Correlates and Employment Consequences." Ph.D. dissertation, The Ohio State University, 1987.

Gitter, Robert G., Lois B. Shaw, and Mary G. Gagen. "Early Labor Market Withdrawal." In *Midlife Women at Work: A Fifteen-Year Perspective*, ed. Lois B. Shaw. Lexington, MA: D.C. Heath, 1986.

Gold, Michael Evans. *A Debate on Comparable Worth*. Ithaca, NY: ILR Press, 1983.

Gregory, R. G., and R. C. Duncan. "Segmented Labor Market Theories and the Australian Experience of Equal Pay for Women." *Journal of Post-Keynesian Economics* 3 (Spring 1981), pp. 403–28.

Haefner, James E. "Race, Age, Sex and Competence as Factors in Employer Selection of the Disadvantaged." *Journal of Applied Psychology* 62 (1977), pp. 199–202.

Hanoch, Giora, and Marjorie Honig. "Retirement, Wages, and Labor Supply of the Elderly." *Journal of Labor Economics* 1 (1983), pp. 131–51.

Harlan, Sharon L. "Federal Job Training Policy and Disadvantaged Women." In *Women and Work: An Annual Review*, Vol. 1, eds. Laurie Larwood, Ann H. Stromberg, and Barbara A. Gutek. Beverly Hills, CA: Sage, 1985.

Haurin, Donald R. "Women's Labor Market Reactions to Family Disruptions, Husband's Unemployment, or Disability." In *Midlife Women at Work: A Fifteen-Year Perspective*, ed. Lois B. Shaw. Lexington, MA: D.C. Heath, 1986.

Holden, Karen C. "Work after Benefit Receipt: Do the Characteristics of Jobs Make a Difference?" Discussion paper, Institute for Research on Poverty, University of Wisconsin, 1987.

Iams, Howard M. "Employment of Retired-Worker Women." *Social Security Bulletin* 49 (March 1986), pp. 5–13.

Johnson, George, and Gary Solon. "Pay Differences Between Women's and Men's Jobs: The Empirical Foundations of Comparable Worth Legislation." National Bureau of Economic Research Working Paper No. 1472, 1984.

Jones, Ethel B., and James E. Long. "Part-Week Work and Human Capital Investment by Married Women." *Journal of Human Resources* 14 (Fall 1979), pp. 563–77.

Jusenius, Carol L., and Herbert S. Parnes. "Introduction and Overview." In *Dual Careers, Volume 4*, R and D. Monograph 21, U.S. Department of Labor, Employment and Training Administration, 1976.

Kahne, Hilda. *Reconceiving Part-Time Work: New Perspectives for Older Workers and Women*. Totowa, NJ: Rowman and Allanheld, 1985.

Kanter, Rosabeth Moss. *Men and Women of the Corporation*. New York: Basic Books, 1977.

Livernash, E. Robert, ed. *Comparable Worth: Issues and Alternatives*. Washington: Equal Opportunities Council, 1980.

Madden, Janice F. "The Persistence of Pay Differentials: The Economics of Sex Discrimination." In *Women and Work: An Annual Review*, Vol. 1, eds. Laurie Larwood, Ann H. Stromberg, and Barbara A. Gutek. Beverly Hills, CA: Sage, 1985.

McCarthy, David. "Private Pension Benefit Levels." In *The Handbook of Pension Statistics 1985*, eds. Richard A. Ippolito and Walter W. Kolodrubetz. Chicago: Commerce Clearing House, 1986. Pp. 119–76.

McConnell, Stephen R. "Age Discrimination in Employment." In *Policy Issues in Work and Retirement*, ed. Herbert S. Parnes. Kalamazoo, MI: W.E. Upjohn Institute for Employment Research, 1983.

Mincer, Jacob, and Haim Ofek. "Interrupted Work Careers: Depreciation and Restoration of Human Capital." *Journal of Human Resources* 17 (Winter 1982), pp. 3–24.

Mincer, Jacob, and Solomon Polachek. "Family Investments in Human Capital: Earnings of Women." *Journal of Political Economy* 82 (March/April 1974), pp. S76–S106.

――――. "An Exchange: The Theory of Human Capital and the Earnings of Women: Women's Earnings Reexamined." *Journal of Human Resources* 13 (Winter 1978), pp. 118–34.

Morgan, William R. "Returning to School at Midlife: Mature Women with Educational Careers." In *Midlife Women at Work: A Fifteen-Year Perspective*, ed. Lois B. Shaw. Lexington, MA: D.C. Heath, 1986.
Mott, Frank L., and David Shapiro. "Continuity of Work Attachment Among Young Mothers." In *The Employment Revolution*, ed. Frank L. Mott. Cambridge, MA: MIT Press, 1982.
Mott, Frank L., and Lois B. Shaw. "The Employment Consequences of Different Fertility Behaviors." In *Midlife Women at Work: A Fifteen-Year Perspective*, ed. Lois B. Shaw. Lexington, MA: D.C. Heath, 1986.
Myrdal, Alva, and Viola Klein. *Women's Two Roles*. London: Routledge and Kegan Paul, 1956.
O'Brien, Carolyn Taylor, and Demetra Smith Nightengale. "Programs for Displaced Homemakers in the 1970s." Discussion paper. Washington: The Urban Institute, 1985.
O'Neill, June. "Role Differentiation and the Gender Gap." In *Women and Work: An Annual Review*, Vol. 1, eds. Laurie Larwood, Ann H. Stromberg, and Barbara A. Gutek. Beverly Hills, CA: Sage, 1985.
Oppenheimer, Valerie Kincade. *The Female Labor Force in the United States*. Berkeley: Institute for International Studies, University of California, 1970.
Parnes, Herbert S. "The National Longitudinal Surveys: New Vistas for Labor Market Research." *American Economic Review* 65 (May 1975), pp. 244–49.
Polachek, Solomon W. "Occupational Self-Selection: A Human Capital Approach to Occupational Structure." *Review of Economics and Statistics* 63 (February 1981), pp. 60–69.
_____. "Occupational Segregation Among Women: Theory, Evidence, and a Prognosis." In *Women in the Labor Markets*, eds. Cynthia B. Lloyd, Emily S. Andrews, and Curtis L. Gilroy. New York: Columbia University Press, 1979.
Pursell, Donald E., and Willard D. Torrence. "The Older Woman and Her Search for Employment." *Aging and Work* 3 (Spring 1980), pp. 121–28.
Remick, Helen, ed. *Comparable Worth and Wage Discrimination*. Philadelphia: Temple University Press, 1984.
Reskin, Barbara F., and Heidi I. Hartmann. *Women's Work, Men's Work: Sex Segregation on the Job*. Washington: National Academy Press, 1986.
Roos, Patricia A., and Barbara F. Reskin. "Institutional Factors Contributing to Sex Segregation in the Workplace." In *Sex Segregation in the Workplace: Trends, Explanations, Remedies*, ed. Barbara F. Reskin. Washington: National Academy Press, 1984.
Rosenbaum, James E. *Career Mobility in a Corporate Hierarchy*. Orlando, FL: Academic Press, 1984.
Sandell, Steven. "Women and the Economics of Family Migration." *Review of Economics and Statistics* 59 (November 1977), pp. 406–14.
Sandell, Steven, and David Shapiro. "The Theory of Human Capital and the Earnings of Women: A Reexamination of the Evidence." *Journal of Human Resources* 13 (Winter 1978), pp. 103–17.
Schuster, Michael, and Christopher S. Miller. "An Empirical Assessment of the Age Discrimination in Employment Act." *Industrial and Labor Relations Review* 38 (October 1984), pp. 64–74.
Schwab, Donald P., and Herbert G. Heneman III. "Age Stereotyping in Performance Appraisal." *Journal of Applied Psychology* 63 (1978), pp. 573–78.
Shaw, Lois B. "Introduction and Overview." In *Midlife Women at Work: A Fifteen-Year Perspective*, ed. Lois B. Shaw. Lexington, MA: D.C. Heath, 1986a.
_____. "Looking Toward Retirement: Plans and Prospects." In *Midlife Women at Work: A Fifteen-Year Perspective*, ed. Lois B. Shaw. Lexington, MA: D.C. Heath, 1986b.
_____. "Determinants of Wage Growth after Labor Market Reentry." Special Report to the U.S. Department of Labor. Columbus: Center for Human Resource Research, The Ohio State University, 1984.
_____. "Causes of Irregular Employment Patterns." In *Unplanned Careers: The Working Lives of Middle-Aged Women*, ed. Lois B. Shaw. Lexington, MA: D.C. Heath, 1983a.

_____. "Effects of Education and Occupational Training on the Wages of Mature Women." Special Report to the U.S. Department of Labor. Columbus: Center for Human Resource Research, The Ohio State University, 1983b.

_____. "Effects of Age, Length of Work Interruption, and State of the Economy on the Reentry Wages of Women." Special Report to the U.S. Department of Labor. Columbus: Center for Human Resource Research, The Ohio State University, 1982.

_____. "A Profile of Women Potentially Eligible for the Displaced Homemaker Program under the Employment and Training Act of 1978." Special Report to the U.S. Department of Labor. Columbus: Center for Human Resource Research, The Ohio State University, 1979.

Shaw, Lois B., and Theresa O'Brien. "Introduction and Overview." In *Unplanned Careers: The Working Lives of Middle-Aged Women*, ed. Lois B. Shaw. Lexington, MA: D.C. Heath, 1983.

Shields, Laurie. *Displaced Homemakers: Organizing for a New Life*. New York: McGraw Hill, 1981.

Smith, Shirley J. "New Worklife Estimates Reflect Changing Profile of Labor Force." *Monthly Labor Review* 105 (March 1982), pp. 15–20.

Snyder, Donald C. "Work After Retirement." Unpublished manuscript, 1987.

_____. "Pension Status of Recently Retired Workers on Their Longest Job: Findings from the New Beneficiary Survey." *Social Security Bulletin* 49 (August 1986), pp. 5–21.

Stone, Robyn, Gail Lee Cafferta, and Judith Sangl. "Caregivers of the Frail Elderly: A National Profile." *The Gerontologist* (1988).

Tittle, Carol Kehr, and Elenor Rubin Denker. *Returning Women Students in Higher Education: Defining Policy Issues*. New York: Praeger, 1980.

Treiman, Donald J., and Heidi I. Hartmann. *Women, Work and Wages: Equal Pay for Jobs of Equal Value*. Washington: National Academy Press, 1981.

U.S. Bureau of the Census. *Characteristics of the Population Below the Poverty Level, 1984*. Current Population Reports, Series P-60, No. 152. Washington: U.S. Government Printing Office, 1986.

U.S. Congress, Office of Technology Assessment. *Displaced Homemakers: Programs and Policy—An Interim Report*. Washington: U.S. Government Printing Office, 1985.

U.S. Department of Health and Human Services, Social Security Administration. "Increasing the Social Security Retirement Age: Older Workers in Physically Demanding Jobs." *Social Security Bulletin* 49 (October 1986), pp. 5–23.

_____. *Income of the Population 55 and Over, 1984*. Washington: U.S. Government Printing Office, 1985.

U.S. General Accounting Office. *Pension Integration: How Large Defined Benefit Plans Coordinate Benefits with Social Security*. Washington: 1986.

Vanski, Jean E., Demetra Smith Nightengale, and Carolyn Taylor O'Brien. "Employment Development Needs of Displaced Homemakers." Final Report to the U.S. Department of Health and Human Services. Washington: The Urban Institute, 1983.

Waite, Linda, and Sue E. Berryman. "Occupational Desegregation in CETA Programs." In *Sex Segregation in the Workplace*, ed. Barbara F. Reskin. Washington: National Academy Press, 1984. Pp. 292–307.

Walshok, Mary L. *Blue Collar Women*. Garden City, NY: Anchor Books, 1981.

CHAPTER 4

Functioning Ability and Job Performance as Workers Age

MONROE BERKOWITZ

Rutgers University

Aging is a complex process involving the deterioration of human capital stock and changing valuations of income and leisure, as has been noted by Clark, Kreps, and Spengler (1978, p. 930). The deterioration of human capital can derive from the obsolescence of skills and from the decline in what may be referred to generally as "health." Functioning ability is obviously related to a worker's health but is quite separate from it.[1] Job performance and functioning ability are also related, but their relationship is mediated by a host of intervening variables.

It seems pointless to try to define precisely concepts which are used quite loosely in the literature and in everyday conversation. But this is an area surrounded by a great deal of confusion and some time must be devoted to explaining, if not defining, various concepts and, in particular, the various meanings of "health." Individuals age, albeit at different rates, and as the years progress there is some deterioration in body systems. Such deterioration might be viewed as normal in some sense, as opposed to the onset of disease or pathology which may affect anyone, regardless of age, but which may affect older persons at some differential rate. But

---

[1] There is no general agreement as to how to conceptualize "health." Grossman (1972a, 1972b) presented health as a stock of capital which is desired by individuals for the services it yields. Berkowitz, Fenn, and Lambrinos (1983) have extended the Grossman model to take into account not only the impact of "days of sickness" but also impairments and functional limitations on consumption and productive activity. Their model recognizes that the debilitating effect of poor health on earnings and labor supply is simply not a matter of the decrease in healthy days, but the lessened ability to produce at the job due to limitations in mental and physical fitness. In their empirical work, their health capital variable consists of some functional limitation measures derived from self-reported data.

As we will see, in much of the literature which discusses health and aging, the analysis seems to proceed on some ad hoc basis without benefit of much in the way of theoretical models. This causes some confusion, especially when it comes to a discussion of trends in "health."

87

whether a person's body system has deteriorated, or whether that person has some disease as he or she ages, may be quite separate and apart from the issue of whether the person's functioning is affected. In turn, the concept of functioning—being able to make certain movements on some continuing basis, being able to see, hear and communicate, to choose particular examples—is related to but is quite separate and apart from whether a person does or does not work or engage in whatever their major activity might be.

The distinctions cry out for explication and example. The human eye might serve as an example. As a person ages, his or her eye is not exempt from the aging process. According to a National Academy of Sciences report, as persons age there is some reduction in pupil size together with a loss in accommodating capacity (National Research Council, 1987). In light-adapted conditions, the 20-year-old eye receives about six times more light than the 80-year-old eye, and in dark-adapted conditions, about 16 times more light: "In comparison to younger persons, it is as though older persons were wearing medium density sunglasses in bright light and extremely dark glasses in very dim light. Thus for any detailed visually guided tasks on which performance varies with illumination, older workers require extra lighting" (National Research Council, 1987, p. 4).

Presbyopia is the most common visual disorder in later life and it is this lack of accommodative ability that limits the range of usable work distances. Apparently bifocals and trifocals are not a complete answer, and the National Academy of Sciences report concludes that when the task involves moving, climbing, or otherwise navigating under conditions of precarious stability, the presbyope may be a hazard to himself as well as to others. The National Academy inquiry speaks of such lens and accommodation changes as naturally occurring with age in contrast with the disease-related visual disabilities such as cataract, macular degeneration, other retinal pathology, and glaucoma. But for the subject under examination in this chapter, it is not the occurrence of the disease which is of prime interest, but the functional consequence: "Such eye diseases have major functional consequences resulting from a loss of visual field or contrast sensitivity. Objects, obstacles, and hazards in the periphery become undetectable and mobility (either ambulatory or vehicular) becomes unsafe, particularly in congested and complex environments" (National Research Council, 1987, pp. 5–6).

Whether the impairment results from a "natural" aging process or is the result of some pathology, the results for functioning ability may be the same. Some aspect of vision is affected whether that is visual acuity, contrast sensitivity, limitation in the range of usable working distances, or color vision. Appropriate tests can measure this loss of function in these several areas. But it is necessary to go further and to inquire about the relationship of these losses of function to the ability of the affected person to work. Obviously, whether the visual incapacity has any effect on the person's performance will depend on job duties and requirements.

Confusion in this area is compounded when considerations of health enter, especially when the concept is not precisely defined. Some persons stop working once they have cataracts for some period of time. When asked why they retired, they might well reply that it was because of the cataracts, and hence the surveyor checks off "ill health" as the reason for not working. It may be nitpicking to note that it was not the cataracts, the pathological condition per se, but rather the loss of visual acuity brought on by the disease combined with the necessity of having a particular level of vision in the job the person was in that probably prompted the decision to withdraw from the labor market. It is perhaps less trivial a distinction if we choose the example of a person with low back pain or some other muscular impairment. The relationship of the impairment to work cannot be understood without some measurement of the degree of functional limitation brought on by the back condition and, of course, the relationship between the functional loss and the requirements of the job.

These subtle and not so subtle distinctions among the health condition, the possible resulting impairment, any functional limitation, and its possible effect on the person's participation in work frustrate our search for clear answers to some obvious questions relating to workers' performance in the labor market as the years go by. So much of the information we have is about disease and health conditions when we really want to know about functioning ability and its relationship to worker performance on the job.

Cross-Sectional and Time-Series Data

We are able to report on some reliable relationships between age and these separate measures. We can examine cross-sectional data to show the sharp age gradient exhibited by disability as measured by a person's self-definition. In similar fashion we can note the increase in functional limitations in older age groups as compared with their younger counterparts. Measures of medical conditions exhibit the same pattern. Thus the data will show that, as of a moment in time, older persons are worse off no matter which of the measures are used. They are less healthy, more impaired and functionally limited, and more disabled. These data can be made to appear less foreboding by noting that there are individual exceptions, that chronological age is not the best indication of the degenerative process for any particular individual, and that individuals might well compensate for these conditions or limitations in a variety of ways. As Robinson (1986, p. 6) notes, cross-sectional data present problems because of the confounding of two kinds of age effects. One is the individual aging effect and the other is the different generational experience and the survival effects. Nonetheless, the evidence we have seems obvious and overwhelming. People change as they age. They may improve in knowledge and wisdom, but not in measures of health or functioning. We examine the evidence in the next section.

The evidence from time-series data is ambiguous. We have seen dramatic improvements in longevity that are especially striking at older ages. The 65-year-old person in 1980 could look forward to 16.4 more years as opposed to an average expectancy of life at that age in 1940 of 12.8 years. But questions remain: With improved mortality rates, have morbidity rates also declined? Has there been a concomitant decrease in impairments and functional limitations? Has there been the same improvement in health as in mortality rates? Alternatively, as mortality rates improve, should we not expect that more and more of the older survivors will suffer from the same functional limitations and the same range of impairments characteristic of their cohorts? There are no definitive answers, but there is a substantial amount of evidence accumulating on this issue and we will discuss what there is.

The evidence on job performance and productivity is even more tenuous than that dealing with aging and the various measures of health. A spate of studies in the 1960s and 1970s seem to show that in spite of the deterioration in human and health capital as persons age, their productivity is not necessarily affected. Many of these studies are univariate and fail to control for other relevant factors.

While the literature relating age to job performance may leave much to be desired, we review studies which link age and variables such as absences, accidents, and turnover, which affect job performance.

Cross-Sectional Data

Age and Functional Limitations. The third-wave supplement to the 1984 panel of the Survey of Income and Program Participation (SIPP) (U.S. Bureau of the Census, 1986) conducted during the May-August period contained information on the several aspects of disability, including questions on functional limitations. Surveyors asked all persons 15 years of age and over about their ability to perform a set of sensory and physical activities, including (1) seeing, (2) hearing, (3) speaking, (4) lifting or carrying, (5) walking, (6) using stairs, (7) getting around outside, (8) getting around inside, and (9) getting into and out of bed. Except for speaking, persons who reported difficulty in performing an activity were asked whether they could perform the activity at all.

As seen in Table 1, only 5.2 percent of persons in the youngest age group, 15–24 years, reported any functional limitation and less than 1 percent reported a severe limitation, i.e., that they were unable to perform the activity at all or if they needed the help of

TABLE 1

Functional Limitation Status, by Age
(Persons age 15 and over. Numbers in thousands)

| | | With a Functional Limitation | | | |
| | | Total | | Severe | |
Age	Total	Number	Percent	Number	Percent
Total	180,987	37,304	20.6	13,537	7.5
15–24 years	39,297	2,054	5.2	346	0.9
25–34 years	40,464	3,049	7.5	596	1.5
35–44 years	30,480	4,074	13.4	890	2.9
45–54 years	22,264	5,110	23.0	1,431	6.4
55–64 years	22,060	7,552	34.2	2,734	12.4
65 years and over	26,422	15,465	58.5	7,539	28.5
65–69 years	8,928	4,052	45.4	1,682	18.8
70–74 years	7,378	4,078	55.3	1,691	22.9
75 years and over	10,116	7,335	72.5	4,166	41.2

Source: U.S. Bureau of the Census, 1986.

another person to perform the activity. The table shows further that the percentages increase regularly and quite dramatically with age. Nearly three-quarters (72.5 percent) of all persons 75 years and over reported some functional limitation and 41.2 percent reported a severe limitation.

It seems to make little difference as to which of the activities is under consideration: the older age groups fare worse. If we contrast the age group 15–64-years-old with the group 65 and over, the percentage functionally limited among the older group will be five or more times the percentage in the younger group. Whereas 4.6 percent of the 15–64-year-olds reported difficulty in seeing, 21.7 percent of those 65 and over answered that they had this difficulty. This information about the relationship between age and functional limitations replicates the data reported in earlier disability surveys conducted for the Social Security Administration in 1966, 1972, and 1978.

Age and Disability. SIPP also has questions about self-perceived work disability. Respondents were asked if they were limited in the amount and kind of work they could do or if they were prevented from working by their condition. Among the population ages 16–64 (the usual age group covered in disability surveys which focus on labor force participation), 12.1 percent reported they had a work disability and 5.3 percent answered that they were prevented from working. SIPP also surveyed the older age group, 65–72 years of age, and it is not surprising to find that 39.2 percent of the older population responded that they had a work disability, with 29.5 percent reporting that they were unable to work at all. The concept of work disability may have little meaning in the upper portion of the age distribution, but data are readily available showing the disability age gradient among the labor force age groups.

Table 2 shows the work disability information available from the 1982 Current Population Reports (U.S. Bureau of the Census, 1983). In the youngest age group, 16–24 years of age, only 3.3 percent reported a work disability and that percentage increases steadily with 24.1 percent of the group 55–64 years of age reporting a work disability.

These age gradients seem to have changed little over the years. Using the earliest of the Social Security surveys of disabled adults (1966), Haber (1970, p. 170) notes that the rate of disability increases at an increasing rate with age: ". . . [P]revalence was twice as high

TABLE 2
Prevalence of Work Disability, March 1982
(Persons 16-64 years old. Numbers in thousands)

| | With a Work Disability | | | | | |
| | Both Sexes | | Male | | Female | |
Age	Total	Percent	Total	Percent	Total	Percent
16-24 years	37,011	3.3	18,338	3.4	18,674	3.1
25-34 years	38,703	5.0	19,090	5.4	19,613	4.7
35-44 years	27,400	7.1	13,404	7.4	13,996	6.8
45-54 years	22,321	12.3	10,761	12.8	11,561	11.7
55-64 years	21,870	24.1	10,198	26.2	11,672	22.3

Source: U.S. Bureau of the Census, 1983.

among those 35-44 as among adults 18-34, three times as high among those 45-54, and five times as high among the population aged 55-64."

Age and Condition Classification. As early as 1970, Haber pointed out several findings about the complex interrelationships among physical condition, illness, and disability that are essential to our understanding of the relationship between functional capacity and aging. For one thing, the condition classification or the major disabling condition (diseases classified in accordance with the International Classification of Disease codes) failed to explain the relationship of aging to disability. Also, the presence of a condition cannot be construed as a measure of "health" or "sickness" since the condition may be stable or acute, active or dormant. The 1966 survey did have data on the days of hospitalization, but hospital days increased only slightly with age, indicating that disabled older men were not, to any great extent, more "actively" sick than the younger men (Haber, 1970, p. 174).

The severity of disability was directly related to the extent of functional limitations, with the proportion severely disabled increasing consistently as the extent of limitation increased. Although this same tendency held true for each age group, a higher proportion of older men were severely disabled regardless of the extent of functional limitation (Haber, 1970, p. 175).

Haber concludes (p. 178) that examination of the data on the relationship between age and the factors affecting the severity of disability provides substantial support for the hypothesis that chronological age is a significant status characteristic for the evaluation of capability.

The Independent Effect of Age. We know from countless inquiries that many factors influence whether persons will report that they are disabled, i.e., prevented from working due to their physical or mental condition. We have looked at age and condition classification, age and impairments, age and disability itself. The question is whether the apparent relationship between age and any of these outcomes survives once other determinants of disability are controlled for. The answer is that it does.

Age is a significant variable in multivariate regressions seeking to explain the determinants of disability. A recent study by Chirikos (1986), designed primarily to examine the growth of disability prevalence over time, used cross-sectional data from the 1978 Social Security Survey of Disability and Work to estimate the net effects of various determinants of disability. The dependent variable was assigned a value of one if health limited the amount or kind of work the individual could do or if it prevented the person from working at all, and the value of zero if it did not. Explanatory variables included a set of health-related characteristics ranging from condition classifications to various impairment ratings as well as a set of demographic and socioeconomic characteristics. The respective effects of these explanatory variables on the probability of reporting a work disability were estimated by maximum likelihood (logistic) techniques. Age, as expected, exerts a significantly positive effect on disability, with relative risk increasing by about 5 (4) percent each year men (women) grow older.

These findings confirm the independent effect of age on disability. The relationship holds almost regardless of the measure of disability used and quite apart from the method of measurement.

Time-Series Data

Thus far all of the evidence reported is from cross-sectional studies. At any given moment of time, older age cohorts experience higher rates of disability, whether due to individual aging effects, generational differences, or selection and survival biases. A different question is whether, say, as the present generation of prime-age workers mature, they will experience the same rates of disability as the current generation's older workers, or whether their disability rates will lessen or increase. Will disability rates follow the marked improvement in mortality rates, or will increased longevity mean more disabled persons?

The question was of prime interest to the Social Security planners who recommended an increase in the normal retirement age. The Social Security amendments of 1983 provide for a phased-in increase in the normal retirement age from 65 to 67 between the years 2000 and 2027. Should we expect that change to have any effect on disability insurance applications? Will the presumed increase in longevity carry with it implications for the incidence and prevalence of disability among older persons?

The Increase in Longevity. As noted by Ycas (1987), after a decade and a half of stability, mortality rates began an unexpected and sustained decline in 1968. With the near total elimination of deaths from acute infection (written in the pre-AIDs era) and parasitic diseases, the main causes of death have become the chronic degenerative conditions such as heart disease, cancer, and stroke. By 1985 about 85 percent of deaths occurred at ages of 55 or later and 70 percent at age 65 or more.

The current decline in mortality rates seems to be due primarily to falling cardiovascular disease rates and declines in deaths due to other chronic causes. The question is whether the steady rise in life expectancy since 1968 signals a fairly substantial improvement in the health of older persons.

The Decline in Labor Force Participation. Over the years the labor force participation rates of workers have fallen precipitously. The trend is particularly dramatic in the case of men. In 1965, some 84.6 percent of men ages 55–64 were in the labor force; by 1982 that percentage had declined to 70.2 percent. But we can hardly take the decline in labor force participation as evidentiary proof of increasingly poor health among the survivors.

Labor supply decisions are affected by a whole host of variables. Health is one of the significant variables, but researchers disagree as to its importance, in part because they conceptualize and operationalize health in different ways, including several types of mortality measures, condition classifications, functional limitation measures, and simple disability measures such as the person's perception as to whether he or she is able to work

(Leonard, 1986). Health, no matter how measured, can affect labor supply by diminishing productivity and affecting market wages and by its effect on the worker's relative valuation of work and leisure or nonmarket activities (Crawford and Lilien, 1981; Burtless and Moffitt, 1984; Sammartino, 1987).

The studies on work and disability make abundantly clear that, even if health remained constant over time, there are other important influences on labor force participation. As an example, one important factor is the availability of benefit programs, particularly the disability insurance program under Social Security (Parnes, Chapter 5 in this volume). But it is difficult to use the trends in the number of benefit awards under that program as an indicator of what has been happening to the older worker. For one thing, the program has exhibited puzzling trends. In the decade after 1965, program participation increased markedly, only to reverse itself as unexpectedly as it began. The number of persons receiving benefits peaked in 1978, fell until 1982, and now seems to be rising once again. (We explore some of the other effects of health on labor market activity below and note that there may be similar trends in some of the health series.)

The Failure of Success. Possibly the common sense interpretation is that health should improve with falling death rates. But the elimination of infectious disease may have fundamentally changed the meaning of mortality as a health measure (Ycas, 1987). We are left with two polar positions, one maintaining that the postponement of death to older ages has left an increasing number of older healthier workers. Since deaths are postponed but not eliminated, we are confronted with a "compression of mortality." And since it is not only deaths but illnesses and diseases that are postponed, this point of view is sometimes referred to as the "compression of morbidity," but the basic idea is the same. The opposite view is that the decline in mortality rates has left in its wake an increasing number of infirm workers, and hence the term "the failure of success." As is often the case, neither of the polar extremes may be entirely satisfactory. There is a middle position, commonly referred to as "dynamic equilibrium," which is difficult to characterize in a few words since it depends on the often complex interactions among health conditions and work disabilities.

Gruenberg (1977) maintains that we may be suffering from the "failures of success." Mortality has been postponed, not by curing the underlying causes of death, but by curbing the lethality of their side effects and sequelae, such as pneumonia. Those who are alive today who would have died in an earlier era are not healthy; they are sick persons whose problems can be kept under control at a level of severity short of death. It is not the incidence of disease which is important, but the prolongation of survival at the individual level, and this has raised the general prevalence of most chronic diseases. Kramer (1980) points out that most chronic conditions have higher age-specific rates among the elderly than the younger age groups, which accounts for the pandemic of chronic physical and mental diseases as the average age of the population increases.

Ycas comments that there may be flaws in Gruenberg's thesis. Some of the conditions with which Gruenberg makes his point most forcefully have fairly low prevalence rates (Down's syndrome) and cannot have made a major contribution to changes in mortality or retirement. When it comes to a major killer disease whose decline has affected the lowering of the death rate, such as heart disease, hypertension, and strokes, for example, modern medicine has been more successful in mitigating or controlling their effects than in preventing or curing them. According to Ycas, it is the extent of the mitigation that is crucial. As we have emphasized above, it is not the severity of the condition which is important, but the extent of the functional incapacity to work, given a particular range of jobs for which the person is qualified. For purposes of extending or restoring the ability to work, complete cures are not necessary, and some conditions, such as high blood pressure, respond well enough to treatment to allow the person to work.

The Compression of Mortality and Morbidity. The polar viewpoint is that both morbidity and mortality are becoming compressed near the upper end of the natural potential lifespan (Fries, 1980; Fries and Crapo, 1981) with an increasing part of the natural lifespan being spent in good health. Newquist (1984) notes that Fries's 1980 *New England Journal of Medicine* article involves predictions about the health of the older population based on an examination of health trends coupled with a theoretical position about the length of the human lifespan. Fries contends that the length of the human life is fixed and that even if all diseases were conquered, people would still die after having lived a certain number of years. The increase in life expectancy is due primarily to progress in the elimination of premature death, resulting in increasing "rectangularization" of the survival curve, fewer people dying at younger ages. Chronic disease has supplanted acute disease as a population health threat. Chronic disease is responsible for more deaths today than in the past, but some chronic diseases can be prevented and, in others, the disabling and symptomatic aspects can be postponed through improved health behavior and better medical care.

Newquist argues that Fries is essentially making a prediction about future trends based on his assumptions. Fries provides no data as to trends in morbidity or disability, and his thesis rests on some questionable assumptions about the length of the natural lifespan.

Dynamic Equilibrium. The third competing notion, which we have identified as a middle position, is set forth by Manton (Manton, 1982; Manton and Stallard, 1982; Wing and Manton, 1981) and is commonly referred to as a "dynamic equilibrium" model. It recognizes some of the complex interactions among disease, severity of the disease, the duration of the disease, and work disability.

Manton and others have examined the system of death reporting to test the compression of mortality and the failure of success theories and find that the results are not entirely consistent with either. They point out that most diseases are becoming more frequently mentioned as associated (present but not lethal) rather than underlying (present and lethal) causes of death. As Ycas (1987) notes, other things being equal, most diseases are increasingly prevalent but decreasingly severe in their impact: "This is at odds with both the compressed-morbidity assumption that increased vitality is delaying the onset of disease and the failure-success assumption that the onset or progress of disease continues unaffected, with only the lethal side effects under increased control" (p. 14).

In Manton's view, the incidence of disease, prevention, and control of effects interact dynamically to determine trends in illness and death. Still we are left with little to relate the disease and mortality trends to work disability. Thus we can only conclude that none of these positions is satisfactory and that if the object is to shed light on what is happening to the number of work-disabled persons as the population ages, it is necessary to at least look at some measures of health and what Ycas refers to as activity limitations over time.

Problems in Discerning Trends in Health and Disability Data. The empirical information in this area is limited and each data source has its own limitations. The Social Security disability surveys conducted in 1966, 1972, and 1978 have an orientation toward work disability, but are limited to persons under the age of 65 and sample sizes become rather small if only older workers are examined. The National Health Interview Survey (NHIS) depends on persons' perception of their health status and their ability or inability to carry on their major activity. There are also other problems related to changes in how the questions have been asked over the years. The National Health and Nutrition Examination Survey (HANES) has the advantage of not relying on self-perceived health status since the data are based on actual examination by health professionals, but it, too, has its limitations when used to measure changes over time. Rather few points in time have been observed, giving rise to some curve fitting problems as discussed below; the number of clinical variables are limited; and there have been changes in laboratory techniques and diagnostic techniques.

Newquist (1984) uses NHIS data to illustrate the increasing number of older persons over the years who report that they are unable to carry on their major activity (Table 3). With the exception of females 65 years of age and over, the trends are steadily upward with the greatest increase evident in the case of men ages 45-64.[2] Although it is possible that some of the methodological changes over the years have affected the results, it is not likely that they have had differential effects on one group relative to others.

---

[2] These NHIS data have to be treated with some circumspection. They are not easily compared with labor force data. For one thing, the question asked is whether the person is limited in his or her major activity, and for women one of the options is housework. A woman may have dropped out of the labor force due to some impairment and now reports that she is not limited in her major activity which is housework. Beginning in 1982, NHIS asked a specific work-limitation question of both men and women.

Men may choose reporting retirement for health reasons and retirement for other reasons, but in one year, 1969, these are combined.

Prior to 1969 the survey asked for information about illness and then probed for disability information through follow-up questions. In 1969 the "person approach" was introduced in which information about disability was first asked and then questions about the condition or illnesses responsible for the disability elicited additional information. The change resulted in an increase in the number of persons reporting a severe disability, but not in the percent reporting any activity limitation.

TABLE 3

Percent of Persons Age 45 and Over Unable to Perform
Their Major Activity Due to a Chronic Condition,
by Sex and Age: United States, 1960–1981

Year	Persons Aged 45–64		Persons Aged 65 and Over	
	Males	Females	Males	Females
1960–61[a]	4.4%	1.5%	22.6%	9.6%
1962–63[a]	4.4	1.4	21.8	10.3
1966–67[a]	4.5	1.2	21.6	7.7
1969	7.2	1.9	26.1	8.8
1970	7.4	1.7	27.6	8.3
1971	7.6	1.7	27.5	9.1
1972	7.6	1.7	28.3	7.7
1973	8.6	2.2	27.5	8.0
1974	9.4	2.1	29.8	8.2
1975	9.4	2.1	29.2	8.8
1976	9.9	2.3	29.9	9.0
1977	10.7	2.2	30.3	8.0
1978	10.1	2.5	28.7	8.1
1979	10.8	2.5	28.7	8.7
1980	11.0	2.3	29.2	8.8
1981	11.5	2.5	30.7	8.4

Source: Newquist (1984). Based on unpublished tabulations, National Center for Health Statistics, National Health Survey, and Wilson and Drury (1981).

[a] Average annual estimates of two fiscal years.

There is also evidence derived from the several Social Security disability surveys showing an increasing number of older workers reporting themselves as unable to work regularly (severely disabled) or limited in the amount and kind of work they can do (Newquist, 1984). In her analysis of the NHIS data on chronic conditions, Newquist examines the trend between 1957 and 1979, among persons ages 45 years and over, in the prevalence of arteriosclerosis, cerebrovascular diseases, hypertension, heart disease, hemorrhoids, arthritis, diabetes, visual impairments, hearing impairments, paralysis, impairments of the back or spine, and impairments of the lower extremities or hips. In almost all cases prevalence rates have increased and in some cases quite dramatically.

Some data on hypertension, available from HANES, have the advantage of being confirmed by a physician's diagnosis and are not dependent upon self-reporting. Only two points in time are present, but these show definite increases in prevalence when the 1960–1962 period is compared to the 1971–1975 period. On the basis of her examination of the NHIS and HANES data, Newquist concludes: "Overall this analysis suggests that the prevalence of chronic conditions has risen within the more mature population. These trends lend support to the position that disability has risen due to increases in the prevalence of chronic conditions. They also challenge the view that the health of the population is improving" (p. 41).

Newquist also examines a number of other measures and concludes that none of these can be interpreted as supporting the assertion that the health of the older population is improving. The prevalence of reported disease, impairment, restricted activity, and disability has risen in most cases. In only one measure, the number of days causing bed disability, has the incidence remained about the same over the period of years examined. Although the prevalence of chronic conditions has risen in most cases, she cannot find any increase in disease severity.

Newquist does not look at any nonmedical factors. Whatever behavioral changes may have been brought about by the ratio of benefits to earnings, for example, are beyond the scope of her analysis. The effects on disability prevalence of such nonmedical factors as benefit levels and administrative stringency in benefit programs are probably great. More problematical is their influence on the incidence of disease, impairments, and functional limitations. At first glance, the influence of these factors would seem to be minimal, but impairments and functional limitations are the necessary prerequisites for a disability benefit application and it may be that conditions that are tolerated and not reported at one time are brought to the fore when a disability application is in the offing.

Even within the limits of her analysis, Newquist finds that although the data do not support the improved health and vitality argument, neither do they totally support the health deterioration argument. The main reason for the latter conclusion is that it does not appear that severity of disease has increased, and there may be some evidence that it has declined in some cases. Also, Gruenberg's (1977) assertion that lower mortality leads to increased prevalence of diseases and that this explains declining levels of health is not fully supported. Increased prevalence is found among nonlethal as well as lethal conditions.

Manton's (1982) analysis has similar results. However, he assumed that disease severity was positively associated with disability so that reduced disease severity would lead to reduced disability. The Newquist analysis, in contrast, suggests that reductions in disease severity may not be accompanied by increases in functional level. Newquist recognizes that disability increases may be strongly influenced by behavioral responses to illnesses at the same time that these illnesses are on the rise. We would simply suggest that the illnesses themselves may be due to behavioral responses in anticipation of disability benefits.

Bearing in mind that nonmedical factors are not included in the analysis, Newquist does note that the older populations may restrict their activities in the face of a chronic condition in order to avoid more serious illness consequences. She calls this behavior "health preservation" and maintains that when health preservation is combined with increased awareness of disease, preventive disability may rise as the older population increases.

Verbrugge (1984) suggests that such basic health preservation behaviors were practiced among the older population. Noting that the decline in incidence of acute conditions has not been accompanied by a decline in short-term disabilities, she concludes that older persons are reducing activities more than ever before for acute conditions. Several studies support the notion of the increased willingness of persons diagnosed as having certain conditions or diseases to restrict their activities (Haynes et al., 1978), and of course to the extent that such restrictions take the form of a reduction in work, it must be influenced by the availability and generosity of benefits.

A Reexamination of Trends. The matter could possibly be left at that. Upward trends in acute conditions, self-perceived disease states, and disability could be attributed to greater awareness, greater willingness to adopt the sick role, in the sociologists' terms, and greater reliance on increasingly available benefits. But Ycas (1987) casts some doubt on some of the trends in the data. Looking at measures of functional limitations, restricted activity days, hospital utilization, and similar measures, this analyst finds not one, but two trends during the years 1969 to 1981. Agreeing that in the first half of the 1970s the trend was generally toward worsening health in the age groups near retirement age, Ycas contends that during the later 1970s the trend was toward stable or perhaps even improving health. This would be similar to the trend in the disability programs.

Ycas notes that if the trend did reverse, then, despite the contradictory trends since the late 1960s, there could be a direct (though lagged) link between lower age-specific mortality and better health in the long run. Studies that compared health measures at points before and after the turnaround may have been somewhat misled by trends moving in opposite directions and misjudged the direction and the amount of the change.

When these ideas are tested by fitting linear and quadratic models to the data, the conclusion is that there has been a real change in trend from worsening to improving health at some point roughly midway between 1969 and 1981 among persons aged 55-70. Ycas realizes that the models used (a curve-fitting system of equations which tests the patterns appearing within the health measures) cannot be used to project the health much beyond the period from which it was derived. Although the finding is that health has been improving in recent years, there is no reason to conclude that the trend would accelerate indefinitely in the future.

Some Hesitant Conclusions

Perhaps one way to conclude what has been a rather involved and complex discussion is to note that in none of this literature do we find good theoretical models seeking to explain the determinants of what is referred to as "health." To the outside observer, investigators seem to be examining masses of data relating to all of the complex dimensions of health, ranging from medically defined conditions to behaviorally driven definitions of disability, without the benefit of any guiding models or agreed-upon methods of analysis. As Ycas points out, perhaps the important conclusion is not that the trends toward declining health among the older age groups seem to be reversing, but how cautiously the conventional wisdom on morbidity and mortality should be accepted.

Job Performance

Much of the literature on health and the aging worker seems to beg the question of the relationship between some of the health measures and the job performance of older workers. Whatever has been happening to the health of the older worker over the years, it is clear that, on the average, the older worker does not do as well as the younger worker when it comes to almost all of the measures, whether these are concerned with pathology, impairments, or functional limitations. It seems reasonable to suppose that, on the average, the older worker should not do as well on measures of job performance.

We began our discussion of the health issues by citing the evidence relating to the aging of the human eye. After noting the deterioration of the eye as workers age, the conclusion was: "Viewed in the context of employment, reduced visual functioning need not have any effect on job performance" (National Research Council, 1987, p. 41). One can only wonder why that should be so. If a worker cannot see as well as another worker, or as well as that person was able to see when he or she was younger, why should that not affect productivity and job performance? As it turns out, the key word is "need" in the sentence quoted above. Granted that there may be some jobs in which visual acuity is irrelevant, reduced functioning *need* not have any effect provided the employer undertakes a vision-based employment program with attention to special devices for lighting and the introduction of keyboards and panels which offer greater contrast between symbols and their background.

What, then, is the fair measure of the older workers' productivity and job performance? Is it appropriate and fair to compare older and younger workers regardless of task, occupation, or types of accommodation? Or should one standardize for these factors as much as possible? If it is age and job performance with which we are concerned, it seems appropriate to compare performance at literally the same job. Needless to say, that is usually not done, which makes the comparisons most confusing. It is probably begging the question to say that all workers, young or old, could probably benefit from better lighting and signs with greater contrast. Yet it raises an issue. If we are to standardize for jobs or tasks, do we standardize on the basis of older workers' jobs or younger workers' jobs? It may well be that older workers do as well as younger workers at jobs for which the desirable accommodations have been made. We recognize that this is not only a matter of selective placement by the employer, but also some degree of self-selection by the older worker. Those workers who survive on the job may be particularly suited for the work at hand.

The Job Performance Studies

Our task is not to look at aging and job performance, but to examine the impact of age on health or functioning and thus the impact on job performance. The question is, as Robinson (1986, p. 63) put it, "Is the job performance of middle-aged and older workers adversely affected by age-related health factors?"

If that is the question, the answers are not easy to come by. In some studies (Shephard, 1969) where samples are drawn from working populations, various test results show declines in aerobic power and an increase in excessive weight as persons age, but no evidence as to the relevance of these factors for individual productivity. Another study by Shephard (1983) did relate the decline in aerobic power to the arduous tasks of inspecting marine vessels and cargo, but even here reliance was on impressions of performance and logical deductions rather than work performance records.

Robinson (1986) notes that the reviews of the limited empirical literature on age and productivity (Baugher, 1978; Kelleher and Quirk, 1973; Meier and Kerr, 1976; Rhodes, 1983; Robinson, 1983) have been inadequate for drawing useful generalizations. However, she notes that, in general, variability in performance within age groups outweighs differences among age groups, but that age differences can be observed more readily in some occupations than in others. But again it is noted that the processes of self-selection and termination tend to reduce age differences in performance among the surviving work force.

Doering, Rhodes, and Schuster (1983) review several studies of the age-job performance relationship. In very general terms, they find that the studies provide mixed results. A considerable number of studies showed a nonsignificant relationship, several studies showed some older workers' performance to be better in terms of accuracy and steadiness of work output and work level, and others showed that performance declined with age.

Among the studies that showed an improvement with age was one of salespersons by Maher (1955) and Holley et al.'s (1978) study of paraprofessionals. Older clerical workers were found to be more accurate and to have greater steadiness of output, with performance declining only for those 65 years of age and older (Kutscher and Walker, 1960). Eisenberg (1980) found that older examiners and materials handlers in a garment manufacturing plant had higher productivity, whereas the productivity of older sewing machine operators was lower, as measured by piece-rate earnings.

Decreases in performance were reported in 15 studies covering such diverse occupational groups as printers, male production workers, factory workers, mail sorters, and air traffic controllers. For scholars, engineers, and scientists, the studies showed essentially an inverted U-relationship between age and performance.

Doering, Rhodes, and Schuster (1983) note that the limitations in the literature were the use of primarily bivariate analyses and cross-sectional data. With multivariate analysis, it would be possible to determine the effects of experience, motivation, and workplace climates. Cross-sectional studies obscure the heterogeneity within age groups and do not allow for changes over time, assessments of generational effects, or of the "survivor" effect which can result in the older workers being those whose performance continues to be acceptable, or those whose performance has declined but who are retained by their employing organizations until retirement.

Since our interest is in the relationship of age-related health changes and productivity, some light on this subject might be shed by examining earnings, which we assume are related to productivity. Joseph M. Davis (1972) used data from the National Longitudinal Survey (NLS) to compare the earnings of healthy and disabled men 45–64 years of age. Unfortunately, the measure of disability used was a self-reported limitation on the amount or kind of work the person could do. Not surprisingly, Davis found that "poor health" negatively affected annual earnings through both total hours worked and hourly rates of pay. He concluded that the lower wage rates could be due to lower productivity or to discrimination, but he was unable to separate the two possible explanations.

Absenteeism

Obviously, the studies relating health, aging, and work performance leave a great deal to be desired. Absent good controlled studies relating these factors, can we find some acceptable substitutes? Robinson (1986) reports on the data collected regularly by Metropolitan Life showing the short-term (1 to 26 weeks) absences from work due to illness. The incidence of these illnesses among men was 81 per 1,000 for the very youngest group, ages 17–24; 74 for the 25–44-year-olds; 180 for the 45–54-year-olds; and 191 for persons aged 55–64 years. The pattern was the same among women except that the youngest age group showed fewer absences than any of the others. As for duration of disability, in general older employees were absent for longer periods of time than were younger employees.

Robinson notes that these data stem from a specific and occupationally homogeneous population drawn from office and sales personnel who would be expected to be much less restricted from performing their jobs for reasons related to health than employees in more physically demanding jobs. Hence, these data could be taken as a conservative estimate of the effects of age on health-related absences.

Doering, Rhodes, and Schuster (1983) summarize the studies relating absences and age, but do not provide a classification by health-related and non-health-related reasons for the absences. They do classify the studies according to "avoidable" and "unavoidable" reasons for absences. Sickness is among the reasons included in the unavoidable category. Of 23 studies among men, 12 found no relationship, seven a positive relationship, three a negative one, and a single study reported a U-shaped relationship. They speculate that the higher rates of unavoidable absences (when compared to the avoidable) may be associated with deteriorating health and the onset of chronic illness together with a longer recovery period for older workers.

Accidents

We do have some reliable data on the relationship between age and accidents from workers' compensation information. The evidence indicates that younger workers have higher injury frequency rates than do older workers (Dillingham, 1981; Kossoris, 1940), although the earlier study failed to control for experience which is a powerful influence on accident frequency rates. While older workers may have lower frequency rates, their severity rates tend to be higher. Older workers apparently have more serious injuries and lose more work time per injury (Dillingham, 1979). Males less than 25 years of age had a frequency rate of 22.3 per unit of exposure (500 workers) in contrast to a rate of 10.9 for those ages 25–44 and a similar rate for those 45 years old and over. Both the compensation cost per injury and per unit of exposure was considerably more for the older worker. For the three age groups, the compensation cost per injury was $789 for the youngest group, $1,421 for the middle group, and $2,072 for the oldest. The higher frequency rate among the youngest workers made the compensation cost per unit of exposure higher for them ($18,732) than for the middle group ($17,585), but the cost was greatest for those 45 years of age and over ($22,550) (Dillingham, 1983).

Occupation exerts a strong influence on accident rates and costs. Table 4 shows these costs by sex, occupation, and age. For males, there is a strong age profile, but it is less clear cut in the case of females except in the white-collar and service occupations.

Given the finding that severity of accidents increases with age, it should not be surprising to find that there is an age profile for the most severe injuries—those that result in death. Kossoris (1940) found that the death rate for the over-50 worker was twice that of the 21–25-year-old worker and that the over-60 death rate was three times that for the 21–24-year-old category. Root (1981), using workers' compensation data from more states than were available to Kossoris, substantiates the nature of the relationship between fatal accidents and age.

Conclusions

Our task was to explain functioning ability and job performance as workers age. We interpret the topic broadly to include the effects of health on performance as workers age. The difficulty is not that the concept of health is not defined, but that there are various definitions, conceptualizations, and uses of the term. We first examined the evidence available from cross-sectional data and what emerges clearly is the deterioration of health as workers age. At any given moment in time, workers in the older age groups will be less healthy than those in the younger age cohorts. Such a relationship holds true regardless of the measure of health used, whether it be condition classifications, indices of functional limitations, or self-perceived classifications of disability.

The intriguing issue has to do with trends over time. As mortality declines and longevity increases, will the increasing numbers of older workers be healthier than ever, or will the survivors, who in an

TABLE 4

Compensation Cost per Unit of Exposure by Age, Sex, and Occupation, 1970

Occupation	Males			Females		
	Less Than 25 Years Old	25–44 Years Old	45 Years Old and Over	Less Than 25 Years Old	25–44 Years Old	45 Years Old and Over
Professional, technical, managers, administrators, sales workers	$ 2,403	$ 3,240	$ 4,758	$2,093	$ 2,932	$ 5,413
Clerical workers	8,023	6,109	7,487	935	2,213	4,518
Craftsmen	19,512	21,168	32,786	8,385	4,367	11,817
Operatives	30,680	30,419	42,695	9,316	14,150	11,675
Laborers	52,829	68,884	98,233	4,353	9,310	6,442
Service workers	13,549	14,184	21,401	6,921	15,439	18,711

Source: Dillingham (1983).

earlier era would have died, now face deteriorating health? The
question is of prime policy importance since we have already made
the decision to postpone the retirement age. If the older group will
become increasingly unfit to work, we should look forward to a
burgeoning of the disability rolls. If, on the other hand, health is
improving, then the new retirement age should not bring about any
significant changes so far as disability programs are concerned.

The question is also interesting from a methodological point of
view. It exposes the paucity of data on health measures, especially
when collected for a long enough time period and for a group
distributed widely enough so that age-specific information can be
relied upon. One objective of this chapter was to present enough of
the controversy so that the reader might choose the side of the issue
that appears to be more convincing. I believe the weight of
evidence is that the health status of the older worker was
deteriorating but that recent years have witnessed what appears to
be a change of direction toward improving health.

If it seems ridiculous that such issues are decided as a matter of
choosing sides, as it were, it points to the difficulties of dealing with
matters of health and work. Our obvious interest is in the labor
supply of the older worker and the demand for their services by
employers or by the market generally if they are self-employed.
Health exerts obvious effects on labor supply by changing market
wages and by changing relative valuations of consumption and
nonmarket goods. It is in the context of such labor supply models
that health factors become important. Over the years the levels of
benefits available have changed, as has the nature of the work
opportunities and compensation levels. Each of these factors is
important, and health exerts its influence in the context of all other
factors. If that is so, it would probably be wise to examine the health
effects only in the context of some model where the independent
effects of the health measure can be assessed.

The role of health in the case of the demand for the work of
older persons is also crucial. Given the cross-sectional evidence that
the older cohort of workers are less well off when it comes to any
of the health measures, one can understand the fears and
apprehensions of employers in hiring the older worker. There
would seem to be some basis, of a statistical nature, for
discrimination. But we have entered into a societal decision not to
discriminate on the basis of age, which means that these age-related

decrements in health must be accommodated in some fashion. Fortunately, accommodation seems possible and a good deal takes place through self-selection and intelligent placement of workers at jobs which can maximize their residual capacities.

Much more research remains to be done in this area. Certainly we need better conceptual models which seek to explain the basic determinants of health, but perhaps most of all we need better measures of health which can be used in labor supply and demand models. Since our interest is in health and work, we are less interested in medically defined conditions than we are in functional limitations—or functional capacities, to use the more positive version. We seek measures that can be administered in large-scale surveys, measures that can be converted to scales useful in multivariate equations, and measures that are reliable and consistent over time and over populations. It is discouraging to report that such measures do not yet exist. Nor are there good alternatives— mortality measures and disability measures each have their own problems. We have already noted the ambiguities in the relationship between mortality and health, and self-reported measures of disability can be tautological when used to determine work status.

The catalogue of what is wrong with existing measures is easy to compile. The task ahead is to get on with testing new measures and, I would say, new measures of functional limitations that are relevant to work and that incorporate measures of duration, pain, and stress as well as the ability to make certain motions or relate to others on the job. One of the problems with existing measures is their apparent instability over time (Chirikos and Nestel, 1981).

The literature on the effects of health and aging on job performance does not yield the answers we seek in an unambiguous fashion. Apart from the measurement problems, the studies fail to control for relevant factors, although there is hardly agreement on what is and what is not relevant in this context. The generalizations which seem to hold are that the older worker has assets or experience and reliability which may compensate for the deficits in physical functioning. When it comes to accidents and absences, distinctions must be made between frequency and severity. The older worker may tend to be absent less frequently, at least in nonillness situations, but the duration of the absences that do take place are longer. In much the same way, accident frequency rates are lower for the older worker, but severity is higher and hence the duration of the absence is also higher. The accident literature, especially that on fatalities, confirms the argument which is evident in the entire examination of all aspects of health, functioning, and the older worker. The key is intelligent placement which makes the most of the residual functioning capacity of those older workers who remain in the labor force.

References

Baugher, D. "Is the Older Worker Inherently Incompetent?" *Aging and Work* 1 (1978): pp. 242–50.
Berkowitz, Monroe, Paul Fenn, and James Lambrinos. "The Optimal Stock of Health with Endogenous Wages." *Journal of Health Economics* 2 (August 1983), pp. 139–47.
Burtless, Gary, and Robert Moffitt. "The Effects of Social Security Benefits on the Labor Supply of the Aged." In *Retirement and Economic Behavior*, eds. Henry J. Aaron and Gary Burtless. Washington: The Brookings Institution, 1984.
Chirikos, Thomas N. "Accounting for the Historical Rise in Work-Disability Prevalence." *The Milbank Quarterly* 64, No. 2 (1986), pp. 271–301.
Chirikos, Thomas N., and Gilbert Nestel. "Impairment and Labor Market Outcomes: A Cross-Sectional and Longitudinal Analysis." In *Work and Retirement*, ed. Herbert S. Parnes. Cambridge, MA: The MIT Press, 1981.
Clark, Robert, Juanita Kreps, and Joseph Spengler. "Economics of Aging: A Survey." *Journal of Economic Literature* 16 (September 1978), pp. 919–62.
Crawford, Vincent P., and David M. Lilien. "Social Security and the Retirement Decision." *Quarterly Journal of Economics* 96 (August 1981), pp. 505–29.
Davis, Joseph M. "Impact of Health on Earnings and Labor Market Activity." *Monthly Labor Review* 95 (October 1972), pp. 46–49.
Dillingham, Alan. "The Injury Risk Structure of Occupations and Wages." Ph.D. dissertation, Cornell University, 1979.
———. "New Evidence on Age and Workplace Injuries." *Industrial Gerontology* 4 (1981), pp. 1–10.
———. "Demographic and Economic Change and the Costs of Workers' Compensation." In *Safety and the Work Force*, ed. John Worrall. Ithaca, NY: ILR Press, 1983.
Doering, Mildred, Susan R. Rhodes, and Michael Schuster. *The Aging Worker.* Beverly Hills, CA: Sage Publications, 1983.
Eisenberg, J. "Relationship Between Age and Effects Upon Work: A Study of Older Workers in the Garment Industry." *Dissertation Abstracts International, 1980.*
Fries, James F. "Aging, Natural Death and the Compression of Morbidity." *The New England Journal of Medicine* 303, 3 (July 17, 1980), pp. 130–35.
Fries, James F., and L. Crapo. *Vitality and Aging: Implications of the Rectangular Curve.* San Francisco: W. H. Freeman, 1981.
Grossman, Michael. "The Demand for Health: A Theoretical and Empirical Investigation." New York: National Bureau of Economic Research, 1972a.
———. "On the Concept of Health Capital and the Demand for Health." *Journal of Political Economy* 80 (March/April 1972b), pp. 223–55.
Gruenberg, Ernest M. "The Failure of Success." *Milbank Memorial Fund Quarterly/Health and Society* 55 (Winter 1977), pp. 3–24.
Haber, Lawrence D. "Age and Capacity Devaluation." *Journal of Health and Social Behavior* 11 (March 1970), pp. 167–82.
Haynes, R. Brian, David L. Sackett, D. Wayne Taylor, Edward S. Gibson, and Arnold L. Johnson. "Increased Absenteeism from Work After Detection and Labeling of Hypertensive Patients." *The New England Journal of Medicine* 299, 14 (October 5, 1978), pp. 741–44.

Holley, W. H., Jr., H. S. Feild, and B. B. Holley. "Age and Reactions to Jobs: An Empirical Study of Paraprofessional Workers." *Aging and Work* 1 (1978), pp. 33-40.
Kelleher, C. H., and D. A. Quirk. "Age, Physical Capacity and Work: An Annotated Bibliography." *Industrial Gerontology* 19 (1973), pp. 80-98.
Kossoris, Max D. "Relation of Age to Industrial Injuries." *Monthly Labor Review* 51 (April 1940), pp. 789-804.
Kramer, M. "The Rising Pandemic of Mental Disorders and Associated Chronic Diseases and Disabilities." *Acta Psychiatrica Scandanavica*, Supplement 285, 62 (1980), pp. 382-96.
Kutscher, Ronald E., and James F. Walker. "Comparative Job Performance of Office Workers by Age." *Monthly Labor Review* 83 (January 1960), pp. 39-43.
Leonard, Jonathan S. "Labor Supply Incentives and Disincentives for Disabled Persons." In *Disability and the Labor Market*, eds. Monroe Berkowitz and M. Anne Hill. Ithaca, NY: ILR Press, 1986.
Maher, Howard. "Age and Performance of Two Work Groups." *Journal of Gerontology* 10 (October 1955), pp. 448-51.
Manton, Kenneth G. "Changing Concepts of Morbidity and Mortality in the Elderly Population." *Milbank Memorial Fund Quarterly/Health and Society* 60 (Spring 1982), pp. 183-244.
Manton, Kenneth G., and Eric Stallard. "Temporal Trends in U.S. Multiple Cause of Death Mortality Data: 1968-1977." *Demography* 19 (November 1982), pp. 527-47.
Meier, Elizabeth L., and Elizabeth A. Kerr. "Capabilities of Middle-Aged and Older Workers: A Survey of the Literature." *Industrial Gerontology* 3 (Summer 1976), pp. 147-56.
National Research Council. *Work, Aging and Vision: Report of a Conference.* Washington: National Academy Press, 1987.
Newquist, Deborah. "Trends in Disability and Health Among Middle-Aged and Older Persons." Unpublished paper. Los Angeles: Andrus Gerontology Center, University of Southern California, June 1984.
Rhodes, Susan L. "Age-Related Differences in Work Attitude and Behavior: A Review and Conceptual Analysis." *Psychological Bulletin* 93 (March 1983), pp. 328-67.
Robinson, Pauline K. *Organizational Strategies for Older Workers.* New York: Pergamon Press, 1983.
————. "Age, Health and Performance." In *Age, Health and Employment*, eds. James E. Birren, Pauline K. Robinson, and Judy E. Livingston. Englewood Cliffs, NJ: Prentice-Hall, 1986.
Root, Norman. "Injuries at Work Are Fewer Among Older Employees." *Monthly Labor Review* 104 (March 1981), pp. 30-34.
Sammartino, Frank J. "The Effect of Health on Retirement." *Social Security Bulletin* 50 (February 1987), pp. 31-47.
Shephard, Roy J. "The Working Capacity of the Older Employee." *Archives of Environmental Health* 18 (1969), pp. 982-86.
————. "Equal Opportunity for a Geriatric Labor Force: Some Observations on Marine Surveying." *Journal of Occupational Medicine* 25 (March 1983), pp. 211-14.
U.S. Bureau of the Census. *Disability, Functional Limitation, and Health Insurance Coverage: 1984/1985.* Current Population Reports, Series P-70, No. 8. Data from the Survey of Income and Program Participation. Washington: U.S. Government Printing Office, 1986.
————. *Labor Force Status and Other Characteristics of Persons With a Work Disability: 1982.* Current Population Reports, Series P-23, No. 127. Washington: U.S. Government Printing Office, 1983.
Verbrugge, Lois M. "Longer Life but Worsening Health? Trends in the Health and Mortality of Middle-Aged and Older Persons." *Milbank Memorial Fund Quarterly/Health and Society* 62 (Summer 1984), pp. 475-519.

Wilson, Ronald W., and Thomas F. Drury. "Factors Affecting the Use of Limitation of Activity as a Health Status Measure." *Silver Anniversary of the National Health Survey Act.* Washington: National Center for Health Statistics, 1981.
Wing, Steve, and Kenneth G. Manton. "A Multiple Cause of Death Analysis of Hypertension-Related Mortality in North Carolina, 1968-1977." *American Journal of Public Health* (July 1981), pp. 823-30.
Ycas, Martynas. "Recent Trends in Health Near the Age of Retirement: New Findings from the Health Interview Survey." *Social Security Bulletin* 50 (February 1987), pp. 5-30.

CHAPTER 5

The Retirement Decision

HERBERT S. PARNES[*]
The Ohio State University

A burgeoning literature on the factors affecting the decision to retire has been produced during the past two decades. The reasons for the substantial research interest are fairly clear. In part it stems from a natural curiosity about a phenomenon that has become a major economic institution over a relatively short period of time (Atchley, 1982). In the early 1900s a substantial majority (65 percent) of men 65 and over were in the labor force, and even as late as midcentury this proportion was almost one-half, in contrast to only 16 percent by 1986; over the latter 36-year period the participation rate of men ages 55 to 64 dropped from 87 to 67 percent. For both the individual and society these trends carry one set of implications if retirement represents largely unconstrained choices, but quite another to the extent that it is induced by poor health, arbitrary age limits for employment, or unfavorable labor market conditions.

An even more immediate explanation of the surging research effort on the determinants of retirement status lies in demographic factors: the prospective increase in the proportion of the over-65 population (from 11 percent in 1980 to 17–20 percent in 2025), together with the trend toward earlier retirement, threatens significantly increased financial burdens in the future. Reasons for retirement must be understood if policy measures directed at this problem are to be effective.

This chapter reviews and evaluates the recent body of research on the reasons individuals retire, making liberal use of previous reviews of segments of the literature by Aaron (1982), Danziger,

[*] I am grateful to Joseph F. Quinn for his careful review of an earlier draft and for his contribution to its improvement.

115

Haveman, and Plotnick (1981), Gratton and Haug (1983), Mitchell and Fields (1982), Morgan (1981), Sammartino (1987), and Thompson (1983). It begins with a description of the nature of this research effort, including the methodological problems confronting researchers. This is followed by a summary and synthesis of findings. A brief concluding section comments on some implications of research findings for policy issues and suggests the directions future research should take.

Character of the Research

Major Research Questions

The Predictors of Retirement. Researchers attempting to identify the factors underlying the withdrawal of elderly workers from employment have approached the issue in a variety of ways. The most general and straightforward approach has been a multivariate analysis of variables that predict the act of retirement. However, this statement of the problem conceals a wide variety of specific research designs.

For one thing, there has been variation in the designation of the dependent variable. A few studies have used the *intention or plan* to retire rather than *actual retirement* as the criterion. Moreover, there is diversity among those that have used actual behavior as the dependent variable: some have explored the probability of retiring over a specified period of time, others have examined the probability of retiring "early" (generally before age 65), while still others have analyzed age of retirement as a continuous variable. Finally, there are different ways of defining the term "retirement," a matter to be considered below.

Perhaps the most serious impediment to a synthesis of research findings has been the wide diversity in the specification of multivariate models with respect to both the variables included and the time frame covered. To illustrate, at one extreme stand the models used by some economists that have included only monetary values (e.g., earnings and private and public pension income), and have (theoretically, if not always empirically) expressed these variables as discounted present values of income streams over the remaining lifetime, on the assumption that individuals attempt to maximize *lifetime* utility (e.g., Fields and Mitchell, 1984). At the other extreme are studies that have used a more extensive list of variables and have measured them at a single point in time—generally the base year (e.g., Morgan, 1981).

Reasons for Retirement. A second approach to uncovering the nature of the retirement decision has sought to identify the principal reasons for retirement. Of course, valid predictors of retirement *are* the "reasons" for retirement, but some studies have attempted to categorize retirees according to the major reason for their withdrawal from the labor market (e.g., poor health, mandatory retirement, labor market "discouragement," simple desire to leave work). They have generally relied on tabulations of retrospective responses of retirees (e.g., Sherman, 1985) but at least one (Parnes and Less, 1985) has used longitudinal records of the experience and attitudes of a sample of retirees *prior* to their retirement. Some of the studies of reasons for retirement have focused on "early retirees," raising the question whether such "premature" withdrawals from the labor market are explained primarily by deterioration in health or by economic considerations (Anderson and Burkhauser, 1985; Bazzoli, 1985; Kingson, 1981a).

Effect of Social Security on Labor Supply. Finally, the chief orientation of a number of studies has been to ascertain the effects of the Social Security system on labor supply generally and on retirement behavior in particular (see review by Aaron, 1982). Included in this part of the literature is the debate engendered by work of Parsons (1980a, 1980b, 1981, 1984) purporting to show that the historical trend toward earlier retirement and the pronounced racial difference in the declining labor force participation rates of older males can be explained by liberalization of the disability provisions of the Social Security Act.

Principal Data Sources

Research on the retirement decision has been substantially facilitated by the development over the past two decades of several longitudinal data bases for representative national samples of individuals, many of whose members moved from employment into retirement over the period covered by the data collection process. A brief description of these data sources is essential to an understanding of the strengths and limitations of the research based upon them.

The national data bank most specifically designed for the study of retirement is the Social Security Administration's Retirement

History Survey (RHS). The RHS sample consisted of somewhat over 11,000 men and nonmarried women between 58 and 63 years of age who were interviewed for the first time in 1969 and biennially thereafter until 1979. Information was collected on past and current labor market activity, attitudes toward and expectations regarding retirement, expected retirement income from Social Security, pensions, and other sources, and health condition.

The National Longitudinal Surveys of the Labor Market Experience of Mature Men (NLS), conducted by the Ohio State University Center for Human Resource Research and the United States Bureau of the Census under contract with the U.S. Department of Labor, involved a sample of slightly more than 5,000 men between the ages of 45 and 59 in 1966, with a deliberate overrepresentation of blacks. Originally designed as a five-year study of the "preretirement years," the surveys were ultimately extended to cover the 17-year period 1966 to 1983 (Parnes et al., 1985). Questions relevant to research on the retirement decision were rather similar to those of the RHS.

The Panel Study of Income Dynamics (PSID) of the University of Michigan Institute for Social Research was begun in 1968 with a national sample of 5,000 families disproportionately representing those in poverty. Because the sample increases as members split off to marry, the sample had grown to about 7,000 family units containing over 20,000 members by 1987. The data bank includes information that permits basically the same type of analysis of the retirement decision as is afforded by the RHS and NLS. Current funding arrangements will permit continuation of the annual interviews through 1991.

Other longitudinal data banks have been used to study the retirement process (Streib and Schneider, 1971; Palmore et al., 1985), but none of these involves a representative national sample. None of the data sources that have been described provides the detailed information about pension plans required to test life-cycle economic models. Accordingly, Fields and Mitchell (1984) have made intensive use of the Department of Labor's Benefit Amounts Survey (BAS), which in 1978 collected detailed information on pension formulas in a sample of firms. Information was also available from these firms on the birthdates and dates of retirement of all pension recipients, and these data were merged by the Social

Security Administration with demographic and individual earnings records for such retirees (Fields and Mitchell, 1984, p. 35).

Methodological Problems

Research on the retirement decision has been plagued by several generally acknowledged methodological problems. While these have been handled with greater sophistication in some studies than in others, they have been nowhere completely overcome.

Definition of Retirement. Perhaps the most obvious, even if not the most important, of these has to do with the way in which "retirement" is to be operationalized. Fields and Mitchell (1984, p. 4) list six definitions that have been used in various studies: subjective (respondent's own perception of status); complete withdrawal from labor force; reduction in hours of work below some specified level; leaving the "main employer," even if another job is subsequently taken; receiving an employer-provided pension; receiving Social Security. Even this list is somewhat oversimplified. For example, in the RHS data the subjective criterion is derived from the respondent's report as to whether he considers himself "retired, completely retired, or not retired at all." In the NLS, on the other hand, respondents are asked "At what age do you expect to stop working at a regular job?" and those who respond "I've already stopped" are conceived to be (subjectively) retired.

Parnes and Less (1985, p. 58) have shown that the subjective criterion in the NLS data is the most comprehensive in the sense that it is less likely than either of two others (receipt of Social Security or pension income and working less than 1,000 hours per year) to be the sole indicator of the retired status. Also using NLS data, Gustafson (1982) reports variation in regression results depending upon the criterion of retirement that is used. Along similar lines, Gustman and Steinmeier (1984) have used RHS data to show that estimates of retirement behavior using a dichotomous dependent variable are sensitive to how the partially retired are categorized. Using the same data base but different methods, Honig and Hanoch (1985) produce evidence showing that partial retirement is a distinct form of retirement behavior that needs to be modeled separately. Indeed, there is increasing interest in exploring a variety of labor market behaviors that cannot be captured by a single dichotomous variable (Sueyoshi, 1986; Rust, 1987).

Measuring Health. A more serious methodological problem in research on retirement relates to measuring health. The most commonly used measures have been either self-ratings of health or responses to questions whether health condition limits the amount or kind of work a respondent can do. Some writers (e.g., Myers, 1982) have criticized as unreliable any self-reports of health obtained through surveys, although Sammartino (1987, p. 42) has called attention to the high correlations between self-reported and medically-determined health status, and suggests that the former may be a superior measure of an individual's ability to work because it doubtless takes into account the physical demands of the person's job.

However, when self-reported health ratings or work limitations are obtained at the same time as retirement status is observed, both have been criticized as perhaps being post hoc rationalizations of the retirement rather than real explanations of it (e.g., Myers, 1982; Bazzoli, 1985). Moreover, questions on work-limiting health conditions have been criticized as being tautological because the evidence of poor health is in a sense merely descriptive of the behavior being explained—i.e., not working (Chirikos and Nestel, 1981, p. 95). Bazzoli's (1985) experimentation with different health measures leads her to conclude that the work-limitation measure has tended to overstate the influence of health in the retirement decision, a conclusion that is supported by the work of Anderson and Burkhauser (1985, p. 324) and of Butler, Burkhauser, Mitchell, and Pincus (1987).

A number of expedients have been used to overcome these difficulties. One has been to use a health measure reported while all members of the sample were employed to explain *subsequent* retirement behavior (e.g., Quinn, 1978). Another has been to use other proxies for health, including total hours of illness in a given year (e.g., Boskin, 1977), retrospective mortality experience (e.g., Parsons, 1981), and an index of functional limitations (Chirikos and Nestel, 1981). While some of these may represent improvements over simple work-limitation measures taken concurrently with retirement status, each probably leaves something to be desired relative to objective clinical information about health.

Measuring Economic Variables. Finally, research designs that have been based upon life-cycle theory have found it next to impossible to develop adequate measures of the necessary monetary values. In the life-cycle perspective, the individual is assumed to choose the optimal amount of work to do in the remaining years of his life. In this context, "optimal" is defined as the labor supply path that maximizes lifetime utility, a function of consumption and leisure (Mitchell and Fields, 1982, p. 116). A fully specified life-cycle model, therefore, must include the discounted present value of six income streams: the net earnings in current job, the net earnings in alternate job(s), net private pension benefits, net Social Security benefits, private pension contributions, and Social Security taxes. Merely to list these variables is to highlight the impossibility of obtaining precise measures from any existing (or indeed conceivable) data sets. It also, of course, raises some questions about the relevance of a theoretical framework that assumes individuals are inclined and able to make these kinds of calculations—including, incidentally, the required assumption of date of death.

Research Findings

Predictors of Retirement

As has been noted, the wide variety of models that have been used make a systematic summary of research findings on the predictors of retirement difficult. Most of the studies have focused on health and economic variables, but there is also ample evidence of the influence of social psychological variables—especially work commitment and degree of satisfaction with current job.

Health. Almost all analyses that have incorporated a health variable have found some measure of poor health to be related to earlier retirement, although there have been several exceptions to this generalization (Boskin, 1977; Burkhauser, 1979). On the basis of his review of the literature, Sammartino (1987, p. 41) concludes that workers in poor health are likely to retire from one to three years earlier than otherwise comparable workers in good health.

Perhaps the clearest indication of the effect of varying specifications of the dependent variable and of different data sources is provided by Palmore and his associates (1985), who used the same theoretical model to explain four measures of retirement: (1) probability of objective retirement among men who had reached their late sixties, (2) probability of early retirement (prior to age 65), (3) annual number of hours worked (among men in their late sixties), and (4) age at retirement (among NLS men age 68–69 in 1976). This model included demographic characteristics, measures of SES, health condition, and job characteristics (including pension coverage); all regressions (except age of retirement) were run using each of two data sets—the NLS and RHS. The health variable was not significant as a predictor of either objective retirement or of annual hours of work in the NLS sample and only marginally so in each case for the RHS. On the other hand, in both samples poor health was found to bear a positive relationship to the probability of early retirement and an inverse relationship to age of retirement (pp. 30–34).

As has been noted, much of the evidence of a relationship between health and early retirement is suspect because most studies have used contemporaneous measures of health and retirement status. However, there is abundant evidence that self-reported health condition among nonretired men is an independent predictor of the likelihood of *subsequent* early retirement (Barfield and Morgan, 1969; Parnes and Nestel, 1975; Quinn, 1978) and of the expectation of early retirement (Parnes and Nestel, 1975). Using age of retirement as the dependent variable, Fields and Mitchell (1984) likewise find that prior health is a significant predictor. On the other hand, in her experimentation with different health measures, Bazzoli (1985) obtained mixed results for the effect of a baseline measure of health on subsequent retirement, obtaining a statistically significant regression coefficient for one of her health measures but not for the other.

The significance of health in affecting retirement decisions has also been shown in studies of the relationship between men's retirement *plans* and their ultimate retirement *behavior*. For example, Beck (1983) has found that poor health decreases the probability of retiring when planned. Anderson, Burkhauser, and Quinn (1986) report that deterioration in health increases the probability that actual retirement will occur earlier than had been anticipated and decreases the probability that it will occur later than had been expected. Improvement in health, on the other hand, does not have analogous effects.

To summarize, it appears that poor health is a significant element in the explanation of early retirement but has much less to do with retirements occurring at age 65 or later. However, even the association between poor health and early retirement is susceptible to alternative explanations. For instance, the documented association between early acceptance of Social Security benefits and the probability of early death has been interpreted differently by the Social Security Administration (1982) and by Wolfe (1983). The Social Security Administration suggests that mortality is a proxy for poor health, and that its association with early acceptance of benefits reflects the influence of poor health on retirement. While acknowledging the possible legitimacy of this interpretation, Wolfe sees the association primarily as a vindication of the life-cycle model: "perceived longevity plays a role in the decision when to begin receipt of Social Security benefits" (p. 580).

Wages or Earnings. One might suppose that if it were possible to control completely for all other factors, the likelihood of retirement would be inversely related to the financial rewards of working. However, economic theory teaches that two counteracting forces operate on a utility-maximizer: an increase in wages increases the price of leisure (substitution effect), which favors more work (later retirement); but the higher wage also increases the individual's wealth (income effect), which leads to the purchase of more leisure (earlier retirement). Thus, the effect of earnings on retirement is theoretically ambiguous.

Moreover, analyses of wage-effects on retirement rarely control perfectly for all other factors. Two decades ago Gallaway (1965, pp. 11-13) pointed out that the *gross* relationship between earnings and retirement is affected by two offsetting intercorrelations. First, high earnings are associated with high savings and liberal pensions, which he believed increase the propensity to retire. Second, high earnings create the desire for high levels of post-retirement consumption, which would operate in the opposite direction.

In addition to the factors that Gallaway mentioned, it is clear that high earnings are also associated with other elements of job satisfaction that are likely to affect retirement behavior and that have only rarely been included in regression analyses. For all of these reasons, in addition to the fact that earnings have been defined and measured in different ways by different investigators, it is hardly surprising that research findings on the relation between wages and retirement behavior have varied widely. On the basis of their painstaking examination of the conflicting evidence, Mitchell and Fields (1982, p. 146) have concluded that when statistically significant results have been obtained, they have more frequently shown that *higher* wages (or wage streams) result in *later* retirement.

However, Anderson and Burkhauser (1985) have suggested that the reason for the frequent finding of only a small or even a nonsignificant effect of wage on the retirement decision is the fact that the health variable may be picking up part of the influence of wage. The problem arises from treating health as an exogenous variable; if a substantial portion of variation in health is attributable to choice, so that preference for work is correlated with preference for good health, "then the estimated impact of health on retirement may be too large, and the estimated effect of wages on retirement may be too small" (p. 316). The results of their analysis are consistent with this hypothesis.

Social Security and Pension Income. Research on the effect of Social Security on the retirement decision has taken two interrelated thrusts. One examines the effect on retirement of the level of Social Security benefits to which an individual is entitled; the other addresses the question whether the system as a whole, or specific aspects of it, have had an effect on the labor supply of the elderly. The latter issue is treated later; here the issue is whether the level of anticipated Social Security benefits and/or other pension income affects an individual's choice of retirement age.

The review of the literature on this subject prior to their own pathbreaking empirical work led Mitchell and Fields (1982, p. 147) to assert that "no empirical conclusion can be drawn about the effects of Social Security on retirement." They point out that the studies that had been made of this issue frequently used as the Social Security variable only the level of benefits for which the individual was currently eligible (or simply the fact of eligibility), rather than the theoretically correct *anticipated income stream* from Social Security. Nevertheless, there were conflicting findings even within each of these specifications.

Mitchell and Fields show that theoretically, for a utility-maximizer in a life-cycle framework, age of retirement is expected to be positively related to the base level of pension (or Social Security) benefit, but that the relation between the prospective annual rate of increase in pension income and the age of retirement is ambiguous because of offsetting income and substitution effects (pp. 137–39). Studies prior to their own had generally not taken account of the entire stream of pension income; most had used simply pension eligibility, while others had used level of current benefits. While findings were not consistent, they generally showed that higher current benefit levels tend to encourage retirement (p. 149).

The extensive research of Fields and Mitchell on this issue is summarized in their *Retirement, Pensions, and Social Security* (1984), a volume remarkable not only for its methodological and analytical rigor, but for its lucid and graceful prose, which makes at least its major thesis accessible even to noneconomists. As has been noted, the authors believe that the most useful theoretical approach is to postulate a utility-maximizer operating in a life-cycle framework. Utilizing RHS data for white married men ages 59–61 employed as wage and salary workers in 1969, the "game" is to assume that these individuals are making their retirement decisions at that time, and that they select a retirement age by calculating which will yield the greatest combination of income and leisure.

They are successful in utilizing three of the six economic variables that they believe are relevant to choosing the optimal retirement age (see pp. 120–121, above): anticipated net earnings stream in current job, estimated stream of Social Security benefits for husband and wife, and estimated stream of net private pension benefits. These three income streams are discounted to produce the present discounted value of income (*PDVY*) for each possible retirement age between 60 and 68. The basic model, then, uses two economic variables based on these data: (1) the level of *PDVY* if retirement were to occur at age 60 (the intercept), and (2) the rate of increase in this value if retirement is deferred to age 65 (the slope). A health variable also appears in the RHS data; when BAS data are used because of the greater reliability of the pension data, no measure of health is available. Finally, in an alternative discrete choice model, it is possible explicitly to introduce a leisure variable (years in retirement).

The authors hypothesize a negative relationship between retirement age and base-year level of *PDVY* simply because wealthier people should wish to consume more leisure. Despite the theoretical ambiguity, they hypothesize a positive sign for the slope variable, expecting that the greater the financial gains to postponing retirement, the later it will take place. There is strong support for both hypotheses in both the RHS and BAS data sets, and across four different types of model.

Four additional major conclusions are yielded by the Fields and Mitchell work. First, while evidence of the impact of the economic variables on the retirement decision is clear, the elasticities—i.e., the responsiveness of retirement age to moderate changes in the economic variables—are not large. For example, their analysis indicates that raising the normal retirement age from 65 to 68 would delay retirement on average by only about 1.5 months (pp. 120–23). Other investigators have reached similar conclusions; the estimate of Burtless and Moffitt (1984, p. 166) (produced by quite different methods) amounts to well under half a year.

Second, there is wide variation in the characteristics of private pension plans, some rewarding early retirement and others making later retirement more attractive (pp. 53–61). The influence of pension characteristics on retirement had, of course, been well recognized even prior to their work. Whether or not one regards pensions as implicit contracts between employers and workers (Lazear, 1979; Clark and McDermed, 1986; Ippolito 1986), it is clear that employers understand the utility of pension arrangements in encouraging or discouraging retirements (Meier, Chapter 7 in this volume; Gravitz and Rumack, 1983).

Third, as would be expected, the variation in pension plans is accompanied by differences in average retirement age across plans. However, not all of this difference in retirement age can be accounted for by differences in the structure of incentives incorporated in the plans; an even larger part of the difference apparently stems from differences in the tastes of the workers (pp. 107–108).

Finally, the authors' major conclusion is that "choice, rather than compulsion, plays a significant role in the retirement decision, in ways consistent with economic theory" (p. 129). Specifically, they reject mandatory retirement rules and poor health as significant influences. This is a matter to which we return below.

Unemployment. It is clear from a variety of types of evidence that unemployment may induce a decision of older workers to leave the labor market (Rones, Chapter 2 in this volume). Quinn (1985) has found that residing in an area of high unemployment increases the likelihood of retirement. Shapiro and Sandell (1984) report that 60-year-old job-losers are three times as likely as other men of the same age to retire. Moreover, labor market adversity is among the reasons for retirement that retirees report retrospectively or that can reasonably be inferred from their employment histories (see p. 134, below).

Inflation. It is curious that life-cycle theorists appear not to have tested empirically the impact of inflation on retirement, although the subject has received a fair amount of comment during the late 1970s and early 1980s, including empirical studies of the effect of inflation on retirement wealth (Clark and Sumner, 1985; Quinn, 1985). Some observers saw signs that inflation might slow or perhaps even reverse the trend toward early retirement (Sheppard, 1981; Clark and McDermed, 1982; Quinn, 1985); others, while recognizing the possibility, pointed to evidence that questioned that conclusion (Morgan, 1981; Parnes, 1981).

The point, of course, is that while Social Security benefits are fully tied to the Consumer Price Index (CPI), private pension plans typically are not, although they have been shown to be more responsive to inflation through ad hoc increases in benefits than many observers had believed (Allen, Clark, and Sumner, 1984, 1986; Clark and Sumner, 1985). Life-cycle theory—and, indeed, even the conventional wisdom of laypersons—would predict that unanticipated increases in the rate of inflation, other things being equal, should have the effect of discouraging retirement. However, while economic theorists have examined the effects of unanticipated increases in Social Security benefits (Hurd and Boskin, 1984; Burtless, 1986; Anderson, Burkhauser, and Quinn, 1986), I have seen no analogous empirical work by persons of that theoretical orientation on the effect of inflation.

While admittedly not conclusive in the absence of controls for other factors, the best available evidence that inflation has not had the impact on retirement decisions that many had anticipated (and that theory would predict) are the continued downward trends during the 1970s and 1980s in labor force participation by older men and in the increasing proportion of early retirements under Social Security (Table 1). The CPI rose by 31 percent in the 1960s, by 112 percent in the 1970s, and by 33 percent in the first six years of the 1980s. During the decade of the 1960s the rate of labor force participation of men 65 years of age and older dropped 19.1 percent, as compared with 28.7 percent in the 1970s and 16.2 percent in the first six years of the 1980s. The corresponding figures

128   THE OLDER WORKER

TABLE 1

Inflation Rate, Labor Force Participation Rates for Older Men,
and Proportion of Male Social Security Awards at Age 62,
Selected Years

Year	Change in CPI from Previous Year	Percent in Labor Force		Percent of New Retirement Awards at Age 62
		Age 55–64	Age 65+	
1960	1.0	86.8	33.1	—
1970	5.9	83.0	26.8	18.4
1975	9.1	75.6	21.6	25.8
1976	5.8	74.3	20.2	27.4
1977	6.4	74.0	20.1	26.6
1978	7.6	73.5	20.5	28.6
1979	11.2	73.0	20.0	27.7
1980	13.5	72.3	19.1	30.1
1981	10.4	70.6	18.4	30.8
1982	6.1	70.2	17.8	34.4
1983	3.2	69.4	17.4	35.8
1984	4.2	68.5	16.3	36.4
1985	3.6	67.9	15.8	n.a.
1986	1.9	67.3	16.0	n.a.

Source: Bureau of Labor Statistics and Social Security Administration.

for men 55–64 years of age are 4.4 percent, 12.9 percent, and 6.9 percent. Over the entire period 1975–1984 the ratio of retirement awards at age 62 to all male Social Security retirement awards rose almost continuously from 26 percent to 36 percent.

Social Psychological Variables. Even if one accepts the utility-maximizing rationale of economic theory, it stands to reason that differences in "tastes" among individuals should have independent effects upon retirement behavior. However, virtually none of the empirical work published in economic journals has explicitly introduced such attitudinal variables.

An analysis of NLS data covering the period 1966–1971 showed that commitment to the work ethic and degree of satisfaction with current job were statistically significant predictors of both the expectation of early retirement as of 1971 and the likelihood of actual early retirement during the period of the study (Parnes and Nestel, 1975). Barfield and Morgan (1969) and Morgan (1981) have also found factors of this kind to be significant determinants of early retirement, but attach considerably less importance to them than to economic factors. Palmore et al. (1985) found attitude toward retirement to be a significant predictor of all four of their measures of retirement, but of lesser importance than their "structural variables" (SES and job characteristics, including pension coverage).

Rather than examining job satisfaction, Quinn (1978) has analyzed the relationship between job characteristics and the likelihood of early retirement among close to 5,000 white married males. He found that early retirement was more likely from jobs with undesirable attributes (e.g., high stress, monotony, great physical demands). Moreover, men in poor health were more sensitive than other men to the character of the work environment.

Gender. Far less attention has been paid to the retirement behavior of women than of men, primarily because of the traditionally low labor force participation rate of women approaching retirement age, the widespread presumption that employment does not represent for them the "central life interest" that it does for men (Szinovacz, 1982, p. 17), and the fact that labor force participation rates among elderly women have not shown the precipitous decline that is evident for men (Shaw and Shaw, 1987). Reflecting these basic factors, there has been no data set for women comparable to the NLS and RHS for men. The NLS sample of the cohort of "mature" women has only recently entered the "pre-retirement years" (Shaw, 1984); the RHS sampled only *unmarried* women, although it did obtain limited information about the wives of the married men in the sample (Henretta and O'Rand, 1980; Pozzebon and Mitchell, 1987).

Whether men and women differ in the factors affecting their decisions to retire has only very recently begun to be explored. The nearest approach to the issue prior to the 1980s was Bowen and Finegan's (1969) classic study of the determinants of labor force participation of a number of male and female age groups. Most of the recent studies of unmarried women based on the RHS have found predictors of retirement that do not differ much from those that have been found for married men (Gratton and Haug, 1983, pp. 67–68). Hanoch and Honig (1983) use RHS data to make explicit comparisons of extent of work activity between white married males and white unmarried females. Most of their results for both men and women conform to theoretical expectation and the findings of other studies; in labor force participation equations for men and women the same variables are statistically significant and the explained variance is almost identical. Honig (1985) has shown that partial retirement is a significant status for unmarried women, as it is for men, and therefore deserves separate treatment in modeling their retirement behavior.

Other studies of unmarried women alone have shown that both health and eligibility for Social Security and/or pension income are significant determinants of retirement (O'Rand and Henretta, 1982) or retirement plans (Hall and Johnson, 1980; Shaw, 1985), as they appear to be for men. The study by O'Rand and Henretta also produced evidence that delayed entry into the work force and having children reduce the likelihood of early retirement both directly and indirectly (by affecting pension coverage). The study by Palmore et al. (1985, p. 116) diverges from these other studies in finding a substantial difference between men and unmarried women in the predictors of retirement.

Several studies have examined the relationship between the retirement behavior or plans of husbands and wives (Clark, Johnson, and McDermed, 1980; Anderson, Clark, and Johnson, 1980; Henretta and O'Rand, 1983; Shaw, 1984; Shaw and Gagen, 1984). These have generally shown that each member of the pair is influenced by the plans or behavior of the other (Gratton and Haug, 1983, p. 68). Henretta and O'Rand (1983, p. 515), for example, conclude on the basis of their study of the retirements of 1,868 white married couples for whom RHS data were available that ". . . retirement is . . . a process that involves the family unit."

Only two studies of the predictors of actual retirement for a national sample of *married* women have come to my attention (Henretta and O'Rand, 1980; Pozzebon and Mitchell, 1987). Henretta and O'Rand used RHS data for working wives in 1969 and contrasted those who stopped working with those who continued to work until 1971 or 1973. They found that current support of a child or an aged parent was associated with continued presence in the labor market. For older women (age 58 or older), coverage by a pension plan and husband's poor health were each associated with a reduced probability of remaining at work.

Pozzebon and Mitchell also used RHS data for the wives (age 54 to 62 in 1969) of white men in family units in which both partners were employed as private-sector wage and salary workers and were included in all five interviews between 1969 and 1979. These restrictions yielded a sample of 139.

The authors employ a life-cycle framework identical to what Fields and Mitchell (1984) used in analyzing the RHS male sample, but with a somewhat different explanatory model because they "postulate that married women's retirement behavior is a more complex phenomenon, affected by both economic and family considerations" (p. 1). The regression results are very different from what the results for males would have led one to expect. Neither of the two economic variables based on the woman's own income is significant. Moreover, contrary to expectation, the husband's income stream is positively related to woman's retirement age. The "family responsibility" variables are of greater influence. Husband's poor health tends to delay the woman's retirement; a large age difference between husband and wife tends to result in earlier retirement, which can be interpreted as pointing to a desire to share leisure time.

Race. There has been very little research that has attempted to compare the retirement behavior of blacks and whites. A study based on the NLS data for 1966–1971 (Parnes and Nestel, 1975) used pooled data for blacks and whites after finding no significant interaction between race and other explanatory variables. No significant differences existed between whites and blacks either in the probability of their actual retirement over the period 1966–1971 or in the frequency of their 1971 expectation to retire early.

Morgan (1980), using PSID data, likewise found no racial differences in retirement intentions. Burkhauser's (1980) study of the decision of males to accept Social Security benefits at age 62 found no significant racial difference. Parsons (1981) found that racial differences in labor force participation among men 45–59 in 1966 disappeared when controls were introduced for demographic factors as well as for the ratio between potential transfer income and wages.

On the other hand, Burkhauser (1979) found that whites were more likely than blacks to take early pensions, but cautioned that the sample that he used (auto workers) was not representative of the entire population of older males. In stratified regressions for blacks and whites using both NLS and RHS data, Palmore and his associates (1985) found that far fewer of the explanatory variables were significant for blacks than for whites, but that the pattern was not consistent as between the NLS and RHS. It is difficult to know what to make of these findings, however, in view of the severe specification problems that appear to plague the analysis (Pampel, 1986; Mitchell, 1987).

Other Variables. A host of other variables have been used in models designed to explain retirement behavior, but it is difficult to summarize and interpret findings relating to them because so much depends upon the nature of the study and the specification of the model. A perfect illustration of the point is *age.* In a study using labor force participation as the dependent variable, one would expect age to be a significant explanatory variable even for a relatively restricted age group of men, and this is precisely what Hanoch and Honig (1983) find in a study of the RHS sample. On the other hand, in the study where age of retirement is the dependent variable and where the model assumes that the decision is being made by all persons at age 60 (Fields and Mitchell, 1984), age clearly does not enter the picture as an explanatory variable.

As another example, when occupation and/or education are used to explain some measure of retirement behavior, both the results and their interpretation depend upon what other variables are in the model. Either of these variables may proxy for earnings, likelihood of pension eligibility, level of expected pension, and degree of satisfaction with job. In addition, educational attainment may reflect a "taste" for work. Burkhauser (1980), for example, found years of schooling to be negatively related to the probability of accepting early Social Security benefits in one of his two samples despite careful controls for economic variables. Hall and Johnson (1980) found a similar relationship between educational attainment and retirement plans.

Among additional factors that have been found in at least one study to be associated with a tendency of men to retire or to plan to retire early are being unmarried (Parnes and Nestel, 1975; Morgan, 1980; Diamond and Hausman, 1984; Palmore et al., 1985); having few or no dependents (Parnes and Nestel, 1975); and being a wage and salary earner rather than self-employed (Hall and Johnson, 1980; Morgan, 1980; Quinn, 1980; Palmore et al., 1985). Hayward and Hardy (1985) have explored occupational differences in early retirement by estimating a model with conventional explanatory variables for a variety of job families. They find that explanatory variables vary considerably across their occupational categories. Another study by Hardy (1985), however, reports fairly consistent determinants of retirement behavior across occupational categories when differences in retirement age are controlled.

Reasons for Retirement

Classifications of retirees according to the reasons for their retirement have generally had the objective of determining the relative importance of voluntary versus involuntary withdrawals from the labor force by the elderly. Data have come from a variety of sources: the Current Population Survey (CPS) of the Census Bureau, the Social Security Administration's Survey of New Beneficiaries (SNB), retrospective questions asked of respondents in sample surveys (e.g., NLS and RHS), and inferences based on longitudinal records from the NLS (Parnes and Less, 1985).

In its study of early retirement, the General Accounting Office (1986) presents CPS data on reported reasons for not working for individuals 50 years of age and over who did no work at all in 1983, classified by pension status. The data for men show that the proportion attributing nonwork to health or disability bears a strong inverse relation to age, falling from 65 percent of those in their early fifties to 14 percent of those 65 and over. Conversely, the proportion citing "retirement" rose from only 13 percent of the youngest group to over four-fifths of the oldest. In every age category the proportion citing "retirement" is higher (and the proportion citing health is lower) for persons receiving pensions than for those who are not. Unemployment accounts for less than 5 percent of the responses of all the groups of men except nonrecipients of pensions under age 62; for those in their early fifties without pensions the proportion reaches almost one-fifth.

Interviews with newly entitled Social Security beneficiaries in 1982 asked respondents who were not working why they had left their last job. The most common reason among the men was simply a desire to retire (40 percent), with health problems accounting for 27 percent. Business adversity or loss of job accounted for 10 percent of the total, while compulsory retirement was reported by 7 percent (Sherman, 1985).

Analogous to the CPS data, the SNB also shows that health reasons are more frequently the reason for early retirement than for retirement at age 65 or older. Among men who entered the Social Security rolls at age 62, one-third reported health as the reason for leaving last job, as compared with 24 percent of those 63–64 and 15 percent of those 65 or older. It should be noted in this connection that three-fourths of the men began drawing benefits before age 65, and that almost one-half began at age 62. Other recent survey data

on reasons for retirement report distributions that differ somewhat
from those of the SNB (Parnes and Nestel, 1981, p. 161; Palmore
et al., 1985, p. 69); to what extent this results from differences in
definition of "retirement," differences in classification systems, or
differences in time period cannot be said with confidence.

Inferring reason for retirement from the entire longitudinal
record of each retiree *prior to his retirement*, Parnes and Nestel
(1981. pp. 160-61) compared the resulting classification with the
retrospective reports of the same respondents and found evidence
to support their a priori belief that the retrospective reports might
suffer from post hoc rationalization. The classification system that
they ultimately developed included four categories of "routes to
retirement": mandatory, health, discouragement (labor market
adversity), and voluntary. Included in the first of these were men
who had indicated being covered by a mandatory retirement plan,
who retired at the mandatory age, *and* who in the survey preceding
retirement had indicated that they would have preferred to work
longer. In other words, in the absence of health or unemployment
problems the authors classified as voluntary retirees men under a
mandatory plan who retired earlier than they had to or at the
mandatory age if they gave no evidence of wanting to work longer.

Of the more than 2,100 men in the NLS sample who had retired
by 1981, only 3 percent had been unwillingly removed from jobs by
the operation of mandatory retirement plans. A larger proportion,
at least 5 percent and perhaps as many as 10 percent, appear to have
retired as a consequence of labor market adversity. Far more
important than both these factors combined in forcing individuals
into retirement was poor health, accounting for about 35 percent of
the total. However, for a majority of the retirees—almost three-
fifths of the total, retirement seems to have been completely
voluntary (Parnes and Less, 1985, pp. 70-73).

There are pronounced differences in these proportions
according to race and to age at retirement. Blacks are much more
likely than whites to have retired for health reasons; health
retirements are also more frequent among very early retirees—47
percent of those who retired prior to age 62 as compared with one-
fourth of those retiring at 62 or later.

Returning for a moment to self-reports of reasons for retirement,
a very interesting trend is discernible both in Social Security
Administration and in CPS data. When the results of the 1982 SNB

are compared with a similar (though not identical) survey of new beneficiaries in 1968 (SNEB), there is a pronounced reversal in the proportions reporting voluntary versus health-induced retirements; in the earlier survey more than one-half of new male beneficiaries 62–64 years of age attributed their retirement to health problems in contrast to fewer than one-third for the same age group in the later one (Sherman, 1985, p. 25). CPS data also show a substantial decline between 1973 and 1983 in the proportion of men 55 and over who cited health or disability as the reason for not working during the year (General Accounting Office, 1986, p. 43).

It may be tempting to attribute this difference to an intercohort improvement in health, especially in view of the clear evidence of improvements in mortality over time. The problem with this interpretation, however, is that that although the evidence on improvement in mortality is definitive, there is considerable ambiguity about the trend in morbidity and disability (Berkowitz, Chapter 4 in this volume). Their careful review of the evidence on this issue has led Chapman, LaPlante, and Wilensky (1986) to conclude that health status of the elderly has deteriorated over the past two decades, while mortality has improved, and Ycas (1987) finds evidence of the same trend at least through 1981 in data from the National Health Interview Survey. Further, while some of this may be attributable to a greater willingness to "adopt the sick role" than in the past because of the greater availability of social and economic supports, part of it is also real and reflects the influence of increased survival (Chapman, LaPlante, and Wilensky, 1986, p. 44).

If the trend in reported reasons for retirement is real, and if it cannot be explained in terms of improvements in the health of successive cohorts of retirees, an alternative explanation is cultural. That is, the institutionalization of early retirement and its greater social respectability may have operated to reduce the tendency of men to resort to a "poor health" explanation of early withdrawal from the labor market—an "excuse" that has always been acceptable.

Intercohort trends in the health of the elderly may have another implication. Wolfe (1985) has argued that it is possible for average retirement age to fall even as the health of the elderly improves as the result of mid-life investments in health (through retirement). Thus, the health of older persons, he suggests, may improve largely *because* of earlier retirement.

Health versus Economic Variables. Much of the research on the reasons for retirement and, indeed, on the retirement decision generally, has focused on the relative importance of poor health and of economic incentives in explaining the withdrawal of elderly males from the labor market. Especially has this been true in analyzing the determinants of early retirement. Early studies by the Social Security Administration tended to emphasize involuntary factors (Campbell and Campbell, 1976).

Exactly how the issue is to be interpreted, and what kinds of evidence ought to be sought to provide an answer, are questions whose answers are not immediately apparent. On the one hand, it is clear that some persons are forced out of the labor market by disabilities so severe that economic rewards or penalties may be completely irrelevant. On the other hand, it is equally obvious that many persons with no manifestations of health problems retire at relatively early ages just because they are financially able to do so. But for most persons there is surely some interaction between the two variables such that identical health impairments will produce different retirement decisions depending upon financial resources, and that identical financial resources will produce different decisions depending on health condition. Some evidence for this a priori inference is Quinn's (1978) finding that the effects of eligibility for Social Security and for other pensions in inducing early retirement are much greater for white married men with health problems than for those without such problems. Bazzoli (1985, p. 225), on the other hand, found no such interaction in the case of any of her four health measures, and she calls for more research on the issue. Diamond and Hausman (1984, p. 113) estimate that the onset of bad health "causes the same percentage rise in the probability of retirement as an increase in a pension equal to about $6,500 a year."

A particularly vigorous debate on the question of the role of health in explaining early retirement was generated by Kingson's research (1981a, 1981b) on *very* early retirees (i.e., men retiring prior to age 62). Finding very little difference in health condition between Social Security disability benefit recipients and nonrecipients who had reported work-limiting health problems, Kingson urged that consideration be given to changing the eligibility requirements for disability benefits. These findings were challenged by Myers (1982) both on the grounds of the unreliability of survey data (especially regarding health) and on technical grounds relating to Kingson's treatment of the data. A spirited debate ensued (Kingson, 1982, 1983; Myers, 1983), which prompted Daymont and Andrisani (1983) to subject the Kingson data to further analysis; they concluded that while the two groups that Kingson had compared were not as similar as he had claimed, many nonrecipients of Social Security disability benefits do indeed have health problems severe enough to keep them from working.

Although Fields and Mitchell have not concerned themselves with the specific issue of the Kingson-Myers controversy, they clearly share some of Myers's skepticism about self-reported health as a means of assessing the importance of that variable in accounting for early retirement (1984, pp. 8–9). Their method of approaching the issue is through an analysis of variance that shows that three-fourths of the explained variance in retirement age among members of their sample is accounted for by economic variables and only one-fourth by health variables (p. 69).

While it is true that six different specifications produce results that can fairly be summarized in this way, it is not entirely clear how much light the finding can shed on the underlying question. First of all, the one-fourth/three-fourths split needs to be viewed in the light of the fact that the economic variables in the model used for this part of the analysis explain only 2 percent of the total variation in retirement age (p. 67). Second, the economic variables in the analysis are continuous, while the health variable is dichotomous; thus, since variation in health is in fact as continuous as variation in economic incentives, this procedure gives an "advantage" to the former on purely technical grounds. Finally, the dependent variable is *age of retirement* rather than *probability of early retirement*, and most of the debate about the relative importance of health has centered on the latter issue.

In short, despite the valuable work they have done in exploring the effects of the economic variables on retirement behavior, the Fields and Mitchell findings on the respective role of health versus economic factors in the retirement decision need to be interpreted with considerable care. Certainly they do not mean (nor do the authors claim that they do) that economic factors are in some sense three times as important as health in explaining retirement decisions.

Has Social Security Affected Retirement Trends?

That economists have expended a great deal of effort to find an answer to this question must occasion at least mild surprise among noneconomists, most of whom would doubtless regard an affirmative answer as being among the more obvious aspects of contemporary life (cf., Morrison, 1986). That this considerable effort has produced no generally acceptable answer is perhaps even more difficult to understand.

The reasons both for the substantial effort and for the disappointing results are admirably explained by Aaron (1982). He demonstrates, first, that alternative theoretical formulations lead to different expectations about the effect of the Social Security program on the labor supply of the elderly (and, indeed, the rest of the population as well). Second, he shows that the complexity of the Social Security system, and particularly its many departures from a pure annuity system, introduces ambiguities in expected outcomes irrespective of the theoretical framework used. Finally, available data simply do not permit adequate empirical tests of any of the theoretical frameworks.

Most of the work that has been done on this issue has been guided by the life-cycle model (see pp. 120–121, above). The strength of this approach, according to Aaron, is that "it enables economists to bring the full armory of economic theory to bear on the question of how social security affects economic behavior"; its weakness, on the other hand is "the belief of many economists and the conviction of most others that people do not consistently" behave according to the assumptions of the theory (pp. 23–24).

Aaron acknowledges that most empirical studies have concluded that Social Security reduces the labor supplied by elderly workers, but points out that estimates of the size of the effect have varied and that, moreover, at least four studies have found that Social Security has either *increased* labor supply or has had no significant effect on it. He is clearly not inclined to draw any conclusion on the matter, especially in view of inadequacies in the data on which the studies are based. "The shortcomings are not perfectionist quibbles with which analysts like to deflate the works of competitors, but fundamental inadequacies that . . . undermine the believability of the results" (p. 58).

Thompson's review of the empirical literature (1983) leads him also to call attention to the conflicting results and to conclude

". . . either that the effects are fairly modest or that we have yet to model successfully the complex interactions" (p. 1448). In their examination of the same studies, Danziger, Haveman, and Plotnick (1981, p. 996) conclude that Social Security can account for at most one-half of the decline in older male labor force participation since 1950.

A recent facet of the debate concerns the effect of the substantial increase in Social Security benefits that were legislated in 1969 and 1972. Hurd and Boskin (1984) conclude that the accelerated decline in the labor force participation rate of the RHS sample over the period 1969-1973 can be almost entirely explained by the increase in their "Social Security wealth." Sueyoshi (1986) finds that the benefit increases had differing effects on the probabilities of full and partial retirement, raising the former but lowering the latter. Studying the relationship between retirement plans and actual retirements, Anderson, Burkhauser, and Quinn (1986) found that the unanticipated rise in benefits increased the probability that men would retire earlier than they had previously planned and decreased the probability of later-than-planned retirements. However, applying a model based on the theory of consumer choice to explain retirement ages, Burtless (1986) has concluded that the rising level of Social Security benefits in the 1970s played only a small role in explaining the decrease in the average retirement age of men. Moffitt (1987) comes to the same conclusion on the basis of time series data and, moreover, demonstrates that the *unanticipated* increase in Social Security wealth was actually greater in the 1950s than in the late 1960s and early 1970s.

If the influence of Social Security is denied, how does one account for the undisputed fact that increasing proportions of persons have opted for retirement prior to age 65? Burtless (1986, p. 801) suggests that rising levels of wealth, the higher unemployment rate after 1970, and changing attitudes toward work and retirement have been the major factors at work. Aaron (1982) offers three competing explanations: (1) that higher incomes have induced the "purchase" of more leisure or that the spread of private pensions has induced earlier retirement; (2) that Social Security, despite its actuarial neutrality between ages 62 and 64 *on average*, does allow early retirement to increase the lifetime income for some workers, viz., those with short life expectancies; or (3) that even if the

financial incentives of Social Security are neutral as between early
retirement and retirement at age 65, people might not understand
this and (irrationally) favor the former.

To complicate matters further, disagreement exists as to
whether the Social Security program is in fact actuarially neutral
between 62 and 65. Blinder, Gordon, and Wise (1980) have
produced evidence that leads them to conclude that when the effect
on ultimate benefits of continuing to work between 62 and 65 is
taken into account, it actually pays the average worker to remain at
work, but their calculations have been disputed by Burkhauser and
Turner (1981). Both Burtless and Moffitt (1986) and Sickles and
Taubman (1986) demonstrate that the effects of imperfect capital
markets create a strong incentive for individuals to retire exactly at
age 62, which explains the clustering of retirements at that age.

Even the question of whether the earnings test discourages work
by persons to whom it applies (now those under 70; previously
those under 72) does not have an unambiguous answer, although
both Pellechio (1979) and Burtless and Moffitt (1984, 1986) have
produced what they regard to be supportive evidence. Tracy (1983)
concludes on the basis of an examination of labor force
participation rates in six nations that the elimination or liberalization
of earnings tests (or the imposition of a more restrictive test in one
case) have had no effect on labor supply.

In my opinion, Aaron (1982, p. 64) identifies the principal
problem underlying research on the effect of Social Security on
retirement behavior:

> . . . the likelihood that people understand the complexities
> of benefit recomputation and actuarial adjustment is small.
> If analysts failed until recently to unravel their effects and
> continue to disagree about whether they constitute a
> subsidy or a tax, how likely is it that workers and their
> spouses can find the answer?

In this context, Hamermesh's (1984) study of retirement
behavior among male members of the Terman sample of gifted
individuals is of interest. Hamermesh notes that ". . . these people
presumably have an above-average ability to make the calculations
implicit in that [life-cycle] theory" (p. 356). Finding that differences
in life expectancy are associated with disappointingly small
increases in working life, he notes that "this is inconsistent with the

simplest versions of life-cycle theory," but quickly adds that it may be the result of specification problems in his model that are dictated by the data.

Before leaving this topic, it is of interest to mention that the kind of economic theorizing that underlies most of the research on the effects of Social Security has also led at least one observer to the conclusion that the spread of private pensions may not be responsible for the trend toward earlier retirement. While acknowledging as indisputable the fact that pension plans are designed to penalize departure from the labor force "too early" or "too late," Ippolito (1986) argues that this does not mean that retirement age has been affected. He believes that through such rules pension firms attract workers whose "behavioral inclinations are consistent with these rules." Thus, pensions are more likely to have resulted simply in a "reshuffling of workers, not an alteration in overall mobility and retirement age policies in the economy as a whole" (p. 150). Along somewhat different lines, Owen (1986) raises the question whether pensions have been a truly exogenous factor or simply a response to new demands of workers. "There is good reason to regard higher real wages as a basic factor underlying more retirement leisure" (p. 78).

Whether the *disability insurance* provisions of the Social Security Act (DI) help to explain the declining labor force participation of men prior to their eligibility for retirement benefits is a related question that empirical research has addressed, but this also remains a matter of controversy. Using NLS data, Parsons (1980a, 1980b, 1981) estimated a model of the labor force participation of men 45 to 59 years of age in 1986 that included among its variables the ratio of potential Social Security DI benefits to wage for each individual and the ratio of level of welfare payment to wages in the state.

The statistical results led Parsons to conclude that (1) the relation between what a man can expect in DI benefits and what he can earn in the labor market exerts a powerful influence on his labor force participation; (2) when this factor is controlled, the difference in labor force participation between white and black men disappears; and (3) his model accounts almost perfectly for the actual trend in the participation rates of blacks and whites between 1966 and 1976 (1981, pp. 150–51).

While other studies confirm the relationship that Parsons has found, they generally disagree with its magnitude. Haveman, Wolfe, and Warlick (1984), for example, criticize a number of aspects of Parsons's work, and they conclude on the basis of their own that not more than about one-seventh of the actual decline in the labor force participation of males 55–64 between 1968 and 1978 can be attributed to the increased generosity of disability benefits. While it seems that the Parsons estimates of the effect of DI may indeed have been too high, it also seems too early to conclude that the issue has been definitively resolved (Newhouse, 1984; Haveman and Wolfe, 1984a, 1984b; Haveman, Wolfe, and Warlick, 1984; Parsons, 1984).

Conclusions

Stepping back from the detailed research findings, I should like to conclude with some rather broad personal interpretations of the evidence and what it implies both for policy and for further research on the factors affecting the retirement decision.

1. The most general conclusion is that retirement decisions are obviously complex; they are influenced by a variety of economic and noneconomic factors including current and prospective earnings, assets, prospective retirement income, health, attitude toward work in general, and the degree of satisfaction the individual derives from the job currently held.

2. Despite the attention they have attracted, mandatory retirement rules, even prior to the legislation that first restricted and then prohibited them (Sandell, Chapter 9 in this volume), have accounted for a very small proportion of retirements during the past two decades. Elimination of such rules, while desirable on the grounds of equity, will not substantially affect the labor force participation of older men.

3. The fact that no study has carefully incorporated all of the relevant variables affecting retirement makes literal interpretation of regression coefficients hazardous or downright silly. At least two economists who have done pioneering work in the field have acknowledged that the diversity of the retirement phenomenon "strains the capacities of economic theory and statistical technique" (Aaron and Burtless, 1984, p. 22).

4. While it is not possible to assess in any precise way the relative importance of economic and noneconomic factors in the retirement decision, it is clear that they both play a significant role,

and that the explanatory power of specific factors varies depending on what one is attempting to explain (e.g., the probability of early retirement, age of retirement, etc.).

5. The most obvious example of the foregoing generalization is the greater importance of health problems in explaining early retirement than retirements that take place at later ages. A large proportion of "early" retirees (prior to age 65), and an even larger proportion of "very early" retirees (prior to age 62), have substantial health problems. Policy measures designed to increase the age of retirement must be mindful of the needs of these people.

Specifically, the increase in the "normal" retirement age mandated by the 1983 amendments to the Social Security Act may operate especially harshly relative to the elderly with severe health problems. Even on the assumption that relatively fewer older workers will be unable to work in the future than now, the best available estimate is that the reduction in total income at retirement for workers in physically demanding jobs and/or ill health will be about 6 or 7 percent when the amendment becomes fully effective in 2027 (Social Security Administration, October 1986). In this context, it must be noted that although Social Security is supposed to be only one of the legs on a three-legged stool (employer-provided pensions and individual savings being the other two), it constitutes at least 90 percent of income for one-fourth of all persons 65 years of age or older (Social Security Administration, June 1986).

6. The specific provisions of the Social Security Act have affected the volume and timing of retirements, but probably by less than is popularly supposed. If any credence at all can be attached to the findings of the very careful econometric work that has been done on this subject, it would appear that fairly substantial changes in benefit levels would lead to quite modest changes in retirement *behavior*, which means that retirement *income* would be more substantially affected. This is a conclusion to which income transfer policy must also be sensitive.

7. Pension plans provided by employers vary considerably in liberality of benefits, age and circumstances under which they become available, and degree of "actuarial neutrality." There is abundant evidence that the retirement behavior of workers is affected by these differences and, indeed, that some of the characteristics of pensions are intended to have these effects.

8. If it is desirable to cause workers to delay retirement, this can be accomplished to some extent through appropriate modifications in both Social Security (e.g., the 1983 amendments) and employer-provided pension plans, and in each case both by increasing the penalties for early retirement and by increasing the rewards for later retirement. The potential damage to the economic welfare of retirees—especially those disadvantaged by poor health and poor labor market prospects—is smaller by acting on employer-provided pensions than by acting on the Social Security system, and smaller by operating through rewards for later retirement than through penalties for early retirement.

9. It is clearly more difficult for the federal government to attempt to affect retirement age through private pensions than through amendments to the Social Security Act. Not only would the former involve rather complex regulation, but it is not clear what kind of regulation should be formulated. The requirement for the continued accrual of pension benefits for workers age 65 and over that was enacted in 1986 (Sandell, Chapter 9 in this volume) is patently desirable from this point of view as well as on grounds of equity. However, any general requirement for strict actuarial neutrality might well be counterproductive in existing plans that reward deferred retirement (Fields and Mitchell, 1984, p. 132).

10. Research findings demonstrate the relevance of policy instruments for affecting retirement age other than public and private pensions. In view of the importance of health and job satisfaction in explaining retirement decisions, for example, it is clear that improving both the health of individuals and the quality of their working lives are among the long-run means of keeping older workers in the labor force longer. Continuing and intensifying efforts to eliminate age discrimination are another means of accomplishing the same end, as is improving work opportunities for older workers through counseling and training programs and through increasing opportunities for part-time work (Meier, Chapter 7 in this volume; Buchman, 1983; Knowles, 1983).

Recommendations for Further Research

Confident policy prescription requires greater knowledge than we now have about the factors affecting the labor supply of older workers. A number of general guidelines for improving our understanding of the nature of the retirement decision are fairly obvious.

1. Increased attention needs to be given to the process of retirement for women—particularly married women. A promising beginning has been made, but the major problem has been the absence of an adequate data source. The continuation of the National Longitudinal Surveys of Mature Women should constitute a valuable resource for this purpose; as of the 1987 survey the age span represented by that cohort was 50 to 64 years of age.

2. Data banks need to be developed with better measures of health. While some of the criticism that has been leveled at existing measures of health appear to be overstated, particularly when they have been used to explain *subsequent* retirement behavior, such measures clearly leave much to be desired. If one can assume that modest clinical examination of respondents could be arranged at a cost of, say $50–$75 a person, this would represent only a modest increase in the cost of a 10-year longitudinal study with a sample of about 5,000 persons.

3. Better information about the detailed characteristics of pension plans is also required if further progress is to be made in exploring the effects of economic variables on the retirement decision. Kotlikoff and Wise (1987) have shown that effects of pensions on labor force participation of older workers can be estimated only on the basis of "the precise provisions of individual plans" (p. 3). This is probably a more intractable problem than obtaining better measures of health, since workers are unlikely to be reliable sources of information about the characteristics of the pension plans under which they are (or have been) covered.

4. Greater attention needs to be paid to reasonable specification of models. Generally speaking, economists have been guilty of ignoring what they are fond of calling "taste" variables despite clear evidence that some of them (e.g., job satisfaction) are correlated with economic variables in the model (e.g., wages, liberality of pension). Sociologists and gerontologists, on the other hand, have frequently failed to give sophisticated attention to economic variables whose importance they would acknowledge.

5. As a corollary to the above, economists and gerontologists should read and profit from each others' work. To a considerable extent there are two distinct bodies of literature whose creators appear to be unknown to each other. A dramatic example is the appearance in 1984 and 1985, respectively, of *Retirement, Pensions, and Social Security* by Fields and Mitchell and *Retirement: Causes*

and Consequences by Palmore and his associates. Despite the fact that each volume is based on previously published works by its authors, the list of references of neither book includes any of the authors of the other.

References

Aaron, Henry J. *Economic Effects of Social Security.* Washington: The Brookings Institution, 1982.
Aaron, Henry J., and Gary Burtless. "Introduction." In *Retirement and Economic Behavior*, eds. Henry J. Aaron and Gary Burtless. Washington: The Brookings Institution, 1984.
Allen, Steven G., Robert L. Clark, and Daniel A. Sumner. "A Comparison of Pension Benefit Increases and Inflation, 1973-79." *Monthly Labor Review* 107 (May 1984), pp. 42-46.
_____. "Postretirement Adjustments of Pension Benefits." *Journal of Human Resources* 21 (Winter 1986), pp. 118-37.
Anderson, Kathryn H., Richard V. Burkhauser, and Joseph F. Quinn. "Do Retirement Dreams Come True? The Effect of Unanticipated Events on Retirement Plans." *Industrial and Labor Relations Review* 39 (July 1986), pp. 518-26.
Anderson, Kathryn H., and Richard V. Burkhauser. "The Retirement-Health Nexus: A New Measure of an Old Puzzle." *Journal of Human Resources* 20 (Summer 1985), pp. 315-30.
Anderson, Kathryn H., Robert L. Clark, and Thomas Johnson. "Retirement in Dual Career Families." In *Retirement Policy in an Aging Society*, ed. Robert L. Clark. Durham, NC: Duke University Press, 1980.
Atchley, Robert C. "Retirement as a Social Institution." *Annual Review of Sociology* (1982), pp. 263-87.
Barfield, Richard, and James Morgan. *Early Retirement: The Decision and the Experience.* Ann Arbor, MI: Braun-Brumfield, Inc., 1969.
Bazzoli, Gloria J. "The Early Retirement Decision: New Empirical Evidence on the Influence of Health." *Journal of Human Resources* 20 (Spring 1985), pp. 214-35.
Beck, Scott H. "Position in the Economic Structure and Unexpected Retirement." *Research on Aging* 5 (No. 2, 1983), pp. 197-216.
Blinder, Alan S., Roger H. Gordon, and Donald E. Wise. "Reconsidering the Work Disincentive Effects of Social Security." *National Tax Journal* 33 (December 1980), pp. 431-42.
Boskin, Michael J. "Social Security and Retirement Decisions." *Economic Inquiry* 15 (January 1977), pp. 1-25.
Bowen, William E., and T. Aldrich Finegan. *The Economics of Labor Force Participation.* Princeton, NJ: Princeton University Press, 1969.
Buchman, Anna Marie. "Maximizing Post-Retirement Labor Market Opportunities." In *Policy Issues in Work and Retirement*, ed. Herbert S. Parnes. Kalamazoo, MI: W. E. Upjohn Institute for Employment Research, 1983.
Burkhauser, Richard V. "The Pension Acceptance Decision of Older Workers." *Journal of Human Resources* 14 (Winter 1979), pp. 63-75.
_____. "The Early Acceptance of Social Security: An Asset Maximization Approach." *Industrial and Labor Relations Review* 33 (July 1980), pp. 484-92.
Burkhauser, Richard V., and John Turner. "Can Twenty-Five Million Americans Be Wrong? A Response to Blinder, Gordon and Wise." *National Tax Journal* 34 (December 1981), pp. 458-66.
Burtless, Gary. "Social Security, Unanticipated Benefit Increases and the Timing of Retirement." *Review of Economic Studies* 53 (No. 176, October 1986), pp. 781-805.
Burtless, Gary, and Robert A. Moffitt. "The Effect of Social Security Benefits on the Labor Supply of the Aged." In *Retirement and Economic Behavior*, eds. Henry J. Aaron and Gary Burtless. Washington: The Brookings Institution, 1984.

————. "Social Security, Earnings Tests, and Age at Retirement." *Public Finance Quarterly* 14 (January 1986), pp. 3-27.
Butler, J. S., Richard V. Burkhauser, Jean M. Mitchell, and Theodore R. Pincus. "Measurement Error in Self-Reported Health Variables." *Review of Economics and Statistics* 69 (November 1987), pp. 644-50.
Campbell, Colin D., and Rosemary G. Campbell. "Conflicting Views on the Effect of Old Age and Survivors' Insurance on Retirement." *Economic Inquiry* 14 (September 1976), pp. 369-88.
Chapman, Steven H., Mitchell P. LaPlante, and Gail Wilensky. "Life Expectancy and Health Status of the Aged." *Social Security Bulletin* 49 (October 1986), pp. 24-48.
Chirikos, Thomas N., and Gilbert Nestel. "Impairment and Labor Market Outcomes: A Cross-Sectional and Longitudinal Analysis." In *Work and Retirement: A Longitudinal Study of Men*, ed. Herbert S. Parnes. Cambridge, MA: MIT Press, 1981.
Clark, Robert L., and Ann A. McDermed. "Earnings and Pension Compensation: The Effect of Eligibility." *Quarterly Journal of Economics* 101 (May 1986), pp. 343-61.
————. "Inflation, Pension Benefits, and Retirement." *Journal of Risk and Insurance* 49 (1982), pp. 19-38.
Clark, Robert L., Thomas Johnson, and Ann A. McDermed. "Allocation of Time and Resources by Married Couples Approaching Retirement." *Social Security Bulletin* 43 (April 1980), pp. 3-6.
Clark, Robert L., and Daniel A. Sumner. "Inflation and the Real Income of the Elderly: Recent Evidence and Expectations for the Future." *The Gerontologist* 25 (April 1985), pp. 146-52.
Danziger, Sheldon, Robert Haveman, and Robert Plotnick. "How Income Transfer Payments Affect Work, Savings, and the Income Distribution: A Critical Review." *Journal of Economic Literature* 19 (September 1981), pp. 975-1021.
Daymont, Thomas N., and Paul J. Andrisani. "The Health and Economic Status of Very Early Retirees." *Aging and Work* 6 (1983), pp. 117-35.
Diamond, Peter A., and Jerry A. Hausman. "The Retirement and Unemployment Behavior of Older Men." In *Retirement and Economic Behavior*, eds. Henry J. Aaron and Gary Burtless. Washington: The Brookings Institution, 1984.
Ekerdt, David J., Raymond Bosse, and Robert J. Glynn. "Period Effects on Planned Age for Retirement, 1974-1984: Findings from the Normative Aging Study." *Research on Aging* 7 (No. 3, 1985), pp. 395-407.
Fields, Gary S., and Olivia S. Mitchell. *Retirement, Pensions, and Social Security.* Cambridge MA: MIT Press, 1984.
Gallaway, Lowell E. *The Retirement Decision: An Exploratory Essay.* U.S. Department of Health, Education, and Welfare, Social Security Administration, Division of Research and Statistics, Research Report No. 9. Washington: U.S. Government Printing Office, 1965.
General Accounting Office. *Retirement Before Age 65: Trends, Costs, and National Issues.* Washington: General Accounting Office, July 1986.
Gratton, Brian, and Marie R. Haug. "Decision and Adaptation: Research on Female Retirement." *Research on Aging* 5 (No. 1, 1983), pp. 59-76.
Gravitz, David H., and Frederick W. Rumack. "Opening the Early Retirement Window." *Personnel* 60 (March-April 1983), pp. 53-57.
Gustafson, Thomas A. "The Retirement Decision of Older Men: An Empirical Analysis." Ph.D. dissertation, Yale University, 1982.
Gustman, Alan L., and Thomas L. Steinmeier. "Partial Retirement and the Analysis of Retirement Behavior." *Industrial and Labor Relations Review* 37 (April 1984), pp. 403-15.
————. "A Structural Retirement Model." *Econometrica* 54 (May 1986), pp. 555-83.
Hall, Arden, and Terry Johnson. "The Determinants of Planned Retirement Age." *Industrial and Labor Relations Review* 33 (January 1980), pp. 240-55.

148 THE OLDER WORKER

Hamermesh, Daniel S. "Life-Cycle Effects on Consumption and Retirement." *Journal of Labor Economics* 2 (July 1984), pp. 353-68.
Hanoch, Giora, and Marjorie Honig. "Retirement, Wages, and Labor Supply of the Elderly." *Journal of Labor Economics* 1 (1983), pp. 131-51.
Hardy, Melissa A. "Occupational Structure and Retirement." In *Current Perspectives on Aging and the Life Cycle*, ed. Zena Smith Blau, Vol. 1, *Work, Retirement and Social Policy*. Greenwich, CT: JAI Press, 1985. Pp. 111-46.
Haveman, Robert, and Barbara L. Wolfe. "Disability Transfers and Early Retirement: A Causal Relationship?" *Journal of Public Economics* 24 (June 1984a), pp. 47-56.
———. "The Decline in Male Labor Force Participation: Comment." *Journal of Political Economy* 92 (June 1984b), pp. 532-41.
Haveman, Robert, Barbara L. Wolfe, and Jennifer L. Warlick. "Disability Transfers, Early Retirement, and Retrenchment." In *Retirement and Economic Behavior*, eds. Henry J. Aaron and Gary Burtless. Washington: The Brookings Institution, 1984.
Hayward, Mark D., and Melissa A. Hardy. "Early Retirement Processes Among Older Men: Occupational Differences." *Research on Aging* 7 (No. 4, 1985), pp. 491-515.
Henretta, John C., and Angela M. O'Rand. "Labor Force Participation of Older Married Women." *Social Security Bulletin* 43 (August 1980), pp. 10-16.
———. "Joint Retirement in the Dual Worker Family." *Social Forces* 62 (December 1983), pp. 504-20.
Honig, Marjorie. "Partial Retirement Among Women." *Journal of Human Resources* 20 (Fall 1985), pp. 613-21.
Honig, Marjorie, and Giora Hanoch. "Partial Retirement as a Separate Mode of Retirement Behavior." *Journal of Human Resources* 20 (Winter 1985), pp. 21-46.
Hurd, Michael D., and Michael J. Boskin. "The Effect of Social Security on Retirement in the Early 1970s." *Quarterly Journal of Economics* 99 (November 1984), pp. 767-90.
Ippolito, Richard A. *Pensions, Economics, and Social Policy*. Homewood, IL: Dow Jones-Irwin, 1986.
Kingson, Eric. *The Early Retirement Myth: Why Men Retire Before Age 62*. Report by the Select Committee on Aging, U.S. House of Representatives, 97th Congress. Washington: U.S. Government Printing Office, 1981a.
———. "The Health of Very Early Retirees." *Aging and Work* 4 (No. 1, 1981b), pp. 11-22.
———. "Critique of Early Retirement Study Disputed." *Aging and Work* 4 (No. 1, 1982), pp. 93-110.
———. "Still More on Early Retirement." *Aging and Work* 6 (No. 2, 1983), pp. 111-15.
Knowles, Daniel E. "Keeping Older Workers on the Job: Methods and Inducements." In *Policy Issues in Work and Retirement*, ed. Herbert S. Parnes. Kalamazoo, MI: W. E. Upjohn Institute for Employment Research, 1983.
Kotlikoff, Laurence J., and David R. Wise. "Employee Retirement and a Firm's Pension Plan." National Bureau of Economic Research Working Paper No. 2323, Cambridge, MA, July 1987.
Lazear, Edward. "Why Is There Mandatory Retirement?" *Journal of Political Economy* 87 (December 1979), pp. 1261-84.
Mitchell, Olivia S. "Review" of Palmore et al., *Retirement: Causes and Consequences. Journal of Economic Literature* 24 (September 1987), pp. 1275-76.
Mitchell, Olivia S., and Gary S. Fields. "The Effects of Pensions and Earnings on Retirement: A Review Essay." In *Research in Labor Economics*, Vol. 5, ed. Ronald G. Ehrenberg. Greenwich, CT: JAI Press, 1982. Pp. 115-55.
———. "The Economics of Retirement Behavior." *Journal of Labor Economics* 2 (January 1984), pp. 84-105.

THE RETIREMENT DECISION   149

Moffitt, Robert A. "Life-Cycle Labor Supply and Social Security: A Time Series Analysis." In *Work, Health, and Income Among the Elderly*, ed. Gary Burtless. Washington: The Brookings Institution, 1987. Pp. 183–228.
Morgan, James N. "Retirement in Prospect and Retrospect." In *Five Thousand American Families—Patterns of Economic Progress*, Vol. 8, eds. Greg J. Duncan and James N. Morgan. Ann Arbor: Institute for Social Research, University of Michigan, 1980.
————. "Antecedents and Consequences of Retirement." In *Five Thousand American Families—Patterns of Economic Progress*, Vol. 9, eds. Martha S. Hill, Daniel H. Hill, and James N. Morgan. Ann Arbor: Institute for Social Research, University of Michigan, 1981. Pp. 207–44.
Morrison, Malcolm H. "Work and Retirement in an Aging Society." *Daedalus* 115 (Winter 1986), pp. 269–93.
Myers, Robert J. "Why Do People Retire Early?" *Social Security Bulletin* 45 (September 1982), pp. 10–14.
————. "Further About Controversy on Early Retirement Study." *Aging and Work* 6 (No. 2, 1983), pp. 105–109.
Newhouse, Joseph P. "Discussion" of "Disability Transfers, Early Retirement, and Retrenchment" by Haveman, Wolfe, and Warlick. In *Retirement and Economic Behavior*, eds. Henry J. Aaron and Gary Burtless. Washington: The Brookings Institution, 1984.
O'Rand, Angela M., and John C. Henretta. "Delayed Career Entry, Industrial Pension Structure and Early Retirement in a Cohort of Unmarried Women." *American Sociological Review* 47 (June 1982), pp. 365–73.
Owen, John D. *Working Lives: The American Work Force Since 1920*. Lexington, MA: Lexington Books, 1986.
Palmore, Erdman, et al. *Retirement: Causes and Consequences*. New York: Springer Publishing Co., 1985.
Pampel, Frederick C. "Review" of Palmore et al., *Retirement: Causes and Consequences. Social Forces* 64 (March 1986), pp. 833–34.
Parnes, Herbert S. "Inflation and Early Retirement: Recent Longitudinal Findings." *Monthly Labor Review* 104 (July 1981), pp. 27–30.
Parnes, Herbert S., et al. *Retirement Among American Men*. Lexington, MA: Lexington Books, 1985.
Parnes, Herbert S., and Lawrence J. Less. "The Volume and Patterns of Retirements, 1966–1981." In *Retirement Among American Men*, ed. Herbert S. Parnes. Lexington, MA: Lexington Books, 1985.
Parnes, Herbert S., and Gilbert Nestel. "Early Retirement." In Herbert S. Parnes et al., *The Pre-Retirement Years*, Vol. 4, U.S. Department of Labor R & D Monograph No. 15. Washington: U.S. Government Printing Office, 1975.
————. "The Retirement Experience." In *Work and Retirement*, ed. Herbert S. Parnes. Cambridge, MA: MIT Press, 1981.
Parsons, Donald D. "The Decline in Male Labor Force Participation." *Journal of Political Economy* 88 (February 1980a), pp. 117–34.
————. "Racial Trends in Male Labor Force Participation." *American Economic Review* 70 (December 1980b), pp. 911–20.
————. "Black-White Differences in Labor Force Participation of Older Males." In *Work and Retirement: A Longitudinal Study of Men*, ed. Herbert S. Parnes. Cambridge MA: MIT Press, 1981.
————. "The Male Labor Force Decision: Health, Reported Health, and Economic Incentives." *Economica* 49 (February 1982), pp. 81–91.
————. "Disability Insurance and Male Labor Force Participation: A Response to Haveman and Wolfe." *Journal of Political Economy* 92 (June 1984), pp. 542–49.
Pellechio, Anthony J. "Social Security Financing and Retirement Behavior." *American Economic Review* 69 (May 1979), pp. 284–87.
Pozzebon, Silvana, and Olivia S. Mitchell. "Married Women's Retirement Behavior." Department of Labor Economics, New York State School of Industrial and Labor Relations, Cornell University, May 1987. Processed.
Quinn, Joseph F. "Job Characteristics and Early Retirement." *Industrial Relations* 17 (October 1978), pp. 315–23.

————. "Labor Force Participation Patterns of Older Self-Employed Workers." *Social Security Bulletin* 43 (April 1980), pp. 17-28.
————. "Retirement Income Rights as a Component of Wealth in the United States." *Review of Income and Wealth* 31 (September 1985), pp. 223-36.
Quinn, Joseph F., and Richard V. Burkhauser. "Influencing Retirement Behavior: A Key Issue for Social Security." *Journal of Policy Analysis and Management* 3 (February 1983), pp. 1-13.
Rust, John. "A Dynamic Programming Model of Retirement Behavior." In *The Economics of Aging*, ed. David A. Wise. Cambridge, MA: National Bureau of Economic Research, 1987.
Sammartino, Frank J. "The Effect of Health on Retirement." *Social Security Bulletin* 50 (February 1987), pp. 31-47.
Shapiro, David, and Steven H. Sandell. "Economic Conditions, Job Loss, and Induced Retirement." Paper presented at the Industrial Relations Research Association Annual Meeting, Dallas, Texas, 1984.
Shaw, Lois B. "Retirement Plans of Middle-Aged Married Women." *Gerontologist* 24 (April 1984), pp. 154-59.
————. "Looking Toward Retirement: Plans and Prospects." In *Dual Careers*, Vol. 6, ed. Lois B. Shaw. Columbus: Ohio State University Center for Human Resource Research, 1985.
Shaw, Lois B., and Mary G. Gagen. "Retirement Decisions of Husbands and Wives." Columbus: Ohio State University Center for Human Resource Research, 1984.
Shaw, Lois B., and Rachel Shaw. "From Midlife to Retirement: The Middle-Aged Woman Worker." In *Working Women: Past, Present, Future*, eds. Karen S. Koziara, Michael H. Moskow, and Lucretia D. Tanner. Industrial Relations Research Association Series. Washington: Bureau of National Affairs, 1987.
Sheppard, Harold. "Is Inflation Slowing Retirement?" News release, The National Council on the Aging, 1981.
Sherman, Sally R. "Reported Reasons Retired Workers Left Their Last Jobs: Findings from the New Beneficiary Survey." *Social Security Bulletin* 48 (March 1985), pp. 22-30.
Sickles, Robin C., and Paul Taubman. "An Analysis of the Health and Retirement Status of the Elderly." *Econometrica* 54 (November 1986), pp. 1339-56.
Social Security Administration. "Mortality and Early Retirement." *Social Security Bulletin* 45 (December 1982), pp. 3-10.
————. "Fast Facts and Figures About Social Security." *Social Security Bulletin* 49 (June 1986), p. 8.
————. "Increasing the Social Security Retirement Age: Older Workers in Physically Demanding Occupations or Poor Health." *Social Security Bulletin* 49 (October 1986), pp. 5-23.
Streib, Gordon F., and Clement J. Schneider. *Retirement in American Society: Impact and Process.* Ithaca, NY: Cornell University Press, 1971.
Sueyoshi, Glenn T. "Social Security and the Determinants of Full and Partial Retirement: A Competing Risks Analysis." Preliminary draft, Massachusetts Institute of Technology, 1986.
Szinovacz, Maximiliane. *Women's Retirement: Policy Implications of Recent Research.* Beverly Hills, CA: Sage, 1982.
Thompson, Lawrence. "The Social Security Reform Debate." *Journal of Economic Literature* 21 (December 1983), pp. 1425-67.
Tracy, Martin B. "Older Men's Earnings Tests and Work Activity: A Six Nation Study." *Research on Aging* 5 (June 1983), pp. 155-71.
Wolfe, John R. "Perceived Longevity and Early Retirement." *Review of Economics and Statistics* 65 (November 1983), pp. 544-50.
————. "A Model of Declining Health and Retirement." *Journal of Political Economy* 93 (December 1985), pp. 1258-67.
Ycas, Martynas A. "Recent Trends in Health Near the Age of Retirement: New Findings from the Health Interview Survey." *Social Security Bulletin* 50 (February 1987), pp. 5-30.

Chapter 6

Pensions and Older Workers

OLIVIA S. MITCHELL*
Cornell University and NBER

Over the past 40 years, company-sponsored pension plans have become an increasingly important element of American workers' compensation package, covering more than half of all active employees (Andrews, 1985) and accounting for 4–5 percent of payroll (U.S. Chamber of Commerce, 1986). The value of accrued pension benefits ranges from 20 to 35 percent of total asset accumulation among workers ages 45–65 with pensions (McDermed, Clark, and Allen, 1987). Pensions are also an increasingly important source of retiree income: between one-third and one-half of all retirees currently receive non-Social Security pension income (Andrews, 1985; Ippolito and Kolodrubetz, 1986), and benefits constitute 40 percent of income for pensioners over age 65 (Ellwood, 1985; Upp, 1983). Entitlements to a pension account for 10 to 15 percent of total wealth among those age 65 and older (Allen and Clark, 1986; Avery, Elliehausen, and Gustafson, 1985).

The U.S. pension system is currently in a state of transition. Labor leaders question pension managers' "conservative" investment policies, management representatives decry government restrictions on the operation of pension plans, and conflicts have arisen between young employees, who often desire more current cash, and older retired workers, who seek more generous pension benefits. Congress, too, has stepped up the pace of pension regulation over the past decade, restricting firms' abilities to defer pension vesting, limiting their abilities to halt pension accrual for older workers still on the payroll, and outlawing mandatory retirement for most workers (Salisbury, 1984; Wendling et al., 1986).

* I am grateful for comments from Gene Dykes, Herbert Parnes, Steven Sandell, and Bert Seidman. Financial support for the research was generously provided by Cornell University and the National Institute on Aging (Grant No. 5-R01-AG0-4737). The views expressed herein are mine and not those of the institutions or persons named above.

151

In this chapter we seek to accomplish three things. First, we briefly describe the current status of pensions in the U.S. economy today. Next, we outline theories of employer-provided pensions and evaluate them in light of recent empirical research. Finally, we spell out the labor market implications of several pension policies currently in effect or likely to take effect in the near future. Of particular interest are the implications of pensions and pension policy for older workers.

The Current Pension System

Employer-sponsored pensions in the United States are voluntary rather than mandated. Hence, pension coverage is uneven in the labor market, being most prevalent for government workers (roughly 90 percent are covered), union workers (about 80 percent coverage), employees of large firms (75+ percent covered in firms with 500 or more workers), and high-wage, high-tenure workers in general (Ellwood, 1985). There are two principal types of pensions: *defined benefit plans*, covering three-quarters of all participating workers and about 85 percent of union members with pensions, and *defined contribution plans*, covering the remaining one-quarter of the eligible work force, many of whom are higher income workers (Ellwood, 1985; Kotlikoff and Smith, 1983; Luzadis and Mitchell, 1986).

In a defined benefit pension plan, the sponsoring corporation specifies a benefit formula which determines a life annuity that will be paid to an eligible retiree. If a defined benefit plan terminates and funds in the plan are insufficient to meet promised benefits, workers' nominal benefits accrued to date of termination are guaranteed by the Pension Benefit Guaranty Corporation. This federal pension insurance agency, created under the 1974 Employee Retirement Income Security Act (ERISA), guarantees benefits up to an annual maximum when a terminated plan has insufficient funds to pay benefits. The agency is funded by an annual premium which is not experience-rated—that is, all pension funds pay the same per-worker fee regardless of the plan's financial solvency. Given recent pension default rates, the agency is currently at risk of bankruptcy itself and is seeking increases in premiums as well as new rate structures to enable it to impose a form of experience rating (U.S. General Accounting Office, 1987).

Defined contribution plans, in contrast, are organized so that the sponsoring employer need only specify annual contributions to the plan—generally a function of payroll, profit, or both. Here the size of a retiree's annuity depends strictly on annual contributions and the fund's investment performance. Unlike the defined benefit plans, defined contribution plans can never have too few assets to meet liabilities since, by definition, liabilities are equal to assets. As a result, the Pension Benefit Guaranty Corporation does not insure defined contribution participants' benefits against plan termination.

What Pensions Do

The simplest explanation for what employer-provided pensions do is that they help workers save for old age. Workers may rationally enroll an employer's assistance in establishing a pension because the automatic contribution mechanism eliminates the need to make frequent decisions to save for retirement (Thaler and Shefrin, 1981).

While this motivation for pensions remains an important explanation for what pensions do, there is increasing evidence that pensions also play other roles in the labor market. Analysts have recently identified two additional roles which, for clarity in exposition, are referred to below as (1) the "deferred wages" theory, and (2) the "implicit contract" theory. A description of them provides the groundwork for the following section, wherein current and proposed pension policy is examined for its likely impact on older workers.

Pensions as Deferred Wages

Proponents of the deferred wage theory argue that pensions are "owned" by the workers on whose behalf benefits are accrued. From this perspective, firms manage pensions for their employees because scale economies make it less expensive for groups of workers to invest large sums of money than it would be for individual workers to invest on their own (Mitchell and Andrews, 1981). In addition, the Revenue Act of 1942 greatly increased the attractiveness of company-sponsored pensions by allowing pension contributions and investment earnings on those contributions to be tax-deferred (Munnell, 1982). Therefore, it is argued, pensions constitute deferred pay held by firms but owed to workers. This theory has its roots in the industrial relations literature of the post-World War II period, and it is widely propounded by supporters of organized labor (Allen, 1964).

One set of empirical studies explored the deferred wage theory by searching for evidence of tradeoffs between wages and pension payments. Earlier research concluded that workers "paid" for pensions with lower wages (Schiller and Weiss, 1980), thus supporting the theory. However, more recent work produces only mixed support (Mitchell and Pozzebon, 1986). A second line of empirical research, which examines the relationship between income and pension coverage, provides somewhat more support. These studies tend to find a strong positive relationship between pension contributions and workers' marginal tax rates (Ippolito, 1986b; Mumy and Manson, 1983; Venti and Wise, 1987; Woodbury, 1983). There is also evidence that high-income workers in large firms are most likely to have pensions, even after controlling for other factors (Dorsey, 1982; Luzadis and Mitchell, 1986).

If one views pension funds simply as deferred wages accumulating in a tax-protected environment, it tends to settle the ownership issue on behalf of the saver—in this case, the worker. One problem that supporters of this view must cope with is how to rationalize company policies which reduce workers' chances of actually receiving promised pension benefits. These include restrictive eligibility rules for pension participation, vesting policies that defer workers' legal claims on accrued pensions, and benefit integration provisions wherein pension payments are reduced by a portion of a retiree's Social Security income (Kotlikoff and Smith, 1983; Ippolito and Kolodrubetz, 1986). Another questionable practice from this perspective is pension underfunding, since underfunding undermines the security of the pension promise.

A possible explanation for the persistence of these pension practices within the deferred wage theory is that workers might not recognize how these provisions threaten the deferred promise. In such a case, the employee would then continue to expect full benefits with certainty, even though vesting, underfunding, and other such provisions reduce the value of his promised benefit. Unfortunately, little empirical research on this question exists. One study explored worker information about pension provisions and concluded that employees appear to have quite good information about some aspects of the pension, particularly regarding eligibility and requirements for normal retirement (Mitchell, 1988). However, they seem to have far less information regarding plan type, contributions, and early retirement eligibility and retirement rules.

In general, information is better among unionized than nonunion employees, which may be evidence of scale economies or may indicate that unions may be more efficient at providing pension information. Comparisons of worker estimates of pension accruals with employer data on such accumulations are very preliminary, but thus far seem to indicate that workers may misestimate such amounts (Clark and McDermed, 1982; Gustman and Steinmeier, 1987).

Indirect evidence regarding worker behavior suggests that many, if not most, employees are quite well informed about key pension characteristics. For instance, worker mobility is significantly reduced when a firm offers a pension plan; the data suggest this is because workers perceive that a significant pension loss is imposed on those who leave their jobs prior to retirement (Allen, Clark, and McDermed, 1986; Mitchell, 1982, 1983; McCormick and Hughes, 1984; Schiller and Weiss, 1979). Indeed, Ippolito (1985) estimates that worker tenure at retirement is two to four years higher in firms with pensions as compared to firms with no plans. Other studies have demonstrated that pensions also exert a potent influence on older workers' retirement behavior, inducing job-leaving patterns that differ systematically from one company to another (Burkhauser, 1979; Fields and Mitchell, 1984; Gustman and Steinmeier, 1986; Mitchell and Fields, 1982, 1985). In addition, one study which had good data on pension underfunding (Smith, 1981) was able to show that unionized public-sector workers tend to obtain wage premiums for underfunded pensions, partially offsetting the risk of losing their pensions in the event of bankruptcy. In sum, the available evidence does not prove that workers are systematically and pervasively ignorant of the riskiness of the pension promise, though worker ignorance about pension provisions cannot be entirely ruled out.

Pensions as Implicit Contracts

One problem with the deferred wage theory just described is that pension growth in the past 40 years far exceeded that which would be predicted on the basis of actual changes in marginal tax rates through time (Andrews and Mitchell, 1986; Alpert, 1987). Hence, additional explanations for pensions and pension growth have been sought. A different perspective, called here the "implicit contract" view, recognizes that pension promises embody risks regarding their level and the probability of receipt. Furthermore, this view holds that the risky aspect of pensions may be beneficial not only to the firms offering the pensions, but to the workers as well.

One influential argument along these lines is offered by Lazear (1979), building on earlier work by Ross (1958). This view first asserts that worker productivity is enhanced by deferring part of the worker's compensation until late in his worklife. This may be achieved by making pension receipt conditional on continued worker loyalty and attachment to the firm (among other ways). Cutting job leavers' pensions shifts the risks of shirking and quitting onto workers and away from the employer. The theory thus identifies a productivity-enhancing role for many restrictive pension features, including vesting rules, restrictions against pension portability, and benefit formulas which powerfully reward years of service.

Empirical support for the turnover view is provided by the several studies mentioned earlier as well as by Hutchens (1986), who finds that pensions are most prevalent where on-the-job monitoring is most difficult. However, contrary evidence appears in a recent study by Allen and Clark (1987) who detect no relationship in the aggregate between industries with greater pension coverage and industry-level productivity, profits, and value-added.

A second version of the implicit contract view of pensions focuses not on productivity risk, as described above, but rather on the risk associated with firm profitability. For instance, workers may disagree with shareholders regarding the time horizon over which to maximize profits (Ippolito, 1986b; McMillan, 1984). Consequently, workers may be tempted to take steps to enhance their own income at the expense of the firm's long-term viability. In such a scenario, employee myopia may be corrected with a defined benefit pension intentionally (and perpetually) underfunded. Here the pension promise is honored only as long as the firm remains viable; consequently, employees are induced via the implicit pension contract to focus on the long-term time horizon of the firm. (The pension guarantees implemented since ERISA to some degree undercut this form of risk sharing.)

Empirical evidence on this version of the implicit contract notion is preliminary as yet. Supporting this theory is evidence that pension underfunding appears to be more prevalent in unionized firms where workers most threaten stockholder returns (Ippolito, 1986b). Also supportive is the finding that defined benefit plans are more prevalent among relatively less profitable firms (Luzadis and Mitchell, 1986). However, there is clearly a need for more analysis of the issues.

The implicit contract view of pensions implies a very different role for government regulation, as compared to the deferred wage theory. For instance, the implicit contract approach looks favorably on provisions such as vesting and eligibility requirements which reduce the probability of pension receipt for those who leave their firms. Hence, if such provisions were eliminated legislatively, predictions are that turnover would increase significantly and overall productivity would be reduced. Similarly, proponents of the implicit contract notion would tend not to require full funding, insofar as underfunding is viewed as a way to share profitability risk with labor. In general, this second theory is less sanguine about regulatory interference with company pension provisions (Ippolito, 1986b).

Labor Market Consequences of Pension Policy for Older Workers

Now that we have some understanding of the role of employer-provided pensions in the U.S. labor market, as well as a preliminary notion of each theory's view of regulatory policy, we need to address another important issue: Has pension policy in the United States over the past several years been on net beneficial or detrimental to the labor market in general, and to older workers in particular? Because there is no simple answer to this question, and because the literature is relatively undeveloped at present (Ippolito, 1986a), our discussion is in many regards suggestive rather than conclusive.

As noted earlier, pension regulation in the U.S. is of fairly recent vintage (Munnell, 1982). Many pension plans that flourished unregulated during the early 1900s collapsed during the Great Depression. After World War II, Congress occasionally implemented regulations affecting the tax status of particular benefits, pension plans' ability to integrate benefits with Social Security, and plan responsibilities regarding disclosure of pension information. However, regulation was rather piecemeal until the 1974 Employee Retirement Income Security Act (ERISA) which placed restrictions on multiple aspects of defined benefit pensions and many features of defined contribution plans as well (Coleman, 1985). Following ERISA, regulations multiplied, as new laws were devised almost every year, from the mid-1970s to the present, changing the way corporate benefit plans operate (Rosenbloom and Hallman, 1986; Wyatt Company, 1986).

A review of how such regulations affect labor markets, and particularly labor markets for older workers, is facilitated by focusing on two general categories of regulations: (1) rules regarding contribution levels, benefit accruals, and benefit amounts, and (2) regulations regarding the probability of benefit receipt. In each case we describe the overall thrust of regulatory policy over time, and then go on to evaluate the policy in light of the theories of pensions described earlier.

Regulation Regarding Contribution Levels, Benefit Accruals, and Benefit Amounts

Over the years the federal government has progressively limited the conditions under which pensions may maintain their tax-qualified status (Congressional Budget Office, 1987). The threat of having a plan's tax-qualified status removed by the Internal Revenue Service is therefore one important inducement for pension administrators to design plans in accordance with the rules the government recommends. Other agencies, particularly the Department of Labor and the Equal Employment Opportunity Commission, have also been assigned the responsibility of ensuring that benefit contributions and accruals are managed in a manner consistent with Congressional intent. The primary enforcement mechanisms are withdrawal of tax-qualified status and lawsuits.

Congressional goals in the area of pension contributions and benefits have emphasized continued eligibility for pension accrual at older ages, limits on integration, and nondiscrimination. *Restrictions on age-related benefit provisions* include rules outlawing mandatory retirement and requiring employers to continue pension benefit accrual after workers reach the age of 65. *Integration rules* curtail the firm's ability to reduce pension payments by a portion of a retired worker's Social Security benefits. *Nondiscrimination rules* include ceilings on the amounts that can be contributed each year into a tax-qualified corporate pension plan on behalf of high-wage or high-salaried employees. Congress also limits total benefit amounts that may be received by highly-paid employees.

Assessments of government constraints on pension accrual and mandatory retirement depend on one's conception of what pensions do in the labor market. Thus deferred-wage theorists tend to assert that employees have rights to pensions and compensation accruals after age 65, just as they have prior to age 65. From this standpoint, regulations requiring continued accrual and rules permitting continued work after age 65 are perceived as clearly beneficial to older workers. In contrast, opponents of the rules emphasize that protecting older workers' claims on high-wage, high-pension-accrual jobs raises labor costs, in turn inducing employers to seek less expensive substitutes (Grant and Hamermesh, 1981; Levine and Mitchell, 1988). In this way, what initially appeared to be a rule change benefiting older workers may actually result in unintended disemployment among the very group this rule was intended to help. In addition, those who argue that pensions are part of an optimal risk-sharing arrangement between workers and firms predict that government interference with a privately efficient contract between workers and their employers will have negative effects on production and overall employment (Lazear, 1979).

Rules curtailing pension integration with Social Security benefits also elicit both praise and criticism. On the one hand, these regulations tighten the link between promised pension benefits and benefits actually received, an outcome favored by proponents of the deferred wage theory. On the other hand, some firms use integration to "tilt" pension payments in favor of very valuable workers. Limits on integration hence constrain the ability of such employers to attract and keep these individuals. A related argument from partisans of the risk-sharing view is that pensions should be integrated with Social Security so as to spread the risk of inflation during retirement between employees, their employers, and the taxpaying public (Feldstein, 1983; Merton et al., 1987). Nondiscrimination regulations raise a parallel set of concerns. Rules limiting maximum contributions and benefits are often touted as equitable, but they also impose restrictions on compensation of high-wage workers, and many older workers are among those who are highly paid. If pension contributions are thus curtailed and wages cannot be raised enough to compensate these individuals, the law will most likely induce retirement among some subset of the older work force. Hence, from this perspective, nondiscrimination rules produce an inefficient use of labor resources and may even reduce employment among the older labor force as well.

A more fundamental question raised by current policy is whether pensions merit their continued tax-favored status. The advantage granted to retirement savings is very large—$60 billion in 1988 dollars—and represents the single largest revenue loss to the federal budget of all the "preferences in the individual income tax structure" (Congressional Budget Office, 1987). Continuing their tax-favored status is justified on grounds of encouraging private retirement savings, and the objective has been, in part, attained. On the other hand, the Congressional Budget Office has estimated that the tax advantage benefits high-income groups the most (24 percent among the richest quartile, 14 percent among the poorest elderly couples), while people without pensions gain nothing at all (these tend to be women, nonunion, and low-wage workers). Hence, Congressional efforts to limit the growth of tax-deferred pensions are explained by equity concerns, at least to some extent.

Regulations Regarding Probability of Benefit Receipt

Congress has addressed the problem of benefit nonreceipt several times since the passage of ERISA in 1974. The guiding philosophy behind most of these efforts was to increase the chances that promised benefits are actually paid to covered workers. Congressional creativity in this area has ranged from establishing methods of increasing the chances of vesting, increasing benefit accrual rates, making pension trustees liable for imprudent pension investments, and increasing funding requirements, limiting circumstances under which a firm can avoid paying promised benefits, to setting up the Pension Benefit Guaranty Corporation. In essence, what all of these rules do is provide a legal framework for pension participants' claims on retirement benefits and define the terms under which promises must be backed either by corporate assets (if any) or tax revenue (if assets are insufficient) (Tepper, 1981; Logue, 1979; Ippolito, 1986b).

Once again, an assessment of these provisions regarding pension promises must depend on one's views of the pension as a labor market institution. Partisans of the deferred wage theory believe that such measures are needed both to increase retirees' economic security and to make participants' claim on firm assets credible.

Implicit contract theorists are somewhat more divided in their evaluations of measures reducing pension risk. On the positive side, Ippolito (1986b) notes that the federal government is in a unique position to bear the risk of economy-wide market crashes. Thus, the insurance measures instituted are at least arguably an improvement over the previous status quo. On the negative side, however, the government's current pension insurance structure has many detractors (U.S. General Accounting Office, 1987). First, the Pension Benefit Guaranty Corporation itself is seriously underfunded. Second, the current structure may actually induce more serious funding problems in the pension system than it resolves. In addition, the concentration of underfunding problems in a few sectors of the economy has led some to question the equity of "bailing out" depressed industries at the expense of healthy ones. Finally, those who argue that both firms and workers benefit from the contingent payment aspect of pension promises predict productivity losses as a result of restricting the ways in which such risks can be borne (Lazear, 1983).

Empirical research on these theoretical predictions has been piecemeal to date. The effect of reducing permissible pension vesting rules appears to be relatively small, on average (Andrews, 1985). The outlawing of mandatory retirement has been studied extensively, and the conclusion seems to be that it has been a relatively inexpensive regulation overall, insofar as most workers currently retire well before age 70 (Burkhauser and Quinn, 1983). This overall judgment should not obscure the fact that the law has a significant impact on subsectors of the economy. For instance, it has been argued that retirement rates among older employees at universities have declined in reaction to the ending of mandatory retirement. Also, pension plans appear to have increased their incentives for early retirement, just as the mandatory retirement rules were abolished (Mitchell and Luzadis, 1988; Lazear, 1983).

While there have been studies of a few individual rule changes reported in the literature recently, far less is known about the overall impact of ERISA and the far-reaching pension regulations subsequent to enactment of that law. Some claim that pension termination patterns over time rose as a result of growing regulatory constraints (Cummins et al., 1980; Wendling et al., 1986). However, there are also dissenting opinions (Ippolito, 1986b). Hence, more research remains to be done on these broader regulatory changes.

Discussion and Implications

Employer-provided pensions have come of age in the United States over the past 40 years, and their growth has been accompanied by ever more elaborate regulations aimed at restricting the tax-deferred status of benefits and contributions as well as increasing the probability of benefit receipt. These changing pension rules alter both workers' and firms' perceptions of the costs and benefits of pension coverage.

How these regulatory policies are evaluated of necessity depends on one's theory regarding the economic functions of pensions. Research indicates that pension regulations in general will reduce productivity and/or raise labor costs, inducing employers to modify their pension plans so as to offset the consequences of the rule changes. To the extent that the regulations differentially affect the costs of employing older versus younger workers, they may induce substitution within labor categories—away from high-cost older workers and toward the young. In the long run, firms may terminate their pension plans or replace older workers with capital.

Evidence on pension regulation is still preliminary, yet it is clear that predicting the impact of a specific pension regulation on worker (and retiree) well-being must depend on the regulation in question. Findings to date suggest that pensions are labor market institutions that do, in fact, respond to the economic environment. Hence, restrictive pension policies will probably result in employer efforts to (1) devise novel compensation schemes to accomplish the same ends, (2) offset the regulations by changing work force levels and composition, and/or (3) terminate pension plans. Thus far, most researchers who have studied the issue agree that ending a mandatory retirement policy will have a minimal impact on the current work force, since few workers remained employed beyond their mid-sixties prior to the reform. However, in the long run it may be quite expensive to require firms to retain highly compensated older employees without allowing them to renegotiate wages and working conditions for these people. These new expenses may compel some firms to reduce compensation in other ways (e.g., lower pension accruals) and to seek less expensive substitutes, including younger workers. In this way, what initially appears to be beneficial rule changes may actually produce lower retirement benefits and even disemployment among the older group the rule was intended to help.

Similar problems arise with other rule changes. For instance, some older workers could be deleteriously affected by nondiscrimination requirements limiting pension contributions. If wages cannot be raised enough to compensate them for the pension ceiling, this law will most likely induce earlier retirement. Other pension regulations will also increase the expense of offering a pension plan and might, in some cases, lead to plan termination. Included here are the proposed increases in the premiums charged for federal pension insurance (U.S. General Accounting Office, 1987). Though current law protects accrued pensions for senior workers in the event of company bankruptcy, this guarantee is not a perfect substitute for an ongoing plan since it contains no provision for cost-of-living pension increases (Clark and McDermed, 1982). Hence, efforts to make the pension promise more secure may result in the decrease of pension coverage.

The literature on pensions and older workers is in many ways incomplete. A high priority for future researchers must be to develop more complete theoretical and empirical models of the complex labor market institutions called pensions. One obstacle to applied work in this area is lack of data; typically, the researcher requires information from workers and retirees covered by the pensions, the firms offering the pension plans, and the pension plans themselves. Specific issues requiring additional research include (but are not limited to) investigations of (1) worker knowledge of pension provisions and the implications for behavior; (2) the economic and political determinants of companies' pension offerings; (3) the pension consequences of proposed or actual federal mandates requiring portability, generous accrual rules, pension funding, and other provisions; and (4) the link between pension promises and other employer-provided benefits such as retiree health insurance. A general issue that has not been resolved, but one that must receive further scrutiny, is whether it is socially desirable to continue the tax-preferred status of company-sponsored pensions. This question is especially important in light of the U.S. Treasury's current revenue needs.

References

Allen, Donna. *Fringe Benefits: Wages or Social Obligation?* Ithaca: New York State School of Industrial and Labor Relations, Cornell University, 1964.

Allen, Steven G., and Robert L. Clark. "Pensions and Firm Performance." In *Human Resources and the Performance of the Firm*, eds. Morris M. Kleiner et al. Madison, WI: Industrial Relations Research Association, 1987. Pp. 195-242.
_____. "Unions, Pension Wealth, and Age-Compensation Profiles." *Industrial and Labor Relations Review* 39 (July 1986), pp. 502-17.
Allen, Steven G., Robert L. Clark, and Ann McDermed. "Job Mobility, Older Workers and the Role of Pensions." North Carolina State University. Final report to the U.S. Department of Labor, 1986.
Alpert, William T. "An Analysis of Fringe Benefits Using Time-Series Data." *Applied Economics* 19 (January 1987), pp. 1-16.
Andrews, Emily S. *The Changing Profile of Pensions in America.* Washington: Employee Benefit Research Institute, 1985.
Andrews, Emily S., and Olivia S. Mitchell. "The Current and Future Role of Pensions in Old-Age Economic Security." *Benefits Quarterly* 2 (2nd quarter 1986), pp. 25-36.
Avery, R. B., E. Elliehausen, and T. A. Gustafson. "Pensions and Social Security in Household Portfolios: Evidence from the 1983 Survey of Consumer Finances." Federal Reserve Board, October 1985.
Burkhauser, Richard V. "The Pension Acceptance Decision of Older Workers." *Journal of Human Resources* 14 (Winter 1979), pp. 63-75.
Burkhauser, Richard V., and Joseph F. Quinn. "Is Mandatory Retirement Overrated? Evidence from the 1970s." *Journal of Human Resources* 18 (Summer 1983), pp. 337-58.
Clark, Robert L., and Ann McDermed. "Inflation, Pension Benefits, and Retirement." *Journal of Risk and Insurance* 49 (March 1982), pp. 19-38.
Coleman, Barbara J. *Primer on ERISA.* Washington: Bureau of National Affairs, Inc., 1985.
Congressional Budget Office. "Tax Policy for Pensions and Other Retirement Saving." Washington: U.S. Government Printing Office, April 1987.
Cummins, J. David, John R. Percival, Randolph Westerfield, and J. G. Ramage. "Effects of ERISA on the Investment Policies of Private Pension Plans: Survey Evidence." *Journal of Risk and Insurance* 47 (September 1980), pp. 447-76.
Dorsey, Stuart. "A Model and Empirical Estimates of Worker Pension Coverage in the U.S." *Southern Economic Journal* 49 (October 1982), pp. 506-20.
Ellwood, David T. "Pensions and the Labor Market: A Starting Point." In *Pensions, Labor, and Individual Choice*, ed. David Wise. National Bureau of Economic Research. Chicago: University of Chicago Press, 1985.
Feldstein, Martin. "Should Private Pensions Be Indexed?" In *Financial Aspects of the U.S. Pension System*, eds. Zvi Bodie and John Shoven. National Bureau of Economic Research. Chicago: University of Chicago Press, 1983.
Fields, Gary S., and Olivia S. Mitchell. *Retirement, Pensions and Social Security.* Cambridge, MA: MIT Press, 1984.
Grant, James H., and Daniel S. Hamermesh. "Labor Market Competition Among Youths, White Women, and Others." *Review of Economics and Statistics* 63 (August 1981), pp. 354-60.
Gustman, Alan L., and Thomas L. Steinmeier. "A Structural Retirement Model." *Econometrica* 54 (May 1986), pp. 555-84.
_____. "An Analysis of Pension Benefit Formulas, Pension Wealth, and Incentives from Pensions." Final report to the U.S. Department of Labor, July 1987.
Hutchens, Robert M. "An Empirical Test of Lazear's Theory of Delayed Payment Contracts." Department of Labor Economics, New York State School of Industrial and Labor Relations, Cornell University, March 1986.
Ippolito, Richard A. "Developments in Pension Research." Washington: U.S. Department of Labor, February 1986a. Mimeo.
_____. *Pensions, Economics and Public Policy.* Homewood, IL: Dow Jones-Irwin, 1986b.
_____. "The Economics of Pensions and Mobility." Washington: U.S. Department of Labor, 1985. Mimeo.

PENSIONS AND OLDER WORKERS 165

Ippolito, Richard A., and W. W. Kolodrubetz. *The Handbook of Pension Statistics,
1985.* Chicago: Commerce Clearing House, 1986.
Kotlikoff, Laurence, and Daniel E. Smith. *Pensions and the American Economy.*
Chicago: University of Chicago Press, 1983.
Kotlikoff, Laurence, and David Wise. "Labor Compensation and the Structure of
Private Pension Plans: Evidence for Contractual Versus Spot Labor Markets." In
Pensions, Labor, and Individual Choice, ed. David Wise. Chicago: University of
Chicago Press, 1985.
Lazear, Edward. "Pensions as Severance Pay." In *Financial Aspects of the U.S.
Pension System,* eds. Zvi Bodie and John Shoven. National Bureau of Economic
Research. Chicago: University of Chicago Press, 1983.
_____. "Why Is There Mandatory Retirement?" *Journal of Political Economy* 87
(December 1979), pp. 1261–84.
Levine, P. B., and Olivia S. Mitchell. "The Baby Boom's Legacy: Relative Wages in
the 21st Century." *American Economic Review* 78 (May 1988), pp. 66–69.
Logue, Dennis E. *Legislative Influence on Corporate Pension Plans.* Washington:
American Enterprise Institute, 1979.
Luzadis, Rebecca, and Olivia S. Mitchell. "Defined Benefit, Defined Contribution,
or No Pension?" In Olivia Mitchell, *Explaining Patterns in Old Age Pensions.*
Final report to the National Institute on Aging under Grant No. 5-R01-AG0-4737-
02, 1986.
McCormick, Barry, and Gordon Hughes. "The Influence of Pensions on Job
Mobility." *Journal of Public Economics* 23 (February-March 1984), pp. 183–206.
McDermed, Ann, Robert Clark, and Steven Allen. "Pension Wealth, Age-Wealth
Profiles, and the Distribution of Net Worth." Department of Economics and
Business, North Carolina State University, February 1987.
McMillan, David M. "Nonassignable Pensions and the Price of Risk." Irvine
Economics Paper No. 84-11, May 1984.
Merton, R. C., Zvi Bodie, and Alan J. Marcus. "Pension Plan Integration as Insurance
Against Social Security Risk." In *Issues in Pension Economics,* eds. Zvi Bodie,
John B. Shoven, and David A. Wise. Chicago: University of Chicago Press, 1987.
Mitchell, Olivia S. "Fringe Benefits and Labor Mobility." *Journal of Human
Resources* 17 (Spring 1982), pp. 286–98.
_____. "Fringe Benefits and the Costs of Changing Jobs." *Industrial and Labor
Relations Review* 37 (October 1983), pp. 70–78.
_____. "Worker Knowledge of Pension Provisions." *Journal of Labor Economics*
6 (January 1988), pp. 21–39.
Mitchell, Olivia S., and Emily S. Andrews. "Scale Economies in Private Multi-
Employer Pension Systems." *Industrial and Labor Relations Review* 34 (July
1981), pp. 522–30.
Mitchell, Olivia S., and Gary S. Fields. "The Effects of Pensions and Earnings on
Retirement: A Review Essay." In *Research in Labor Economics,* ed. Ronald G.
Ehrenberg. Greenwich, CT: JAI Press, 1982.
_____. "Rewards to Continued Work: The Economic Incentives for Postponing
Retirement." In *Horizontal Equity, Uncertainty, and Economic Well-Being,* eds.
Martin David and Timothy Smeeding. Chicago: University of Chicago Press,
1985.
Mitchell, Olivia S., and Rebecca A. Luzadis. "Changes in Pension Incentives Over
Time." *Industrial and Labor Relations Review* (forthcoming 1988).
Mitchell, Olivia S., and Silvana Pozzebon. "Wages, Pensions, and the Wage-Pension
Tradeoff." In Olivia Mitchell, *Explaining Patterns in Old-Age Pensions.* Final
report to the National Institute on Aging under Grant No. 5—R01-AG0-4737-02,
1986.
Mumy, Gene E., and William D. Manson. "Payroll Taxes, Social Security, and the
Unique Tax Advantage of Company Pensions." *Journal of Risk and Insurance* 50
(March 1983), pp. 161–65.
Munnell, Alicia. *The Economics of Private Pensions.* Washington: The Brookings
Institution, 1982.

Rosenbloom, Jerry S., and G. Victor Hallman. *Employee Benefit Planning*, 2nd ed. Englewood Cliffs, NJ: Prentice-Hall, 1986.
Ross, Arthur M. "Do We Have a New Industrial Feudalism?" *American Economic Review* 48 (December 1958), pp. 403–20.
Salisbury, Dallas L., ed. *Why Tax Employee Benefits?* Washington: Employee Benefit Research Institute, 1984.
Schiller, Bradley R., and Randall D. Weiss. "The Impact of Private Pensions on Firm Attachment." *Review of Economics and Statistics* 61 (August 1979), pp. 369–80.
_____. "Pensions and Wages: A Test for Equalizing Differences." *Review of Economics and Statistics* 62 (November 1980), pp. 529–39.
Smith, Robert S. "Compensating Differentials for Pensions and Underfunding in the Public Sector." *Review of Economics and Statistics* 63 (August 1981), pp. 463–68.
Tepper, Irwin. "Taxation and Corporate Pension Policy." *Journal of Finance* 36 (March 1981), pp. 1–13.
Thaler, Richard H., and Harold M. Shefrin. "Pensions, Savings and Temptation." Graduate School of Business and Public Administration Working Paper No. 81-26, Cornell University, November 1981.
United States Chamber of Commerce. *Employee Benefits 1985*. Washington: The Chamber, 1986.
United States General Accounting Office. "Pension Plans: Government Insurance Program Threatened by Its Growing Deficit." Report to the Chairman, Subcommittee on Oversight, Committee on Ways and Means, U.S. House of Representatives, HRD-87-42. Washington: U.S. Government Printing Office, March 1987.
Upp, Melinda. "Relative Importance of Various Income Sources of the Aged, 1980." *Social Security Bulletin* 46 (January 1983), pp. 3–10.
Venti, S. F., and David A. Wise. "IRA's and Saving." In *The Effects of Taxation on Capital Formation*, ed. Martin Feldstein. Chicago: University of Chicago Press, 1987.
Wendling, Wayne, C. A. Crabb-Velez, and M. A. Carlsen. *The Regulatory Impact on Pensions*. Brookfield, WI: International Foundation of Employee Benefits, 1986.
Woodbury, Stephen A. "Substitution Between Wage and Nonwage Benefits." *American Economic Review* 73 (March 1983), pp. 166–82.
Wyatt Company. "The Tax Reform Act of 1986." Washington: Wyatt, 1986.

CHAPTER 7

Managing an Older Work Force

ELIZABETH L. MEIER*
Public Policy Institute
American Association of Retired Persons

As fewer young persons enter the labor force, the role of older workers is being increasingly scrutinized. Recognizing the importance of employment in the financial security of midlife and older persons, the American Association of Retired Persons (AARP) organized a Worker Equity Initiative in 1985.

One of the three main thrusts of the Initiative is developing, collecting, and disseminating new information about the capabilities, needs, and rights of older workers. As a result, a number of research projects have been undertaken recently, including two surveys—one of full-time workers age 40 and over, and the other concerning employer perspectives of employees age 50 and over. In addition, the Initiative has sponsored studies of technological changes within the manufacturing and services sectors of the economy and how these changes will affect older workers. This chapter is based on the data obtained in these surveys as well as on other relevant published research.

The following section deals with means of increasing the opportunities for older workers to remain vital participants in the labor force. The third section is an examination of the impact of technological change on training needs of older workers, while the fourth is a discussion of the extent of alternatives to the standard 40-hour week and the reactions of older workers to them. The final section briefly reviews additional research that is required on each of these topics.

---

* The views expressed in this chapter are those of the author and do not necessarily represent formal policies of AARP. Anita Stowell, AARP, contributed materials and ideas for this chapter, particularly the first section.

Management Perceptions of Older Workers and Strategies for Keeping Them in the Work Force

The American business community is changing rapidly. Stories about corporate mergers, hostile takeovers, restructuring, and the layoffs and early retirements which accompany such events are reported almost daily in the business press.

Because of increased competition, both domestic and foreign, cutting costs and increasing productivity are high-priority business objectives of the 1980s. One "mean and lean" approach is through reductions in the work force. An often-used technique is the early retirement incentive program usually aimed at long-term and highly paid employees age 50 and over who have their vested pension benefits "sweetened" if they agree to retire within a limited time period (Meier, 1986).

Even in the short run, this approach is costly as the extra cost of the incentive program must be declared a current expense on the profit and loss statements rather than deferred into the future (Meier, 1986). Moreover, since the early retirement under such programs must be open to all who qualify in order to avoid charges of age discrimination, companies have sometimes lost valued expertise and have had to rehire retirees as consultants. Younger employees find that their mentors are gone and with them the feeling of stability and loyalty. In the longer run, additional reasons why companies may have to reevaluate their early retirement strategies are the inexorable aging of the labor force and the dwindling numbers of new entrants. The business community will have to rely more on middle-aged and older workers, and new operational policies and practices may be necessary.

An AARP study of company executives and their perceptions of workers over age 50 provides some insights into how employers view older workers. Table 1 lists the characteristics of such workers that the executives rated as highly valuable assets to the company, including their experience, seasoned judgment, solid performance, and commitment to quality. Some of the negative perceptions centered around their resistance to change, difficulty in adapting to changing technology, and physical limitations. Resistance to change and physical limitations were the leading weaknesses cited, although they were mentioned by only a minority of the executives—41 and 36 percent, respectively (American Association of Retired Persons, 1986d).

TABLE 1

High Ratings of Older Workers on Selected Characteristics
(Percent of Raters)

Characteristics Rated Excellent/Very Good	All Companies
Good attendance and punctuality	86
Commitment to quality	82
Loyalty and dedication to company	79
Practical, not just theoretical knowledge	79
Solid experience	74
Solid/reliable performance record	71
Someone to count on in a crisis	70
Ability to get along with co-workers	60
Emotional stability	59

Source: American Association of Retired Persons, 1986d.

In addition to these characteristics of older workers as perceived by company executives, there are other factors that need to be kept in mind in developing strategies for retaining, motivating, and maximizing the productivity of older workers. One of these is the fact that, as the result of long service with the company, the older worker may have "plateaued" and may need opportunities for meaningful involvement (Lorsch and Takagi, 1986). Another is that some older workers whose jobs have become obsolete may require skill upgrading and second-career training (Liebig, 1987). Finally, it must be recognized that for many older workers income enhancement may become less critical than other factors in job satisfaction as compared with earlier stages of their careers (Bird, 1987).

Because job satisfaction is an important element in keeping older workers in the labor market, strategies for enhancing the satisfaction of middle-aged and older workers merit careful attention. At least four of these have been identified (Bird, 1987; Lorsch and Takagi, 1986) and are summarized here.

*Providing the Skills, Knowledge, and Support
Required for High-Quality Job Performance*

Midlife and older workers bring a wealth of existing knowledge and skill to a job, having learned through life experience, not just through formal education. Often they have a valuable historical perspective of the business acquired through their long service.

Nevertheless, skill obsolescence is a reality for some older workers, and one that can have adverse effects on both them and their employers. Training opportunities and career counseling can provide such employees with information that will enable them to examine their options in a pragmatic and systematic fashion. They can plan for career advancement or new careers and obtain the needed skills and knowledge to make the transition. The company benefits by channeling capable employees into more productive job slots and, in addition, reduces unnecessary turnover (Cronin, 1985).

Effective performance appraisal is another technique which can be used, for it provides valuable reinforcement for good work as well as information on deficiencies. Used properly, appraisals can create a supportive working environment. The key to success, however, is that performance appraisals should be an on-going activity that is timely, concrete, forthright, and specifically tied to job knowledge and skill requirements (Sterns and Valesek, 1985).

Offering Opportunities to Learn and Grow

Long service with one employer may lead to a career plateau—a position from which a worker may not be promoted and one which may offer fewer and fewer challenges. Yet many opportunities exist for companies to tap the knowledge and resources of such workers. Among the approaches that have been used successfully are job redesign, lateral job options and job rotation, special assignments, sabbaticals or training programs, and mentoring programs.

With job redesign, permanent changes may be made in job descriptions and assignments; new work assignments can be added and others can be eliminated. Lateral job options and job rotation involve reassignment of employees to different jobs at the same level of responsibility. Some companies rotate all employees to different positions at the same level of responsibility after a specified period of time.

Employees also may be asked to undertake special assignments providing leadership or support to a one-time-only project or to serve on committees or task forces. Recognizing the importance of good community relations and the value of improving the quality of life within the community, employers provide financial or in-kind support to community projects. One approach is the loaned executive program. Other community assignments can be less time intensive, such as heading the company's blood donor program or the United Way campaign.

Sabbaticals or training programs allow workers, after a specified period of service, to take a short-term leave of absence to attend an education or training program. Most employers continue to pay the worker's salary and allow the worker to choose the course of study, which need not be work-related. Some employees have used the sabbaticals to train for second careers.

In mentoring programs, the employee is the teacher rather than the trainee. These programs are frequently intergenerational; the older worker works with younger employees of the company or with youth from the community to share skills or to provide counseling or personalized encouragement or reinforcement.

All of the foregoing options have several things in common: they expose the worker to new skills and information; they provide opportunities to gain a broad understanding of the organization and internal and external environments; and they expand the number of people that the employees interact with on a regular basis.

Recognizing Unique Contributions to the Company

In the early stages of a work assignment, most supervisors are careful to monitor their staff's job performance and to commend and reward employees for doing the job well. After a worker has mastered the job, however, many supervisors tend to expect the worker to perform well with a lesser degree of supervision and attention. The worker gets less positive feedback. This situation can be interpreted by the worker as organizational devaluation of his or her job.

Acknowledging the accomplishments and contributions of older workers can be almost as important as income enhancements in motivating the worker (Bird, 1987). Sincere compliments or public comments about the quality of the work are effective. Some companies have taken the process a step further and given tangible forms of recognition such as notices in employee newsletters or performance trophies that are periodically circulated to high performers. These techniques have proven successful with employees regardless of age.

Involving the Worker in Meaningful Activities

At midlife, many workers begin to deal with what sociologist Erik Erikson terms the "generativity issue": "What will I leave behind for the next generation?" (Lorsch and Tagaki, 1986). They begin to examine their work and to make judgments about its meaning and its value to others. Consequently, it becomes important to involve older workers in challenging assignments that enable them to use their skills and knowledge. As importantly, the assignment must be part of the mainstream of the company's activities.

Another successful option is to design mechanisms that enable the long-term employee to play a visible and meaningful role in the decision-making process (Lorsch and Tagaki, 1986)—for example, participation on a task force charged with designing the strategic plans for the corporation. In planning for the future, it is critical to articulate, quantify, and integrate the historical perspective of the organization into forecasts. Tapping the historical memory of long-term workers can have a measurable impact on the reliability of the plan and long-range financial security.

Technological Change and Training

Training is an indispensable part of managing in this era of fast technological change. Both the speed of change and the use of new technologies by our global competitors are impacting on the workplace in an unprecedented fashion. Robots are a reality on the factory floor and video display terminals dominate the automated office. Many segments of the labor force are and will be affected by these changes, including middle-aged and older workers. New skills and knowledge are needed to acquire technological competence not only for new entrants into the work force but for experienced workers.

Technological Impact in Manufacturing

A report prepared for AARP has examined the potential impacts on older workers of technology in the durable goods manufacturing sector (Coberly, 1986). The technologies examined are computer aided design (CAD) and computer aided manufacturing (CAM). Draftsmen and engineers use CAD technology in the design of products, primarily in the automotive, aerospace, and electronics industries. CAM is used on the factory floor and includes the use of robots in the production process, particularly in the automotive industry.

The durable goods manufacturing industry is still an important source of employment for middle-aged and older workers. It employs about 18 percent of male workers ages 45 to 64 and about 8 percent of female workers in the same age cohort. In total numbers, 3.8 million men and women age 45 and older were employed in durable goods manufacturing in 1985. White males are expected to be most affected by changing technologies because of their predominance in this older worker population (Coberly, 1986).

Figure 1 summarizes the expected impact of CAD/CAM technologies on occupations in the durable goods industries. As can be seen, there is considerable potential for job displacement, but the most pervasive impact is expected to be in changing skill requirements. Deskilling, or reducing the skills required to perform the jobs, may occur in occupations such as craftsman, material handler, and operative. Engineers and technicians, mechanics, and

FIGURE 1

Job Impact of CAD/CAM Technologies

CAD:
- renders jobs performed by conventional drafters and designers obsolete
- expands employment opportunities for engineers and engineering technicians

Robots:
- threaten production painters, welders/flamecutters, and machine tool operators; smart robots affect assemblers, inspectors, filers/grinders/buffers, packagers, heat treaters, and electroplaters
- displace some workers and create new jobs for others; 15,000 robots have displaced 20,000 workers; estimates of the jobs created by building and installing robots vary widely

Automated Machine Tools:
- decrease the number of machine tool operators and setters
- increase the need for computer numerically controlled machine controllers and computer programmers

Flexible Manufacturing Systems:
- have reduced plant personnel by as much as half; specific occupational impacts are not documented

Automated Materials Handling Systems:
- reduce the need for handlers of materials, such as conveyor operators, crane/derrick/hoist operators, industrial truck operators, loading machine operators, and order fillers

Source: Coberly (1986).

installers will have to expand their skills by learning to use the CAD/CAM systems and taking on new tasks. Managerial occupations will be restructured and will require different ways to approach the job. How older workers will adjust depends upon their opportunities for retraining and the availability of other opportunities such as early retirement.

Union Training Agreements. Seniority rights and technology-related training agreements can be expected to protect many older workers from displacement. In the automotive industry, management and the United Automobile Workers have negotiated such agreements. For example, the Ford Motor Company is offering both basic mathematical skills and computer training to seasoned workers at its Ypsilanti, Michigan, assembly plant. The average hourly worker has more than 17 years on the job. Free courses at the plant were arranged under a 1982 UAW-Ford agreement (Vobejda, 1987). The need for training was seen in anticipation of a new statistical process control system.

A different type of training was offered to former General Motors workers who were hired by New United Motors Manufacturing, Inc. (NUMMI), a corporate joint venture of Toyota and GM (U.S. Department of Labor, 1987a). NUMMI agreed to hire a majority of its workers from those who had been laid off when GM closed its Fremont, California, plant in 1982 after 20 years of operation. The plant was closed not because of technological obsolescence, but because of a changing market and confrontational relations between the UAW workers and GM management.

When the plant was reopened in 1984 with 85 percent of the work force consisting of former GM Fremont workers, the union agreed to the adoption of the Japanese system which is built on teamwork with flexible work rules. Before reopening, 240 workers and production managers were sent to Japan in groups of 32 for three weeks of classroom and on-the-job training on a Toyota production line. The concept of *kaizen*, or "continuous improvement," was included in the training. After returning from Japan, the union representatives worked with management in establishing the training for the remainder of the team members.

While the joint venture and the cooperative team approach is still considered experimental in this country, the Fremont plant is no longer an industrial battleground and the retrained work force, including many middle-aged workers, has become productive and quality conscious. Production levels rival those of Japan even though NUMMI is less automated than some newer auto plants (U.S. Department of Labor, 1987a).

Updating Older Engineers. Engineers are in demand in high technology manufacturing industries, but older employed engineers may find it difficult to keep current in emerging technologies unless training opportunities are available. A recent conference report on utilization of engineers (sponsored jointly by the National Council on the Aging and the Institute of Electrical and Electronics Engineers) found that small and medium-sized companies often lack the continuing education structure for keeping employees current. Government contractors are also reluctant to invest in education for their employees because of competitive pressures to maintain low overhead rates (National Council on the Aging, 1986).

Colleges and universities do not usually have programs designed to meet the professional needs of middle-aged and older workers. However, there have been instances of universities teaming with industry to provide such programs. One such is the Monsanto Company and Washington University Program for Retraining and Professional Development initiated in January 1977. Selected Monsanto engineers spent a year in St. Louis attending Washington University at the employer's expense. The curriculum included refresher courses, advanced mathematics, and computer science, as well as problem solving. The average participant was age 40–50 and had worked for Monsanto for at least 20 years. Seventy-six of the 81 engineers who entered the program from 1977 to 1981 completed the program successfully (Perry, 1983).

Another example is the Honeywell Company and Arizona State University program which has stressed interaction between the university and the company, including shared laboratories, engineer assignments at the university, and R&D projects. There have also been annual industrial fellows, customized courses, televised courses, technology update programs, and special degree programs. The impact of the information and computer revolution on engineering and the need to maintain the technical vitality of middle-aged and older engineers has given impetus to these programs (National Council on the Aging, 1986).

Another company developed its own training program to supplement its tuition reimbursements for attending local university classes. High-Tec Engineers decided in the late 1970s to retrain their

176   THE OLDER WORKER

older engineers whose skills were becoming obsolete due to changing technologies. A cost study showed a three-to-one cost/ benefit ratio through retraining rather than recruiting new hires. In addition, the company felt a moral responsibility to its employees (Copperman and Keast, 1983).

The training consisted of two half-time courses of 10 weeks and 12 weeks plus a six-week full-time course in custom chip design which was followed by six months of on-the-job training. As managers were asked to select participants who needed skills upgrading, initially the trainees were apprehensive. However, their attitudes became positive as the training progressed, and only one out of 40 engineers selected failed to complete the course successfully. Most participants were in their mid-forties, but some were in their fifties. The successful trainees were promoted into new positions (Copperman and Keast, 1983).

Technological Impact in Service Industries

As has been widely noted and discussed, the U.S. economy has undergone a structural shift from goods-producing industries to service-producing industries. Since 1950, job growth has occurred overwhelmingly in the services sector which now accounts for three-fourths of nonagricultural employment (Committee for Economic Development, 1986).

Table 2 shows the proportion of workers age 45 and over employed in the five broadly defined service categories. The large

TABLE 2

Number of Employed Persons Age 45 and Over,
by Major Service Industry 1985 (thousands)

	45–54		55–64		65+	
Service Industry	Men	Women	Men	Women	Men	Women
Transportation and public utilities	1,047	304	640	156	78	23
Wholesale and retail trade	1,389	1,287	1,082	918	319	251
Finance, insurance, and real estate	517	593	394	324	147	73
Services	1,900	3,046	1,483	1,978	541	483
Public administration	687	322	352	241	72	40

Source: American Association of Retired Persons, 1986c.

miscellaneous services category includes business, personal, entertainment, professional, and related services. Components of the latter are health, education, social, and legal services. The miscellaneous services industries employ the largest number of persons age 45 and over (9.4 million) and more than half (58 percent) are women. Wholesale and retail trade is the next largest employer, with women constituting 47 percent of the 5.2 million older employees.

Much of the work in the service industries is performed in offices which are automated, with employees using personal computers and word processors. As new equipment and applications are continually being introduced, the composition of the automated office is in flux. Desk workstations are being developed which will allow access to data bases, automated filing, computer mail, word processing, data analysis, and other services (National Research Council, 1986). Voice recognition hardware will be widely used in the future, and employees will rely less on paper and more on electronic messages and files (Sterns, 1987).

Information technology is also being introduced in the health services industries. In hospital and other health care settings, automation is used not only for records control, but for activities such as patient monitoring. Computer interest groups have sprung up within the national nursing associations and nurses have become actively involved in the introduction of electronic innovations in patient care (National Research Council, 1986).

Computer Training. Much of the new technology in the service industries is computer-based. Young adults growing up in this age of automation are generally expected to have had more experience with computers than older workers and to be able to adapt more readily to the use of computers in the office.

In order to determine if older adults can master common computer applications, a study was made of groups of older persons (ages 65–75) and younger persons (ages 18–30) who were trained in the use of word processors. The results of the study showed that the older group did not differ from the younger group in the correctness and efficiency of the computer operations. They did require more time to perform the procedures and required more assistance in the editing tasks (Hartley, 1984).

The older group in the study cited above was composed of adults who are usually no longer in the labor force. Only 10.9

percent of those 65 and over were in the labor force in 1986 (U.S. Department of Labor, 1987b). Other studies, both in the laboratory and on the job, have examined a variety of younger and older age groups and have come to similar conclusions regarding the ability of older adults to learn and to absorb training (Meier and Kerr, 1976). One of the principles in retraining older persons is that either the pace of instruction should be slowed or the pace should be under the trainee's control (McFarland, 1973). Among the requirements for retraining mature executives, an experienced trainer recommends "only general guidelines and time schedules for completing projects" (Mintz, 1986).

Another study of technological change used case studies to show that older workers can adapt to automation in an office. Case studies of word processing in an engineering project office and of an on-line computer system in the export section of a company demonstrated that older people were able to develop new skills very effectively, primarily through on-the-job training (Lovelady, 1981).

Age and Training Opportunities

As the report to AARP on manufacturing technology notes, "There is a general perception that older workers are at a disadvantage in training decisions" (Coberly, 1986). The assumption seems to be that employers favor younger workers over their older employees when providing technology-related training opportunities. However, a nationwide survey of full-time workers age 40 and over, conducted for AARP by the Gallup Organization, revealed that half had received some on-the-job training over the previous three years and 22 percent had received job training or education outside of work that had been paid for by the employer (American Association of Retired Persons, 1986a). Nevertheless, Table 3 shows that the proportion of employer-provided training does decline by age within the older worker population. Workers in their forties were more likely to receive training than were those in their fifties and sixties.

The survey by occupation found that those who were classified as manual laborers had the highest percentage of employees who received no training at all (54 percent). When they did receive training, it was on the job. Forty-one percent of the manual workers, compared to 55 percent of the professionals/managers,

TABLE 3

Percent of Older Workers Receiving Training in Past Three Years,
by Source of Training and Age

Training	Total	40–49	50–62	63+
On-the-job training or education provided by employer	50.2	56.9	46.5	36.8
Training or education outside of work paid by employer	21.9	23.4	22.1	15.3
Training or education outside of work paid by employee	14.1	17.0	11.8	11.3
None	34.3	25.9	39.0	50.3

Source: American Association of Retired Persons Older Workers Study, unpublished data, 1985.

had received such training. Comparable figures for employer-paid training outside the workplace were 5 and 32 percent, respectively.

Table 3 shows that on-the-job training is the most prevalent form. Other data show that employers have taken the lead in providing technological training to current employees and that this type of training is gaining in importance (Coberly, 1986).

The Gallup survey also asked the employees if they wanted training opportunities, and a large majority indicated interest in some type of training. Only 10 percent said that they did not want any training, although almost a third of those age 63 and over were not interested (Table 4). The most desired type of training was to

TABLE 4

Types of Training Preferred by Older Workers,
Percent Distribution

Type	Total	Ages		
		40–49	50–62	63+
Update current job skills	39.3	36.9	43.7	34.8
Prepare for a better but similar job	24.3	29.3	22.0	13.3
Prepare for a totally different job	11.2	13.2	10.5	6.0
Not related to job	10.3	11.9	8.6	9.3
None	10.2	4.3	10.4	30.8
Don't know	4.8	4.5	4.8	6.5

Source: American Association of Retired Persons Older Workers Study, unpublished data, 1985.

update current job skills, followed by training for a better job similar to the one currently held. Employees in their forties were more likely to want training to prepare for a better or totally different job, but almost a third of those age 50 through 62 wanted to prepare for another job.

The survey results on training show that a majority of middle-aged and older workers are taking advantage of training opportunities and many of these opportunities are being initiated by employers. This is a positive indicator that those who are affected by technological change in both manufacturing and service industries will adapt and avoid occupational obsolescence. Many employees age 40 and over are interested not only in updating current job skills, but in training for a better job. However, those 63 and over show both markedly less recent experience with training and less interest in it, and manual workers have fewer opportunities for training than do other employees.

Alternative Work Options

With the exception of phased retirement, alternative work options are seen as helpful not only for older workers, but for students, single parents, and households with children where both parents work. Changing American lifestyles, including the increased labor force participation of women and the desire for more free time, have placed greater value on flexible scheduling of work. Nevertheless, many employers and unions are skeptical of alternatives to full-time regularly scheduled work, and the traditional workweek is still the norm for those in the primary work force.

From the standpoint of older workers, alternative work options can provide (1) a transition to retirement, and (2) work opportunities after retirement. Phased retirement, flextime, and part-time work (including job sharing) are options that are often suggested.

Phased Retirement

Phased or gradual retirement is defined, for this discussion, as a program with reduced work schedules *before* leaving a job at an age of retirement eligibility specified by a pension plan or by Social Security. Wages are usually reduced and may or may not be replaced with a partial pension.

Sweden is the country with the most experience with gradual retirement. Legislation enacted in 1976 provided for a partial pension for workers and self-employed persons ages 60–64 if they reduced their work to part time. It is financed through a 0.5 percent tax on gross wages. Work must be reduced by at least five hours per week with a minimum of 17 hours. More than one in five eligible workers ages 60–64 opted to receive a partial pension (Nusberg, 1986).

Few employers in the U.S. offer their employees the opportunity to phase into retirement through a gradual reduction of hours, and in those companies which do, not all employees accept the offer. One nationwide survey of employers found that only 15 percent of the respondents had a "tapering off" program in which some employees could reduce work time as they approached retirement. Another survey of members of the American Society for Personnel Administration defined phased retirement as a policy that allowed a worker to receive a partial pension while receiving partial wages. Only 7 percent of the employers had such a program (Meier, 1980).

Several employer studies have found that older workers would have a strong interest in phased retirement if partial pensions were provided. A study of the desirability of work options by older workers at Lockheed Corporation and the City of Los Angeles found that part-time options were of interest to the workers if they could receive at least part of their pensions. In an analysis of 900 workers over age 50 in a high technology company, 62 percent of them said that they would probably or definitely continue to work part time past their current planned retirement age if they could receive prorated pension benefits (Copperman and Keast, 1983).

In the Gallup survey of workers age 40 and over, workers were asked if phased retirement with decreasing hours would be a major consideration in delaying retirement. No mention was made of partial pensions. A minority—27 percent of those age 63 and over— and 39 percent of those ages 50 through 62 rated phased retirement a major consideration should it be made available (American Association of Retired Persons, 1986b).

AARP has specific examples of employer phased-retirement programs in its National Older Workers Information System (NOWIS). In one company's "40-percent work option," phased retirement was available to selected salaried professionals age 58 or older with 20 years of service. Those selected by management were given the opportunity to retire and collect their pensions while continuing to work two days a week at 40 percent of their preretirement salary. Of the 50 employees given the option, 30 chose to participate (American Association of Retired Persons, 1986a).

Another company offers a reduced workweek with reduced salary to employees 55 and over who intend to retire within two years. No partial pension is offered. As a rule, the reduction consists of a four-day workweek in the first year and a three-day week in the second. About 5 to 10 percent of the eligible employees participate (American Association of Retired Persons, 1986a).

As is illustrated in the case examples cited, phased retirement programs are utilized by some companies, but there is no indication that there is a growing trend toward programs of this type. On the contrary, there is evidence that what might be termed "sudden retirement" is widespread through the use of early retirement incentive programs, particularly in large corporations. These programs typically give eligible employees (usually age 50 and over) a few weeks to decide whether or not to accept liberalized early retirement benefits and leave employment. A 1985 survey of 400 companies found that 41 percent of those with 1,000 or more employees had implemented early retirement incentive programs. The magnitude of the programs can be further assessed by the fact that in one company alone, 11,000 employees retired under an incentive program (Meier, 1986).

Flextime

One of the largest employers to adopt flextime is the federal government. It has permanently adopted both flexible work schedules and compressed workweeks for many of its civilian employees. Under these arrangements, fixed times of arrival and departure may be varied, usually providing that a core of hours is worked, and the length of the workweek may also be changed. The compressed workweek schedules the biweekly 80 hours of work requirement in less than 10 full workdays—for example, the four-day week with eight 10-hour days, or the 5-4/9 plan in which employees work four days one week and five days the next, usually nine hours a day.

The House Committee on Post Office and Civil Service estimated in 1985 that more than 10 million full-time workers had flexible work schedules or compressed workweeks. Its report stated, "These variations from the standard eight-hour workday evolved as a means of coping with social change, particularly the dramatic increase of women in the work force, as well as the desire of all employees for a better accommodation between their working and personal lives" (Bureau of National Affairs, 1986).

Since flextime arrangements do not decrease work hours, and compressed workweeks actually increase the length of the workday, neither can be seen as a way to cut back work in a transition to retirement for older workers. The compressed workweek ranked comparatively low when workers age 40 and over were asked if it would be a major consideration in delaying retirement. Only 30 percent responded affirmatively; of those 63 and over, the proportion was only 21 percent (American Association of Retired Persons, 1986b). A review of the literature on older workers and the compressed workweek concluded that older workers were likely to resist a change to such a schedule because of the increased fatigue of a longer working day (Copperman and Keast, 1983). In any case, the compressed work schedule is offered by few employers. A recent survey by the American Society for Personnel Administration (ASPA) found that only 8 percent of the organizations responding reported use of a shortened or compressed work schedule (1987 ASPA/CCH Survey).

Flextime without the compressed workweek is more popular with older workers. In the older worker survey, 44 percent of those age 40 and over and 32 percent of those 63 and over rated it a major consideration in delaying retirement (American Association of Retired Persons, 1986b). The ASPA survey found that 26 percent of the organizations used a flexible working hour schedule and that its use seems to be growing (1987 ASPA/CCH Survey).

Part-Time Work

In surveys of older workers, part-time work is often cited as a preferred way to remain employed. For example, the 1981 Harris poll conducted for the National Council on the Aging asked current employees working full time or part time if they would prefer to stop working completely or to continue some kind of part-time work "when you retire." About three-fourths of those ages 55–64 and of those 65 and over said that they would like part-time work. Of those who wanted to continue in part-time work, slightly over half of those ages 55–64 and more than 80 percent of those 65 and over wanted the same kind of job (National Council on the Aging, 1981).

Full-time workers age 40 and over were not, however, as enthusiastic about part-time work when they were asked if it would be a major consideration in *delaying* retirement. Two-fifths of the entire age 40 and over group and less than one-third of those 63 and over said that it would be a major consideration (American Association of Retired Persons, 1986b).

As has been discussed, phased retirement with reduced work hours and a partial pension is rare in this country. For those employees who are covered by pensions, reducing work hours to part time for the same employer may not be a viable option since (1) it could reduce the amount of the pension compared to what it would be if full-time work were continued, and (2) if the employee is already eligible for a pension, collecting the full pension and obtaining part-time work elsewhere could be more attractive. As another study of older workers concluded, "If they could not receive all or part of their pension while shifting to part-time work for the firm, most persons interested in part-time work would simply retire completely and seek a job with another employer" (Copperman and Keast, 1983).

Job-Sharing. Most part-time jobs are low-wage, low-skill, and temporary. There is no evidence that the number of permanent job-sharing positions, which are career-oriented and come with prorated salaries and benefits, is increasing. Under this type of arrangement, the duties of one full-time job are split between two persons, each working part time. The recent ASPA survey found that only 4 percent of the firms had job sharing. They reported that the main advantage of job sharing was to accommodate working parents, and no mention was made of older workers (1987 ASPA/CCH Survey).

Part-Time Work After "Retirement." The trend of decreasing labor force participation of men, both before and after age 65, has continued unabated in the 1980s. In the age 65–69 cohort, men's participation decreased from 28.5 in 1980 to 25 percent in 1986; among women, participation declined slightly from 15 to 14 percent. In the age 70 and over group, only about 10 percent of the men and 4 percent of the women remained working or were seeking work by 1986. Many of those who do remain in the labor force after age 65 are working part time (Meier, 1987).

Table 5 shows the amount and proportion of part-time employment for workers age 55 and older for the years 1976 and 1986. The proportion of total employment which is part time is dramatically higher for those age 65 and over than for those in their late fifties or early sixties. In 1986, slightly more than half of the

TABLE 5
Older Worker Part-Time Employment, 1976 and 1986

	1976		1986	
Age and Sex	Number (thousands)	Percent of Total Age Group Employment	Number (thousands)	Percent of Total Age Group Employment
Total				
55–59	721	11	917	13
60–64	698	17	920	20
65+	1,334	49	1,527	52
Male				
55–59	153	4	219	5
60–64	242	9	326	12
65+	750	44	826	47
Female				
55–59	569	17	698	24
60–64	456	29	594	32
65+	583	58	701	60

Source: U.S. Bureau of Labor Statistics, unpublished data.

approximately 3 million persons age 65 and over who were in the labor force were working part time, compared to a fifth of those ages 60–64 and 13 percent of those ages 55–59. A larger proportion of women than of men in each age category were working part time.

Labor Department statistics on part-time employment do not reveal if the workers in these positions have "retired" from full-time jobs. However, the 1981 Harris survey did include workers 55 and over who were already working part time. About half reported that they were "retired" but working part time in their retirement. Eighty percent of them were 65 and older (Sheppard and Mantovani, 1982).

Some firms have a pool of retirees who are familiar with company procedures and can be called back when needed. One large insurance and financial services firm maintains a "retiree job bank" for on-call positions. The average number of hours worked by the retirees per month is 62 (American Association of Retired Persons, 1986a).

A large aerospace company employs some of its retirees on a part-time "casual" basis. They are from every job category, including senior engineering specialists, and they are called in to meet special temporary staffing needs (National Council on the Aging, 1986).

In both of the above cases, however, there are limits on the number of hours that can be worked per year while collecting a pension. In the insurance company it is 960 hours and in the aerospace company 1,000 hours. Many managers limit the number of part-time work hours to less than 1,000 because of the "1,000-hour rule" which mandates pension vesting for employees who work 1,000 hours or more yearly. This rule is mandated by the Employee Retirement Income Security Act of 1974 (Paul, 1987).

Another law which reduced the amount of time that retirees can work is the Social Security earnings test. In a survey of organizations who employed retirees, the managers "expressed frustration in the fact that once retirees who are receiving Social Security earn $6,000 (the 1982 maximum earnings limitation) they usually cease working, or they will limit their work hours, upon re-employment, so as not to exceed the $6,000 limit. This is a particular problem for retirees who command high compensation and thus reach the $6,000 mark very quickly" (Paul, 1987).

Figures on the use of retirees as "nonregular" employees are provided by the ASPA survey, which found that they were used as part-time employees by almost a third of the survey respondents. Employment of retirees was a recent development for many of the organizations, as 58 percent had done so for less than a year (1987 ASPA/CCH Survey). This, coupled with the fact that the primary reason for hiring retirees was to "capitalize on special skills," appears to give some credence to the theory that labor shortages are developing and more employers are turning to older workers for temporary assistance. There is no evidence as yet, however, that older workers are seeking such employment in sufficient numbers to halt the trend toward earlier and complete retirement.

Research Agenda

Research can play an important role in meeting the needs of both management and the older worker in a changing work environment. The following sections are brief summaries of some research needs, based primarily on the work of Needham Porter and Navelli (1986) and Coberly (1986).

Maintaining Work Force Involvement

As has been discussed, the issue of maintaining older workers' involvement in the labor force has received a good deal of attention, but additional information is needed on factors that promote or encourage acceptance of continuing career planning by older workers, the impact of alternative work options on retirement income, and older workers' skills and needs in the context of anticipated trends in employment opportunities.

Economic/Technological Trends

A wealth of information exists on changing demographic trends and the evolving economy, but data on the impact of the new technologies on older workers are sparse. Research is needed on the diffusion of new technologies in specific industries and how these technologies affect older workers in these industries, the types of new jobs being created and the extent to which they will provide opportunities for older workers, the impact on older workers of the "deskilling" of certain jobs, and the relationship between the continuing trend toward early retirement and the adoption of new technologies.

Training

If middle-aged and older workers are to adapt to new technologies, their accessibility to training programs will be crucial. Some training topics that require further investigation are the availability of employer-sponsored training to older employees, an evaluation of alternative training technologies in promoting successful outcomes among older workers, and incentives and disincentives for older workers to take advantage of training opportunities.

References

American Association of Retired Persons. *Managing a Changing Work Force.* Washington: AARP, 1986a.

_____. Work and Retirement: Employees Over 40 and Their Views. Washington: AARP, 1986b.
_____. Workers 45+ Today and Tomorrow. Washington: AARP, 1986c.
_____. Workers Over 50: Old Myths, New Realities. Washington: AARP, 1986d.
Bird, Caroline. "The Shape of Work to Come." Modern Maturity (June-July 1987), pp. 32–45.
The Bureau of National Affairs, Inc. Work and Family: A Changing Dynamic. A BNA Special Report. Washington: BNA, 1986.
Business Planning in the Eighties: The New Competitiveness of American Corporations. Washington: Coopers & Lybrand, 1986.
Coberly, Sally. "Manufacturing Sector Technology Study: Implications for Older Workers." Unpublished report prepared for the Institute of Lifetime Learning, American Association of Retired Persons. Washington: 1986.
Committee for Economic Development. Work and Change: Labor Market Adjustment Policies in a Competitive World. New York: The Committee, 1986.
Copperman, Lois F., and Frederick D. Keast. Adjusting to an Older Work Force. New York: Van Nostrand Reinhold Co., 1983.
Cronin, Carol. "Resources for Managers of an Aging Workforce." In Age Issues in Management—Participant's Manual. Los Angeles: University of Southern California, 1985. Pp. 71–79.
Hartley, Alan A. "The Older Adult as Computer User." In Aging and Technological Advances, eds. Pauline K. Robinson, Judy Livingston, and James E. Birren. New York: Plenum Press, 1984.
Kahne, Hilda. Reconceiving Part-Time Work. Totowa, NJ: Rowman & Allanheld, 1985.
Liebig, Phoebe S. "Impacts of Technology on the Changing Work Place and on an Older and Changing Work Force." Speech, Third Annual Health and Healing Convocation, Technology and Aging, February 26, 1987.
_____. "The Workforce of Tomorrow: Its Challenge to Management." In Age Issues in Management—Participant's Manual. Los Angeles: University of Southern California, 1985. Pp. 16–21.
Lorsch, Jay W., and Haruo Takagi. "Keeping Managers Off the Shelf." Harvard Business Review 64 (July-August 1986), pp. 60–65.
Lovelady, Louise. "Manual, Technical, and Clerical Case Studies on Change Within Employment." In After Forty: The Time for Achievement, eds. Cary L. Cooper and Derek P. Torrington. New York: Wiley, 1981.
McFarland, Ross A. "The Need for Functional Age Measurements in Industrial Gerontology." Industrial Gerontology (Fall 1973), pp. 1–19.
Meier, Elizabeth L., and Elizabeth A. Kerr. "Capabilities of Middle-Aged and Older Workers." Industrial Gerontology (Summer 1976), pp. 147–56.
Meier, Elizabeth L. Early Retirement Incentive Programs: Trends and Implications. Washington: Public Policy Institute, AARP, 1986.
_____. Employment of Older Workers, Disincentives and Incentives. Washington: President's Commission on Pension Policy, 1980.
_____. "The Future of Early and Late Retirement." Business and Health (June 1987), pp. 16–18.
Mintz, Florence. "Retraining: The Graying of the Training Room." Personnel 63 (October 1986), pp. 69–71.
Nardone, Thomas J. "Part-Time Workers: Who Are They?" Monthly Labor Review 109 (February 1986), pp. 13–19.
The National Council on the Aging. Aging in the Eighties: America in Transition. Washington: The Council, 1981.
_____. The Aging Workforce: The Challenge of Utilization. Proceedings of a conference sponsored by the Council in cooperation with the Institute of Electrical and Electronics Engineers, Inc. New York: IEEE, 1986.
National Research Council. Computer Chips and Paper Clips, Vol. 1. Washington: National Academy Press, 1986.

Needham Porter and Novelli. "An Evaluation of Older Persons' Workforce-Related Needs: Developing a Research Agenda." Unpublished paper. Washington: 1986.

The 1987 ASPA/CCH Survey. Chicago: Commerce Clearing House, June 26, 1987.

Nusberg, Charlotte. "Measures that Prolong Work Life." Aging International (Autumn-Winter 1986), pp. 7–25.

Paul, Carolyn. "Work Alternatives for Older Americans: A Management Perspective." In The Problem Isn't Age: Work and Older Americans, ed. Steven H. Sandell. New York: Praeger, 1987. Pp. 165–76.

Perry, Nancy J. "'Recycled' Engineers Provide Talent and Technical Expertise at Monsanto." Aging and Work 6, No. 4 (1983).

Sheppard, Harold L., and Richard E. Mantovani. Aging in the Eighties: Part-Time Employment After Retirement. Washington: The National Council on the Aging, 1982.

Stagner, Ross. "Aging in Industry." In Handbook of the Psychology of Aging. New York. Van Nostrand Reinhold, 1985. Pp. 789–814.

Sterns, Harvey, and Diana L. Valesek. "Performance Appraisal of the Older Worker." In Age Issues in Management—Participant's Manual. Los Angeles: University of Southern California, 1985. Pp. 34–39.

Sterns, Harvey L. "Service Sector Technology and Change: Implication for Older Workers." Unpublished report prepared for the Institute of Lifetime Learning, American Association of Retired Persons, 1987.

U.S. Department of Labor, Bureau of Labor-Management Relations and Cooperative Programs. "New United Motor Manufacturing, Inc., and the United Automobile Workers: Partners in Training." Labor-Management Cooperation Brief, No. 10, March 1987a.

U.S. Department of Labor, Bureau of Labor Statistics. Employment and Earnings (January 1987b).

Vobejda, Barbara. "The New Cutting Edge in Factories: Education." The Washington Post, April 14, 1987, p. 1.

CHAPTER 8

Organized Labor and the Retired Worker

LESTER TRACHTMAN*

Executive Director, PLAN

This chapter focuses on the retired unionized worker, and specifically his relationship to the labor movement.[1] It is an examination of the interest that various unions have shown in their retired members, the structure of retiree clubs, labor's sponsorship of low-cost housing for the elderly, and the ties between the retirees and their unions. The diversity of the labor movement itself is reflected in the vast differences in retiree organizations and attitudes of the international unions to their retirees. In no way is this chapter an attempt to present a definite portrait; rather it is a series of observations, a review of the very limited published material, and a composite picture based on many discussions.

With the increase in age of the average worker, the growing number of retirees, and the problems of organizing in today's changing labor market, organized labor has had to take a hard look at its retired members and ask some basic questions about activities, programs, and organizational structure for this large group within its population.

There are many overlapping interests and motivations involved. There is no doubt that "seniors" are a potent political power, and that is obviously a key issue for labor today. People who can be

* Senior consultant to the National Institute for Work and Learning on "The Older Worker and the Labor Movement" and Executive Director of PLAN. The views expressed are solely those of the author.

[1] Some of the information on which this chapter is based was gathered as part of a larger project, "Older Workers and the Labor Movement," which is being conducted by the National Institute for Work and Learning. The sponsors of that study are the AFL-CIO, 14 affiliated international unions, the U.S. Department of Labor, the Villers Foundation, the Retirement Research Foundation, and the American Income Life Insurance Company. Other information and observations not footnoted are based on work that the author has done with labor organizations, in the retirement planning field, and as a result of many conversations with union officials and experts in senior care. The opinions and interpretations are strictly those of the author.

counted on to vote, sign petitions, attend rallies, and get others to vote are very important. There is also a deep social concern for the older member who has often worked most of his life for a regular paycheck in a factory or at a trade and has held a union card for many years. Often they were also the cadre that helped to build the unions: they walked the picket lines, attended the rallies, and went on strike. The current generation of local and international leaders feels a debt and, more important, a genuine sympathy. However, in terms of union priorities, this concern has generally not been expressed as a top issue deserving of any substantial portion of the limited resources available.

Today, as labor hopes to rekindle the early sense of commitment and dedication that often seems to be lacking in the younger union members, it needs to utilize the historical perspective and first-person accounts of how the old battles were won and individual locals were organized, what it was like before there was a union, and certainly the major accomplishments of the union. The retirees have the potential to provide that linkage.

Another intangible is the deep psychological need that many retirees have for the groups and the people that were part of their working lives. After a lifetime on the job, the workplace and the union have become part of their identity. Together they established the worker's job status, responsibilities, and routines. Although all relationships were not necessarily pleasurable, they may well have created strong bonds that are not easily broken. The often lonely retiree has a need to be known, to feel useful, and to sense that he has accomplished something tangible. The local unions, particularly in nonurban areas, are often social units and their facilities provide the opportunity for socializing and rekindling memories. Union leaders, when discussing the needs of the retirees, often speak of their need to swap stories, get together, and just talk.

The political forces in the country recognize the strength of the retiree vote and lobbying power which has been demonstrated repeatedly in recent years. The senior viewpoint is taken very seriously by the lawmakers. At the same time, the government is worried about the rising costs of health care for older persons and how these costs might be contained. Communities are worried about the increasing numbers of the homebound and the need for low-cost housing for the elderly, nursing homes, senior centers, and services.

Where do the unions come into the picture? Basically, they have always had a strong social concern for the needs of the elderly. They have formed coalitions with senior groups and lobbied on behalf of the seniors. Social and political concerns are a high priority on their agenda. But as far as organizing their own retirees is concerned, their record has been mixed at best, and in terms of developing programs to meet retiree needs, few national unions have gotten very involved. This is an issue that organized labor is now examining.[2]

Organized Labor's Support for Retiree Groups

The National Council of Senior Citizens

The starting point for an examination of labor's efforts to organize retirees and to use their strength and resources is the establishment of the National Council of Senior Citizens (NCSC). This prominent national organization emerged in 1961 out of a small meeting held in Detroit under the chairmanship of a former congressman, Aime J. Forand of Rhode Island, who became the organization's first president (NCSC, 1986, p. 7). The key issue at the time of formation was Medicare, and leading that fight was Nelson Cruikshank, then AFL-CIO Social Security Director, who was also a prime force in the development of the NCSC and later became its third president. Two unions were instrumental in the creation of the NCSC—the United Auto Workers and the Steelworkers. Participation of labor unions has increased steadily since that time, and the labor movement has taken and maintained a prominent role in the direction, support, and membership of the organization. Of the six current officers, the majority, including the president, come from the ranks of labor.

The organization is composed of approximately 4,500 independent clubs. Of that number, it is estimated that "one-third are retiree clubs of organized labor" (NCSC, 1985, p. 7). The remaining two-thirds include clubs related to churches of all faiths as well as community and social welfare groups. There are 12 international unions with a number of affiliates in the NCSC, the most active being the United Auto Workers, the American Federation of State, County and Municipal Employees, the International Brotherhood of Electrical Workers, the International Association of Machinists, the United Steelworkers, and the International Union of Operating Engineers.

---

[2] See Note 1.

The total membership of the clubs that are affiliated with the NCSC is estimated to be several million. However, many of the club members have not individually joined the national organization. Union retirees who hold individual or family memberships are reported to number over 250,000 (NCSC, 1986, p. 7), which is clearly only a small portion of all retired union members.

There are no published figures on union contributions to the NCSC, but it can be assumed that a large portion of the organization's operating funds come from the labor movement. In 1985 the UAW's Retired Workers Department contributed $77,406 to the NCSC (NCSC, 1985, p. 9). The contribution of the AFL-CIO today is also reported to be quite substantial. In the early days of the organization, 90 percent of the funds were from labor organizations. Today 48 percent come from individual memberships (NCSC, 1987, p. 32).

To focus attention and mobilize efforts on behalf of retirees and retiree organizations, the president of the AFL-CIO created the AFL-CIO Executive Council Committee on Retirees (subsequently renamed the Committee on Older and Retired Workers). This committee was first chaired by Douglas Fraser of the UAW and now by William Winpisinger of the IAM. In 1983 the Executive Council issued a statement urging all of the internationals "to establish retired members' clubs and affiliate them with the NCSC; designate one person, preferably on a full time basis, to work on retiree activities; support national, state and community programs providing opportunities for retirees to engage in creative services to the community and nation."[3]

This relationship between labor and the NCSC translates into a strong coalition for action at both the national and local levels. A majority of the NCSC state and local organizations have a strong union tie and many have leadership that comes from the labor movement. This relationship is a natural one. Retirees seek and need organization and the infrastructure provided by organized labor is already in place. Experienced leaders often come from the trade unions. Perhaps more important, attitudes toward senior issues transcend attitudes toward organized labor. The issues are basic to

------

[3] Statement by the AFL-CIO Executive Council, Linthicum Heights, Maryland, May 24, 1983.

all seniors. They are social issues that labor has long championed: the problems of adequate income, low-cost housing, medical care, public transportation, affordable health insurance, and long-term care, among many others. These are basic issues on labor's domestic agenda.

The Current National Union Programs

Surprisingly few international unions have an active national program and structure for their retiree clubs. However, there are many union locals and district organizations with regular programs, meetings, and activities. While the internationals may provide the local club charter, they usually provide little additional financial support, though there are several exceptions.

Often there is a staff person at the national headquarters who has retiree activities among his or her specific assignments. The staffer may be responsible for coordinating with the NCSC, encouraging new clubs, taking a local reading on legislative issues, or dealing with specific benefit problems. Sometimes staff people at the district level have retirees among their responsibilities, though their interaction with retiree groups is usually minimal.

The potential role of retirees in the local union varies surprisingly. In several construction unions, the retirees who pay reduced retiree dues can vote in the election of local officers and on many other items of local union business. In general, however, the unions do not allow retirees to vote on any economic or collective bargaining issue. Yet the fact that retirees can vote in an election of officers in many locals gives them influence in developing union positions on various issues.

Prime Examples

It is instructive to examine the retiree programs and approach of some of the major international unions that are very active in the field—the UAW, AFSCME, ACTWU, ILGWU, and USWA.

The first major union to formally adopt a structure and an approach to organizing its retirees and addressing their needs was the UAW. At its 16th constitutional convention in 1957, the UAW created a special department for retiree programs, allocated a portion of dues money to retiree activities, and called for standing committees on retired workers' programs to be created in each local (Korn, 1976, p. 3).

The structure of the UAW retiree organization consists of local union retired worker chapters and area councils (where no local chapters exist), which are represented at regional retired workers' councils. The top body is the International Retired Workers Advisory Council which is responsible to the Executive Board. The operating arm of the organization is the Retired Workers Department which works closely with the regional councils. There are now about 715 retired workers' chapters and 120 regional area councils (UAW, undated, p. 9).

Today there are approximately 400,000 retirees under UAW negotiated pension plans, and it is reported that 80 percent have agreed to a dues checkoff of $1.00 per month per retiree, which indicates a budget of over $3,800,000 per year for retiree activities (UAW, undated, p. 6). Forty cents of each dollar of retiree dues goes to the Retired Workers Department and area councils, 35 cents stays in the chapters to fund programs, and 25 cents is for the use of the regional councils and for regional programs.

Activities of the UAW include preparing its members for retirement as well as promoting their welfare after retirement. The international has formulated the most comprehensive and elaborate retirement planning program of any of the unions. It includes audio-visual materials, a participant's manual with a set of modules covering all the basic subjects, and an instructor's manual. A considerable amount of information is produced by the Retired Workers Department and is disseminated to the chapters. Chapters usually have monthly meetings that often attract more than a hundred members. These meetings provide an opportunity for members and their spouses to socialize and for the union to communicate with them on issues of concern.

Among the many benefits offered to UAW retirees is the opportunity to stay at a UAW-sponsored retiree "village" of mobile homes near St. Augustine, Florida. Florida was chosen because so many UAW retirees move to that state, and the village is a way of testing their acclimation to the Sunbelt.

Another example of a major retiree program is AFSCME's, which has more than 110,000 dues-paying members in 21 chapters in 15 states and is growing rapidly. Membership in individual retiree organizations ranges from 100 to 40,000, the latter being the retirees of AFSCME Local 1000 in New York state (the State Civil Service Employees Association). Several large chapters have subchapters;

the 13,000-member organization in Washington state, for example, has 40 subchapters. Eligible retirees can become members even if they did not belong to the union when they were working. The minimum dues are $10.20 per year of which $9.00 remains with the local groups and $1.20 is sent to the national organization. Some chapters have dues that run as high as $3.00 to $4.00 per month; several have a checkoff arrangement for their members which creates a major financial resource.

Retiree chapters have a voice at the national level through the Retiree Council, which is composed of all of the chapter presidents. The council meets annually and elects its own chair and vice chair; the chair attends all meetings of AFSCME's Executive Board. Retiree resolutions are first raised in the Retiree Council and then are brought to the Resolutions Committee at the convention. As a result of a new constitutional amendment, each retiree chapter is now entitled to one delegate and one vote at the convention. Since there are 3,000 delegates and only 21 chapters, the retiree voice is limited.

There is an interesting political aspect to the representation question. Since the retirees now have increased membership rights, their participation in the union's Political Action Committee is now allowed by law. Labor's experience has been that a much larger percentage of retirees than of the general membership contribute to the PACs, although they contribute small amounts individually.

The Union Role as a Service Provider

The delivery of specific services to retirees has been a noteworthy characteristic of the needle trades for a number of years. The Amalgamated Clothing and Textile Workers (ACTWU) and the International Ladies' Garment Workers' Union (ILGWU), though faced with major declines in membership, have developed programs and facilities to address the social, psychological, and recreational needs of their members.

ACTWU, through its joint boards, supports 75 retiree clubs and four retiree centers that have facilities to provide a range of weekly activities for local members. These activities include arts and crafts, exercise classes, drama clubs, health education programs, regular trips, potluck lunches, and topical speakers. How these programs differ from those of most other unions is that retiree activities are seen as a necessary service to be provided to the retirees by the union. In many other cases the emphasis is on the need for organization rather than program. ACTWU activities are generally supported in each area by the joint boards of the international union.

The ILGWU has about 127,000 retirees on its rolls and reaches 90,000 of them through its clubs and programs, a remarkable achievement. A major portion of the retirees are organized into 104 clubs, which include groups in Canada and Puerto Rico. Since large numbers of ILGWU retirees have settled in Florida, the international opened and fully staffed an office there which replicates the social welfare orientation of the international.

The strong social service orientation of the ILGWU programs is shown by the presence of several social workers on the staff. The union has also created special programs for retirees to help other retirees, particularly the "Friendly Visitor Service." Under this landmark program, each retiree is visited at least once a year, with follow-up visits as needed. It is designed to provide support, guidance, and companionship for the retirees. The services of friendly visitors and/or social workers are available in communities in nine states. The "friendly visitors" are ILGWU retirees who have received training from social workers.

The ILGWU retiree clubs, with the assistance of the Retiree Service Department, mount special educational, recreational, and cultural programs for their members, including concerts by professional musicians. The clubs are sometimes able to increase their resources by organizing into associations or councils. Some of the ILGWU regional bodies have staff members whose duties include working with retiree groups and keeping them informed of important social and legislative issues.

Communications are facilitated by *Justice*, the international union's regular publication, which has one page in each issue devoted to retirees. In addition, special mailings are often sent out to all the clubs.

Historically, there have not been many major unions like the UAW, ILGWU, ACTWU, and AFSCME which have demonstrated such a strong social concern for their retirees. With the aging of the work force and particularly the union membership, the growing strength of retirees, and the increasing social concerns among the union leadership, many more unions are now beginning to develop programs and services for their retirees.

Some Other Major Union Programs

A number of other large international unions have retiree clubs across the country which vary greatly in size and activity, and efforts are under way to strengthen them. The Communications Workers of America (CWA), for example, reports that it has more than 90 clubs serving 10,000 retirees, primarily telephone workers. Its retiree rolls show about 28,000 names on computer lists. A basis for a national structure exists in the union's eight districts. Each district selects a delegate to participate in a Retiree Members Advisory Committee, which meets annually. The RMAC elects a representative to speak to the convention and makes recommendations to the CWA Executive Board. The union is considering a more active program for its retirees and a new structure to build a stronger organization and to give retirees more of a voice.

The United Steelworkers of America (USWA), a major union decimated by the decline of its industry in the United States, has recently started a major new organization for its retirees, called SOAR—Steelworker Organization for Active Retirees. The union seeks to involve about 400,000 of its retirees as well as spouses, widows, and widowers in the new organization.[4] Retired former officials of the Steelworkers are participating in the effort. The USWA estimates that there are 700 retiree clubs already existing that are eligible to affiliate with SOAR.

Activities of the Retiree Organizations

The majority of local unions do not have their own retiree clubs. Some refer their retirees to district organizations. Whether or not a club exists, many union locals try to acknowledge the role and significance of their retirees in some tangible way. A common approach is to have an annual or semiannual event primarily for retirees. An annual picnic is one popular way to acknowledge the retirees' service to the union, provide information on recent events and benefit changes, and give the retirees a chance to socialize.

Of the many retiree needs, socializing is the one in particular that is recognized by many of the local leaders, and they try to provide the setting for easy conversation and camaraderie. The retirees show their loyalty by their readiness to support the union position in

---

[4] *The Steelworker Oldtimer* 9 (Spring 1986), p. 9.

legislative and election campaigns and by donating time to political activities.

There are probably several thousand clubs of retired union members across the country. While they vary greatly in structure, participation, and activities, they have many common features. Many clubs are primarily social; the retirees get together to exchange news, plan trips, celebrate events, and often just to socialize. There are also many clubs with a strong educational and activist orientation; their emphasis is on speakers on such issues as health care, Social Security, financial planning, and legislative developments, nationally and statewide. The politically active clubs may plan a rally, a bus trip to the state capital, or a petition-signing program, or they may staff phone banks and stuff envelopes.

The active clubs are often led by former union activists—individuals who may want to continue their involvement in social and political issues and need a base of support. These activists may find that their greatest problem is to locate volunteers to work with them. Apparently there is a strong tendency for retirees to avoid "getting involved" and taking on fresh responsibilities.

A related problem is the reluctance of the younger, more recent retirees to join a retiree club. They seem to feel that they are much younger than the "old timers" and have other interests. Yet it is this group of young retirees that the clubs need if they are to get fresh leadership and the momentum to grow and better service their members. Many of the younger group may join eventually, but this often takes years. This issue is one that is important for labor to examine, and one union that is addressing it is the International Brotherhood of Electrical Workers (IBEW), which has recently started a campaign to enlist 300,000 members over age 50 in the NCSC and in IBEW retiree clubs. Retirement planning programs are to be offered as part of this effort.

It appears that more of the individual unions are now recognizing the importance of reaching the older workers through retirement planning programs. Whether these programs will influence the older workers to join union retiree clubs and/or the NCSC remains to be seen.

Retiree Club Format

Retiree clubs usually meet monthly or bimonthly on a set day of the month. The majority meet in the daytime since many seniors try to avoid going out at night. A significant number feature potluck lunches or coffee and doughnuts as a minimum. The local union often will help defray expenses. The club may raise some funds through a small admission charge or by taking a small portion of the winnings from a card or bingo game.

The business meetings of the clubs sometimes have common elements. Often there are one or more club officers concerned with "good and welfare" who report on problems of the sick, travel committees that report on plans for the next club trip, and a program committee that schedules events, including speakers. Clubs like to mark milestones of individual members, such as birthdays, anniversaries, or years in the union.

The clubs frequently are a good base from which to plan political activities. The membership is accessible, tends to understand the issues, and has free time and a sense of commitment. Union retirees are most often actively sought at election time to staff phone banks, get petitions signed, stuff envelopes, and hand out leaflets. Political candidates cultivate the senior vote wherever a meeting is organized and the unions can get the seniors to fill the hall, and several national legislators have said that it was the organized retirees who made the difference in their election. Whether the issue is of special concern to the active union members—"double breasting," for example—or of particular concern to the seniors—for example, Medicare regulations—the retirees will ride buses to the state capital or turn out for local rallies.

Club Finances

Retirees may pay two types of dues—dues to the union and dues to the club. (In several cases one payment covers both.) Dues to the union, which may be passed on in part to the international, range from the Machinists' one-time fee of $5.00 to almost $15.00 per month paid to a major construction local. The unions which have a dues structure for their retired members usually allow them to vote in local elections. However, the UAW, which collects dues through a voluntary checkoff on its members' pensions, does not permit retirees to vote for leaders of the locals, though they have representation on local union executive boards. Several of the construction unions waive retiree dues after 25 or more years of union membership.

Retiree club dues are much smaller than local dues and usually do not exceed $1.00 per member per month. The parent local or district most often covers mailing and administrative expenses and may assist with special needs.

Senior Housing and the Labor Movement

A highly significant and frequently overlooked accomplishment of the labor movement on the agenda of senior issues is its financial support for union housing. With the aid of federal programs, labor has sponsored or supported over 100 different projects across the country that have provided housing primarily for seniors. Unfortunately, aggregate figures are hard to obtain. It is clear that the Reagan administration actively discouraged and tried to eliminate many forms of low-cost housing. Nevertheless, there is a record of labor's accomplishment and involvement in this area which is quite noteworthy.

A 1979 article in *Commonweal* (Fuerst, 1979) reported that there are 20 "astonishingly successful" housing projects around the country sponsored by a wide variety of labor unions. These projects contain about 4,000 units and are subsidized under Section 236 of the federal housing law—that is, they were built for low- and moderate-income families and the elderly. In a broader context, unions operate well over 100 subsidized projects that are devoted primarily to serving the elderly. The variety of unions involved is quite surprising: bartenders, food handlers, plumbers, steel workers, commercial workers, electrical workers, and auto and aerospace workers (Fuerst, 1979). Regional groups of unions in central labor councils and building trades councils have also been actively involved in the Section 202 projects (a direct loan program exclusively for projects for the elderly and handicapped).

The success of these projects, which apparently lacked any central coordination and guidance other than federal regulations, appears well documented. Vacancy rates were very low, rental payments were much better than average in timeliness, and the projects were well integrated racially and were well managed (Fuerst, 1979).

A more recent development affecting housing for the elderly is the growing role of the NCSC and its Housing Management Corporation, NCSC-HMC. This organization is now one of the largest management firms of Section 202 housing in the country. It manages 28 senior housing projects, 21 of which, containing 3,500 units, it owns partially or fully. Four of the projects in which it has a substantial investment are co-sponsored with the UAW, two it co-sponsors with the Steelworkers, and one it co-sponsors with the Maine Federation of Labor.[5] Since the labor movement has a major role in the NCSC, it can certainly take significant credit for the NCSC role in senior housing. There are also many labor-sponsored housing projects that are managed by the unions or local labor councils directly, without NCSC input.

It is interesting to note that the NCSC, as a nonprofit organization with a specific interest in the well-being of seniors, is able to insure a number of amenities in the projects it manages. In terms of public space, there are community rooms, activity rooms, and sun porches, providing space for libraries, arts and crafts, and, of course, card playing and TV. The projects usually provide congregate dining areas, individual kitchens, and medical examination rooms. The care and sensitivity of the management appear to be quite high, as one reviews the detailed activities and the facilities lists, project by project.[6]

Several examples of union-sponsored housing deserve mention, although they are not designed specifically for the elderly. Some of the largest and most notable are those undertaken by the United Housing Foundation in New York, with specific projects sponsored by the International Ladies' Garment Workers' Union and the then Amalgamated Clothing Workers Union (prior to merger with the Textile Workers). The United Housing Foundation has built more than 50,000 housing units, primarily in the New York area. In addition, the ILGWU and the ACTWU have built other housing outside New York City.

One arm of the labor movement—the Housing Investment Trust—was created specifically to stimulate building activities. This organization deals primarily with Federal Housing Authority (FHA) loans, and in recent years it has been particularly active in the construction of nursing homes.

Organized labor is apparently ready to do much more in this field. However, there is a general feeling among union people that

---

[5] National Council of Senior Citizens, "Building Roster," unpublished document, revised May 21, 1987.

[6] National Council of Senior Citizens, "Senior Housing: Meeting the Challenge: A Description and Summary of Housing Projects Managed by the NCSC Housing Management Corporation," unpublished report, 1986. Table 2, "Common Space and Amenities."

the opportunities for senior housing under the Reagan administration were severely limited. They look forward to new legislation, preferably under new national leadership.

Conclusions and Observations

There is a very high degree of sensitivity and concern for the problems of the retirees at the local level. In the majority of situations, this is a natural response of a union leadership that grew up alongside the retirees in the union or on the job and sympathizes with their problems. At the same time these union leaders are faced with many pressures and problems involved in running their locals. If they can't find leadership to start and direct retiree clubs, they may limit their support to one or two annual functions and ad hoc assistance. The internationals, faced with a myriad of problems and often with declining resources, have usually not assigned a high priority to retiree activities. And if they do, they are not clear as to what path they should pursue.

The "real ballgame," in terms of programs and leadership, may be at the local level—in retiree activities of the central labor councils, the district councils, the NCSC chapters, and the state coalitions. To run more effective and popular activities, it would undoubtedly be advantageous to pool the very limited amount of dedicated leadership for retirees that is available to organize events, secure better health care arrangements, and explain the issues. The resources at all levels that are now focused on programs appear limited.

In the political context, the tremendous amount of leverage that retiree groups can exercise has been repeatedly demonstrated at the national and state levels, and there are a number of effective local and statewide retiree bodies. However, it is surprising to find some local union leaders in various parts of the country who have not heard of the NCSC or know of no senior groups that might be of interest to their retirees. A broad educational program on the mutuality of concerns of labor and its retirees is still needed.

A major problem, indeed an inherent problem, faced by retiree organizations is finding and keeping effective, committed leaders. Workers who are retiring at 65 or who are enjoying life in their eighties are often not ready to volunteer and take on responsibilities. The psychological and, perhaps, physical reasons are many. If they have not been leaders for the first two-thirds of their lives, they are reluctant to become activists now. However, the converse offers some interesting speculation. How many retired union leaders, shop stewards, and staff are currently active in retiree groups? These are people who have demonstrated an interest in leading a group, assuming responsibility, and confronting a problem. Very often the leaders of strong organizations were very active in their own unions before retiring, and they want to remain moderately active but with less day-to-day pressure. When retiree organizations exist, these union activists will often gravitate to them and provide some leadership. A systematic campaign to locate former union leaders at all levels and enlist them in leading retiree clubs may uncover talented individuals.

The lengthening age span of retirees is a factor contributing to the difficult task of organizing fresh clubs and revitalizing older ones. Workers retiring at 55 or 62 do not see themselves joining together with retirees in their mid-seventies, although their interests in such issues as improved health care and pension adjustments are certainly similar. Veteran unionists have noted that the younger retirees are not ready to join many of the retiree clubs dominated by people who are 15 years their senior. Perhaps it makes them feel older and more vulnerable to the problems of aging. It is also not clear whether the older adult members would fully welcome them into their cliques.

These intergenerational problems may be a significant hindrance to building retiree clubs in the labor movement. Yet the resources, the energy, and especially the leadership of the younger retirees are needed to build up the clubs and organize new ones. The younger retirees understand the current issues, the key personalities, and the power bases in local elections and legislative campaigns. They know what the major bargaining issues are for the local union and the perceptions of senior issues among the younger workers. Their participation in retiree clubs becomes of critical importance for senior influence on union growth, in community affairs, and in election campaigns at all levels.

One approach to involving them is through the development of retirement planning programs. These sessions can be of tremendous personal benefit to the retiring workers and at the same time give them an understanding of the purpose and activities of the retiree clubs. Indeed, a well-designed retirement planning program can be a major factor in enriching the life of the retiree and smoothing the transition to another lifestyle while showing strong union interest in an enjoyable and productive retirement for its members. In short, the union role in the life of the worker could be projected into the life of the retiree to the benefit of all concerned.

The image of labor, which has become tarnished in recent years, has often benefited from meaningful community service. From responding to natural disasters to building wheelchair ramps for the frail elderly and the disabled, volunteer union labor has won praise in many quarters. Retiree involvement in volunteer service that responds to community needs would seem a natural and logical path for many union retiree groups to follow. There is a wide range of activities where they can be of significant assistance and achieve satisfaction at the same time. The key is organization and networking within the community. There are enough successful local examples across the country for unions to emulate. If the leadership and motivation can be mobilized, the union, the retiree, and the community would benefit.

The labor movement is gradually becoming aware of its problems in reaching the retirees and the tremendous potential that retirees have in helping the unions grow and extend their influence. Organized labor and the retirees need each other, but the initiative has to come from the labor movement. Time will tell whether labor (both nationally and locally) will be able to meet the challenge in an effective and creative manner to the benefit of our aging society, the labor movement itself, and the retired worker.

References

Clague, Ewan, Bolraj Polli, and Leo Kramer. *The Aging Worker and the Union.* New York: Praeger, 1971.

Fuerst, J. S. "Unions and Subsidized Housing: A Hidden Success Story." *Commonweal* (March 2, 1979), pp. 110–15.

Korn, Richard. *A Union and its Retired Workers: A Case Study of the UAW.* Ithaca: New York State School of Industrial and Labor Relations, Cornell University, 1976.

Louis Harris and Associates, Inc. *Study of American Attitudes Towards Pensions and Retirement.* New York: Johnson and Higgins, 1979.

Massachusetts University Labor Relations and Research Center. *An Inter-Union Pre-Retirement Training Program.* Conducted for AOA, U.S. Department of Health, Education, and Welfare. Amherst: 1970.

National Council of Senior Citizens. *Progress Report, 1985.* Washington: NCSC, 1985.

————. *Progress Report, 1986.* Washington: NCSC, 1986.

————. *Progress Report, 1987.* Washington: NCSC, 1987.

Parnes, Herbert S. *Work and Retirement: A Longitudinal Study of Men.* Cambridge, MA: MIT Press, 1981.

United Auto Workers. *Retired Workers Program.* Detroit: undated.

CHAPTER 9

Public Policies and Programs Affecting Older Workers

STEVEN H. SANDELL*

U.S. Department of Health and Human Services

Public policy affecting older Americans' employment has many dimensions. First, Social Security and pensions policies, by affecting older workers' pecuniary gain from additional work as well as their financial resources for retirement, heavily influence the decision to leave the labor force. Second, income security policies, such as the availability of disability insurance and Supplementary Security Income (SSI), may also influence labor supply decisions. Third, direct regulations, especially under the Age Discrimination in Employment Act, affects employment opportunities and conditions for older workers. Fourth, employment and training programs, such as those funded under the Job Training Partnership Act, are meant to improve the employment prospects of distressed workers, including older ones. Finally, a whole range of economic and labor market policies, including minimum wage legislation, unemployment insurance, health and safety regulations, regulation of foreign trade, transfer payments to displaced workers, and even tax and macroeconomic policies can in particular instances have a major effect on older Americans' employment, sometimes through their effects on the policies and practices of private employers.

This chapter selects four topics from among the foregoing for close examination: (1) age-related employment regulation, (2) the effects of government policy on employer-sponsored programs, (3) government employment and training programs, especially those for the economically disadvantaged, and (4) the employment effects of retirement policies. Since the facts relating to the earnings and employment of older Americans have been covered compre-

---

* This chapter was written while the author worked at the National Commission for Employment Policy. He is grateful to Herbert S. Parnes for his extensive comments on an earlier draft. Opinions expressed are those of the author and do not necessarily represent the views of the Commission, the U.S. Department of Health and Human Services, or any other government agency.

hensively by Rones in Chapter 2, that important background information is not repeated here. Similarly, the aspects of pension policy that have been dealt with in Chapters 5 and 6 are consciously ignored.

Influences on Public Policy Toward Older Workers

Before examining specific public policies affecting older workers, it is important to understand the forces that help shape them. Not unlike other areas of government policy, older worker legislation is born more from the interaction of pressures from interest groups than from dispassionate analysis of social problems. Objective analyses are most likely to influence policy when they are used by advocates of specific policies or positions.

Advocates for the aged, business interests, unions, civil rights organizations, and public interest groups (such as the National Alliance of Business, Inc. and the National Governors Association) have demonstrated significant interest in and influence over federal older worker policy. However, older workers are not the primary focus for these groups.

In older persons' organizations, employment is only one of several activities of interest to its members. Income security issues, especially the size of Social Security benefits, volunteer activities, health and health care financing (which by virtue of its expense may be considered a vital part of income security policy), and even travel opportunities often take priority over employment as concerns of members of these organizations.

For example, the American Association of Retired Persons (AARP), a nonprofit, nonpartisan organization of more than 23 million members age 50 and over, runs a Senior Community Service Employment Program. It also sponsors a Worker Equity Initiative which has as its overriding goal "to advance the employment and career goals of middle-aged and older people through information, education and advocacy efforts" (American Association of Retired Persons, 1987, p. 14). However, the diversity of AARP's objectives is indicated by the description of its bimonthly magazine, *Modern Maturity*, which "provides members with a wealth of information and entertainment tailored to their interests and concerns [and] includes articles on finance, pensions, second careers, retirement locations, travel, personalities, food, health and current affairs" (American Association of Retired Persons, 1987, p. 12).

In labor unions the interests of older workers sometimes conflict with those of younger ones and retirees. Furthermore, older workers who are nearing retirement may be more interested in protecting pension and health benefits than preventing age discrimination in employment. Notwithstanding their concern for the unemployed, unions often are more concerned with protecting the jobs of current members than supporting the interests of outsiders, including people unsuccessfully seeking employment.

Moreover, even when unions turn their attention to social problems, the interests of older workers may come behind those of groups substantially more disadvantaged, such as blacks and Hispanics. Thus unions and other public interest and constituency organizations (e.g., the League of Cities) may focus more on the concerns of these groups than those of older workers.

Business groups, such as the U.S. Chamber of Commerce, may consider older worker policy to be one of many policy areas that impact on their members. For example, a mandated increase in health benefits for older workers may be a substantial cost to the organization members. While the effect of a change of the rules on a single firm may not be consequential, the firms taken together may face cost increases large enough for them to mount serious political opposition.

Research is an integral aspect of the policy formation process. Most readers of this volume are committed to the scientific method and are familiar with the nature of academic research. However, "objective" research on older workers, particularly policy-related research, is not read dispassionately by advocates of various interests.

The following statement made by a person whose function is to represent the interest of older workers, made in the course of reviewing an older-worker study, illustrates the point:

> I would argue that research should identify problems that exist, and offer a range of solutions to those problems. Those who would do nothing don't need research to make their case—they will rest on inertia no matter what the evidence. On the other hand, those who would argue for change need accurate information and innovative suggestions to make improvements on the status quo.

My personal belief is that while research should identify and offer a range of solutions to problems, good policy analysis must do a lot more. The causes of the problems must be understood before useful solutions can be designed. Furthermore, in a world with limited resources but unlimited competing problems, policy research should provide a perspective from which to judge the relative importance of the problems.

The Age Discrimination in Employment Act

The Age Discrimination in Employment Act (ADEA), enacted in 1967 and amended in 1978 and 1986, prohibits arbitrary age discrimination in hiring, discharge, pay, promotions, fringe benefits, and other aspects of employment for persons 40 years of age and older. Enforcement of the Act was the responsibility of the U.S. Department of Labor until 1979 when, by Executive Order, it was shifted to the Equal Employment Opportunity Commission.

Difficulty in distinguishing between age discrimination and other causes of employment problems makes examination of the ADEA's effectiveness a perplexing research and policy problem. The fact that most older workers are better off in terms of employment and earnings than their younger counterparts may hide age discrimination. Further, age discrimination is not necessarily the predominant cause of older workers' labor market problems. The problems that older workers may face stem from three separate but not mutually exclusive sources:

- Those unrelated to age, such as living in an area of high unemployment or racial discrimination.
- Those common among, but not unique to, older workers, such as poor health or inadequate schooling or training.
- Age Discrimination

In measuring the magnitude of age discrimination, it is important to distinguish these factors from one another and their effects on employment and earnings. For example, a 60-year-old may have lower pay than a younger worker, not because of age discrimination, but because of fewer years of schooling, which in turn may reflect a lack of educational opportunities when the person was young.

Nonetheless, the existence of age discrimination is undeniable. EEOC and court records attest to the discrimination suffered by some individuals. On the other hand, empirical documentation of pervasive age discrimination in earnings is not available.

The ADEA essentially requires employers' decisions in virtually every area of personnel policy to have a basis other than age alone. The threat of administrative enforcement of these provisions as well as the possibility of private suits appears to encourage employers to examine company policies regarding compliance. However, it is important to note that the Act proffers three exceptions. It is not unlawful for an employer, employment agency or labor organization to:

1. take any action otherwise prohibited where age is a bona fide occupational qualification (BFOQ) reasonably necessary to the normal operation of the particular business, or where the differentiation is based on reasonable factors other than age (RFOA);
2. observe the terms of a bona fide seniority system or any bona fide employee benefit plan such as retirement, pension, or insurance plan which is not a subterfuge to evade the purposes of the Act, except that no such employee benefit plan shall excuse the failure to hire any individual; or
3. discharge or otherwise discipline an individual for good cause. (29 United States Code, 621 et seq., 92 Stat. 189 (1978))

The burden of proof that the bona fide occupational qualification exception is applicable rests with the employer; the implementing regulations provide strict rules for using this defense. "Respondents must show that the age-limit is reasonably necessary to the essence of business, that all or substantially all of the persons within the age groups would be unable to perform the duties in question or that some members of the group possess a disabling characteristic which could not be detected through individual testing." (U.S. Senate, 1982)

In some cases the ADEA regulations appear to contradict the purpose and intent of the Act or to conflict with other legislation. For example, a conflict surfaced between the spirit of Title VII of the Civil Rights Act and the ADEA. Labor Department regulations allowed age limits for admission into bona fide apprenticeship programs, and in July 1981 EEOC reaffirmed that interpretation.

The factor motivating this decision was that lifting the age ban might limit apprenticeship opportunities for minority youth (U.S. Senate, 1982). In 1984, EEOC reversed direction on this issue and published notice of intent to rescind the apprenticeship exception. However, in 1987 the EEOC voted to maintain the exemption of apprenticeship programs from ADEA coverage by stating that the existing interpretation "correctly reflects the original intent of Congress with regard to the ADEA and bona fide apprenticeship programs" (*Employment and Training Reporter*, 1987). This example illustrates the dangers of isolating older worker policies from a broader context that considers the needs of other groups in the labor market.

The number of age discrimination charges filed with the EEOC had grown to over 26,000 annually by 1985, more than doubling from fiscal year 1980. Several factors account for the dramatic increase in the number of age discrimination charges filed with the Equal Employment Opportunity Commission (EEOC) during the 1980s (Fay, 1987). First, passage of time since its 1967 inception meant that the public's awareness of its protections grew. Second, the 1978 amendments expanded the Act's coverage. Third, because the EEOC handles sex and race discrimination as well as age discrimination, multiple charges are sometimes filed. More recently, widespread reductions in force accompanied with "sweetened" early retirement schemes have led to complaints and litigation.

Three trends have been noted in legal decisions with respect to the ADEA (Fay, 1987). First, models of proof developed in cases under Title VII of the Civil Rights Act of 1964 have been used in ADEA cases. Second, group actions have expanded. Third, claims for damages have expanded to "front pay" in lieu of reinstatement (as well as back pay). Liquidated or double damages are available if the violation is deemed to be "willful." One author (Bolick, 1987) warns that, "The potential economic effects flowing from the vastly enlarged reach of the ADEA cannot be overstated."

Most of the setting of age discrimination policy is currently taking place in the courts. At issue in the de facto policy formulation of the courts, aside from the facts of the individual cases, is interpreting Congressional intent and the language of the relevant statutes, not what age discrimination policy should be. Since the

1986 ADEA amendments that removed age 70 as the upper age limit and extended the protection of the Act to almost 800,000 employees age 70 or over, neither the Congress nor the Administration has been developing or debating substantial new policies in this area.

The Effect of Selected Government Policies on Employer-Sponsored Programs for Retirement-Age Workers

Alternative work options and management practices toward older workers, such as those discussed in Chapter 7 by Meier, are affected by government policies. By stimulating their creation and influencing their structure, federal legislation affects not only the implementation of some options but the response to them by older workers and retirees (Paul, 1987). For example, passage of the 1978 amendments to the Age Discrimination in Employment Act influenced some firms to examine the age structure of their personnel and then to establish part-time work programs and to recruit more workers over age 40.

Part-time work may not be the panacea some suggest to dramatically increase employment among older persons. Primarily because most part-time jobs are not well paid, retirees in general will continue to opt for complete retirement instead of part-time work. Social Security benefits, pension income, and savings appear to provide most retirees with a satisfactory alternative to working. The findings of some surveys that many older workers desire part-time jobs reflect interest in working part time at highly paid (career) jobs. Firms and workers might indeed benefit if, instead of complete retirement from long-held jobs, arrangements for working in them part time were more common.

Application of government policy toward this end is limited by the important economic foundation for the fact that part-time work generally pays less than full-time work in comparable jobs. Essentially similar employment costs (such as training) exist whether jobs are full or part time, and imply that higher hourly costs are associated with part-time employees. Employers can recoup these higher costs only by paying less per hour of work to part-time than to full-time employees (Jondrow et al., 1987). Because the government is not an important source of these costs, it cannot play a major role in reducing them.

Specific federal government policies affect the employment of older Americans. The number of hours retired persons work is affected by the Social Security earnings test, which in 1986 reduced benefits by 50 cents for every dollar earned over $7800 for persons ages 65 through 69. The Employee Retirement Income Security Act of 1974 (ERISA) contains a provision commonly referred to as the "1,000 hour rule," which mandates pension credit for employees working 1,000 hours or more during a single year. In response to this provision, management usually restricts annual part-time work hours to fewer than 1,000. Another ERISA provision allows pension benefits to be suspended for retirees who are reemployed for 40 or more hours in a calendar month. This encourages retirees to work less than 40 hours or offer their services through consultant contracts or for a different firm.

Finally, the Tax Equity and Fiscal Responsibility Act of 1982 makes firms which provide health insurance to their employees pay for the cost of health insurance of workers age 65 and over. Before passage of the Act, Medicare was either the first or only payer of health insurance for workers (and their spouses) 65 and over. The change, undertaken as a government cost-savings measure, raises costs for employers of older workers, and creates economic disincentives to their continued employment.

While there are many examples of employer personnel practices that other employers can adopt to increase employment opportunities for older workers, the practices do not meet the needs of large segments of the older population. These programs are least available for blue-collar and unskilled older workers. Employer-sponsored programs have been successful when they have been "symbiotic," i.e., useful to both workers and firms (Root and Zarrugh, 1987). When business conditions are poor, many work-options are no longer offered. The government's role should be to publicize information about these programs so they can be adopted by interested firms.

Employment and Training Programs

It is important to keep in mind that older workers are not a homogeneous group. While many proceed from a successful career in one or more long-held jobs to a desired period of retirement, some have serious labor market problems. Some persons experience unanticipated mid-life events, such as a major health problem or the loss of a long-held job, which disrupt the normal pattern. Other older people never experienced success in the labor market. They have histories of intermittent employment and low earnings and often have severe labor market problems when they reach old age.

Employment and training programs are the primary policy vehicles available to the government to improve the employment prospects of older workers. These include programs specifically designed for the older persons such as the Senior Community Service Program (Title V of the Older Americans Act), as well as programs in which older persons are eligible to participate, such as those financed under the Job Training Partnership Act.

Employment and training programs should be examined by focusing on who is served and what the program's impact is on participants' employment and earnings. The key participation questions are: Is the size of the program adequate? Do older workers in general, and specific subgroups of older workers, receive their fair share of training slots? Impact analysis often implies measurement of net increase in earnings. Separate measurement of the program's effect on rates of pay and employment is desirable. For programs that provide subsidized jobs and other services, measuring the benefits of in-program activities, rather than post-program activities, is important.

The Job Training Partnership Act

Adopted in 1982 as the successor to the Comprehensive Employment and Training Act (CETA), the Job Training Partnership Act (JTPA) is the government's primary legislative vehicle for providing services to persons experiencing difficulty in the labor market. JTPA establishes the framework and funding formula for employment and training programs for economically disadvantaged youth and adults (Title II) and dislocated workers (Title III). The programs are administered by the states and are conducted through Service Delivery Areas. The Act also establishes nationally administered programs for the disadvantaged, including the Job Corps, Native American Programs, and programs for Migrant and Seasonal Farm Workers, and it amends the Wagner-Peyser Act, the authorizing legislation for the Employment Service.

JTPA made significiant changes in the ways in which decentralized programs for the disadvantaged are conducted. These include emphasizing training to increase earnings in unsubsidized jobs, increasing the role of state governments, and providing a partnership with the private sector by giving primary operating responsibility to Private Industry Councils. Changes were made also in the rules governing the use of funds for programs.

In addition to the regular programs, 3 percent of each state's Title II-A allocation is set aside for employment and training services to economically disadvantaged persons age 55 and older. While three-fourths of the states administer these programs through the same units that are responsible for other JTPA programs, one-fifth delegate the responsibility to State Units on Aging (National Commission for Employment Policy, 1987).

Many factors affect participation in Job Training Partnership Act training programs. The eligibility specifications in the legislation allow only economically disadvantaged persons (as defined by the Act) to participate in the main (Title II-A) programs. However, the statutory definition of eligibility is sufficiently broad that a relatively large number of people meet it. Approximately 39 million people or about 20 percent of the population age 14 and over were eligible for JTPA Title II-A based on income in calendar year 1985. Nevertheless, only a small fraction of those eligible actually participate in programs: about 738,000 people or only 2.3 percent of the 31.7 million persons between the ages of 16 and 64 eligible for JTPA received training in program year 1985. Moreover, from the perspective of this chapter, it is important to note that the percentage of eligible persons participating in JTPA declines with age. Specifically, about 4.4 million persons between the ages of 55 and 64 were eligible for JTPA programs based on their 1985 income, but only .4 percent of these eligible persons actually participated (Sandell and Rupp, 1987). The rate for eligible persons ages 55 to 64 is less than one-fifth of the rate for persons 22 to 44.

The dramatically lower participation rate among older eligible persons can be substantially accounted for by the difference in the labor market interest of older compared to other adults eligible for JTPA programs. Essentially all persons who have income below the poverty level or 70 percent of the Office of Management and Budget's lower living standard are *eligible* for JTPA programs. However, to be *interested in participating* in JTPA training or job-search assistance, a person must be interested in obtaining a job. Thus persons who are unemployed *and* income-eligible make up the de facto eligibility pool. Among persons 55 to 64 years of age, about 210,000 persons or less than 5 percent of the eligible

PUBLIC POLICIES AND PROGRAMS 217

population were unemployed. In contrast, more than 13 percent of the eligible population ages 22 to 54 were unemployed in March 1986.

Table 1 shows the number of unemployed-eligible adults and program-participation rates (number of participants per 100 unemployed eligibles) by age and sex. While the program-participation rate for unemployed older Americans is still substantially lower than for other adult men, large differences in participation rates are not observed for older women. The rate for unemployed-eligible men 55 to 64 can still be considered low at 4.4 percent, about half of the rate for unemployed-eligible men ages 22 to 44. The rate for unemployed-eligible women ages 55 to 64 (11.1 percent) is close to that of women 22 to 44 (14.3 percent), and is higher than the 8.7 percent participation rate for women ages 45 to 54. Thus, much of the age-related differences in training program participation is not caused by age discrimination by program operators.

TABLE 1

Eligibility and Participation by Age in Job Training
Partnership Act Programs Among Unemployed Adults in 1985

	Unemployed Men		Unemployed Women	
Age	Number Eligible (in thousands)	Participation Rate (percent)	Number Eligible (in thousands)	Participation Rate (percent)
22–44	1,428	10.2	1,047	14.3
45–54	226	5.3	151	8.7
55–64	146	4.6	64	11.1

Source: Sandell and Rupp (1988).

Moreover, even the remaining age differences in participation cannot be attributed solely to age discrimination. Analysis of the factors that affected participation under the Comprehensive Employment Training Act (CETA) programs, the predecessor to JTPA, can inform discussion of this issue. More than one-third of the difference in the participation rates among adults is explained by factors other than age (Rupp et al., 1987). That is, older persons were more likely than younger persons to have characteristics associated with low program participation.

Eligible single persons, widows, persons in good health, and persons with more years of education were more likely to participate. CETA participation seems also to have been substantially influenced by eligibles' recent employment experience. The stronger the labor force attachment of eligible individuals, the more likely they were to participate in training. Specifically, the more they worked in the past year and the larger the number of weeks they were unemployed as a proportion of weeks in the labor force, the more likely they were to participate in CETA. Higher family income from sources such as the earnings of other family members and nonearned income seemed to discourage participation among those eligible. Available data do not allow for a full analysis of all differences in program participation by age, but it is clear that part of the difference is due to lack of desire on the part of some eligible older workers to participate.

However, the fact that older eligible individuals have lower unemployment rates and participation rates in training programs does not signify an absence of labor market problems among these persons. While seniority affords some protection to older employees, some portion of the lower unemployment rates of older workers is due to what I have called elsewhere "induced retirement" (Sandell and Shapiro, 1987). Some previously employed persons choose to leave the labor force based on their expectations about the difficulty of finding decent paying jobs compared with receipt of pension and/or Social Security benefits that accompanies labor force withdrawal.

Although including discouraged workers and induced retirees increases the measure of older persons with labor market *problems*, these estimates are not particularly useful for evaluating the adequacy of labor market *programs*. An interest in training implies an interest in participation in the labor market, which usually implies meeting the formal requirements of the Bureau of Labor Statistics definition of unemployment—i.e., seeking work. However, if overall economic conditions were better, or if the labor market prospects for older workers were improved, more out-of-work older persons would seek employment, and some might want government-sponsored training.

On the other hand, JTPA does not seem to be a useful vehicle for improving the employment prospects of the working poor. In 1985 more than 7 million men and almost 6 million women between the ages of 16 and 64 were working but lived in families which received food stamps or had incomes below the higher of the poverty line or 70 percent of the lower living standard. Under this definition roughly 600,000 men and 500,000 women between the ages of 55 and 64 could be considered to be working poor. Increasing the earnings of these older people would be laudable, but based on their low participation rates in JTPA, it is unlikely this will be accomplished in government employment and training programs (Sandell and Rupp, 1988).

While data on participation are available, JTPA is still too new to provide data for credible impact studies. However, analysis of CETA programs indicate that JTPA may be useful for solving some older persons' employment problems. Comparing post-program employment and earnings of older participants with the employment and earnings of eligible nonparticipants, even after other factors that affect employment and earnings were taken into account, indicates that participation in CETA led to an increase of 4.5 weeks of employment and a 20 percent increase in the employment rate (Rupp et al., 1987). The program worked for persons 45 and over who participated.

The Senior Community Service Employment Program

The Senior Community Service Employment Program (SCSEP), established by Title V of the Older Americans Act, provides part-time, minimum-wage jobs for low-income older persons in community service agencies. Although some training for subsequent, unsubsidized employment takes place, the emphasis is on providing income support through the participants performing useful community services.

To be eligible for the SCSEP, a person must be 55 or older and have a family income less than 125 percent of the poverty level established by the U.S. Office of Management and Budget. According to estimates by Rupp et al. (1986), 12.7 million persons, 26.4 percent of the population in the age group, met the income criteria for eligibility during 1983 (as reported in the March 1984 Current Population Survey). Slightly under 100,000 persons, or less than 1 percent of the eligibles, participated in the program during program year 1983–1984.

While labor force status is not part of the formal eligibility requirements, most income-eligible persons who are already

employed, or who are out of the labor force, will have little interest
in program participation—the former, because they already have
jobs, and the latter because they are not interested in obtaining
them. The 6 percent of the eligible population (750,600 people) who
have reported experiencing at least one week of unemployment
could be considered to be the population in need of SCSEP
services. Serving 13 percent of this population, the program may be
considered small, but not miniscule.

The Senior Community Service Employment Program is
popular among participants, sponsors, and the agencies that benefit
from the older workers' subsidized employment. Subsidized
employment is an important component of employment policy for
persons with short work-horizons. The programs of the various
national sponsors differ in their emphasis on placement in contrast
to subsidized employment. The National Council on Employment
Policy recommends a new "Older Americans Employment
Program," to provide full-time, year-round employment at the
minimum wage to persons between the ages of 50 and 62 (National
Council on Employment Policy, 1987).

The Employment Service

The Employment Service (ES) has a long history of providing
services to clients of all ages, including older workers. Although a
wide range of services, including job referral, counseling, testing,
job development, and referral to training or supportive services are
provided to some older job-seekers, the only service most jobseekers, young or old, received was job referrals (Johnson,
Dickinson, and West, 1987).

Referrals significantly improved the job search efforts of older
women, but not older men. After the effects of other characteristics
were taken into account, older women with job referrals had seven
fewer weeks of unemployment and annual earnings $570 greater
than older women who did not receive referrals. The increase in
earnings is attributable to the increase in weeks worked. Older men
with referrals received only $77 more per year than otherwise
similar men who did not receive them. The finding of effects for
women and not for men is similar to analysis of other employment
and training programs (e.g., CETA).

Older job-seekers were considerably less likely to receive
referrals than younger job-seekers. During a six-month period

studied, only 15 percent of the men and 22 percent of the women 45 and over received referrals, in contrast to 31 and 34 percent for men and women between ages 25 and 44. The differences could not be explained statistically by group differences in education and other characteristics.

The reasons for the age differences in referral rates are not entirely clear. Since the jobs listed are often low-paying, entry-level jobs, Employment Service offices may not have jobs available that are appropriate to the skills and interests of many older workers, especially those who have been relatively highly paid. Also, older job-losers must register with the Employment Service in order to collect unemployment compensation, even if they are de facto retired and do not intend to take other jobs.

It is possible that if the Employment Service made a concerted effort to place older persons, some improvement could be made in their employment prospects. However, many competing demands are placed on the Employment Service, so it would not be realistic to expect a dramatic change in its efforts. This may explain the emphasis on job search assistance in some programs that serve older workers under JTPA.

State and Local Initiatives

State and local governments, in cooperation with community groups, can develop policy strategies to increase employment options for older Americans. Governance tools can be used to remove disincentives or to establish incentives to employ older workers (Gollub, 1987).

These tools fall into five categories: encouraging public-private collaboration, administrative reform, program innovation, tax policy changes, and regulation and deregulation. Encouraging public-private collaboration implies making use of business philanthropy and the interest of business in public issues. Changing civil service regulations to permit permanent part-time employment is an example of administrative reform. Public seed money can be provided for innovative programs. Tax policies, such as tax credits for employing disadvantaged older workers, can be tried. Regulation, perhaps the most common type of state and local policy, involves using government's police powers to constrain detrimental activities. Examples include outlawing age-based mandatory retirement, prohibiting age discrimination in employment, and regulating worker benefits.

Pension and Retirement Policies

Many retirement policy issues have already been discussed in this volume (Chapters 5 and 6). This section juxtaposes aspects of the research that have a bearing on public policy decisions, highlighting the dangers of overly narrow research or policy perspectives.

Although the applications of economic theory to explain institutional phenomena, such as the implicit contract paradigm to explain the existence of pensions, are often useful, the simplifying assumptions of these models are sometimes overlooked in inferring policy implications. For example, purposeful structuring of pension benefits may well be a useful way to increase productivity by reducing shirking and providing optimal firm attachment. However, the broad principles of implicit contract theory do not limit the use of flexible payment schemes (e.g., deferred cash bonuses) or other possible institutional arrangements to achieve the same objectives.

Many models of how pensions affect retirement ages implicitly assume that pension benefit structures are unilaterally developed by the employer. While this may be the case in some instances, worker preferences as to age at retirement, transmitted to employers directly through their unions in collective bargaining and indirectly through a competitive labor market, are probably equally important. It would be expensive for a firm to establish (through incentives in a pension plan) a retirement age of, say, 62, if the (union) workers wanted to work until age 67.

Several aspects of Social Security benefit rules affect the employment and retirement of older workers. These include benefit levels, age of eligibility for benefits, actuarial adjustments for retirement at different ages, the earnings test, and the availability of disabled-worker benefits. These provisions of Social Security have changed over the years. Although, as Parnes (Chapter 5 in this volume) makes clear, analysts do not agree on the magnitude of the effects these policy levers have on retirement decisions, the probable effects on employment of possible initiatives in Social Security policy are small. Often consideration of the effects on the income of certain groups of retirees, and the effects on the financial health of the Social Security Trust Fund, drives the policy choices.

Policy Interactions

Predictions of magnitudes of the effects of changing policies are based on research conducted on past data; policies, economic environments, behavior, and social mores may have changed. Since the impact of new policies will be in the future, the assumptions used to predict the effect of a policy might not hold. The previously mentioned ADEA amendments of 1986, which uncapped the age 70 limitation in the Act, provide a good example of this phenomenon.

About 800,000 persons over age 70 and now working received the protection of the Act as of January 1, 1987. An additional 200,000 persons are expected to work (U.S. Department of Labor, 1982), based on comparisons of retirement patterns in firms that have had mandatory retirement ages and those that have not. However, the studies on which this estimate is based were conducted in an environment where firms could stop contributing to pension plans at specific normal retirement ages (usually 65), a practice that no longer will be possible in the future because of another change in federal policy. The Omnibus Budget Reconciliation Act of 1986 amended ADEA, ERISA, and the Internal Revenue Code to require continued contributions, credits, and accruals under pension plans for service beyond normal retirement age (usually 65). The effective date is January 1, 1988, or as late as 1990 for collective bargaining agreements (*Daily Labor Report*, 1987). Thus the estimates of the effects of mandatory retirement policies, which implicitly were made under a regime that allowed the accrual of pension benefits to stop at age 65, may not be useful for the future. This increase in total compensation for work after age 65 might induce more people to delay retirement.

Thus, policy changes which in the past, or taken alone, might have been unimportant, may be significant in the future. Policies interact with each other in affecting older workers. Changes in the normal retirement age in Social Security under the 1983 amendments, a policy that by itself is expected to have little effect on actual retirement ages, may be important in the 21st century if the labor market environment is very different. However, unless changes are forthcoming, current integration between Social Security and pension benefits implies that some of the retirement-age-specific reduction in Social Security benefits will be borne by firms via increased retirement-age-specific pension benefits.

As noted in a different context, a major inconsistency in federal policy toward age discrimination in compensation was eliminated in 1986 when the practice of stopping pension contributions at age 65 was restricted. Until then, ERISA regulations had allowed discrimination in total compensation on the basis of age, even though discrimination in pay was explicitly prohibited by the terms of the Age Discrimination in Employment Act.

However, because ERISA allows firms the freedom to establish a variety of benefit structures, employees who differ only in age can accrue actuarially different benefit amounts for a given year of work. Only by changing ERISA to require age-neutral benefit structures or to mandate defined-contribution plans (both unlikely policy initiatives) would age-neutral pensions become a reality.

Economic Conditions, Pensions, and Retirement

Job-losers are much more likely to retire than workers of the same age who have not lost their jobs (Sandell and Shapiro, 1987). In a year when the national unemployment rate was 6 percent, 10 percent of all males age 60 retired, compared with 30 percent of 60-year-old job-losers. Poor economic conditions disproportionately increase the number of job-losers who retire early. Of the 222,000 workers ages 55 to 64 who lost jobs in 1985, 70,000, or about 31 percent, were out of the labor force in January 1986.

"Sweetened" early retirement benefits have become common among companies that have to "downsize" their work forces (Meier, 1986). For many older workers, these additions to expected pension income provide an inducement to leave the firm as well as the means for a more pleasurable retirement. Others may have underestimated the difficulty in finding new jobs at comparable pay and are then sorry they accepted the "golden handshake."

Job displacement at early ages, combined with the impression that job changes will be more frequent for future workers, has heightened concern by policymakers about the portability of pensions. Proposals to improve portability, such as The Pension Portability Act of 1987 (H.R. 1961), basically allow job-leavers to cash out their pensions at the time they leave specific firms. This, under certain proposals such as deposits into Simplified Employee Pensions (SEPs) or qualified Individual Retirement Accounts (IRAs), allows some of the tax advantages of pensions to be maintained by the worker.

However, these proposals do not solve the fundamental problem. Short-tenured employees and those who leave the firm at young ages receive pensions of limited monetary value, even if they are vested. Under many common benefit formulas, pension benefits increase more than proportionately with length of employment and the salary received in the years immediately prior to retirement from the firm. Early job-leavers suffer capital losses in terms of the potential value of pension benefits they would have received if they had not left their jobs. Only if a mechanism is developed to adjust for the effects of inflation on salaries (and hence pension benefits) over time will the loss incurred by workers who leave at young ages be substantially mitigated (Congressional Budget Office, 1987).

Changes in the patterns of employment may reduce the level of pension benefits and the extent of pension receipt among next century's retirees. If changing employers becomes more frequent, or if a greater proportion of the work force is employed in small or medium-sized firms (firms less likely to provide pensions), pension income of future retirees will be reduced.

Conclusions and Policy Recommendations

Older Americans' employment is impeded by age discrimination, poor overall economic conditions, job loss, health problems, pension rules, and inflexible personnel practices (Sandell, 1987). The policy solutions to these employment difficulties include improved economic conditions, training and retraining, improved job search, and vigorous prevention of age discrimination (National Commission for Employment Policy, 1985).

First, many of the labor market problems of older Americans are grounded in causes other than age discrimination. So even if age discrimination is completely eliminated from the labor market, many older workers would continue to experience employment problems.

Second, employment policies and programs must treat directly these other important causes of labor market problems, such as the loss of a long-held job. Job search assistance and training are two examples of useful activities under government employment and training programs such as those funded under the Job Training Partnership Act.

Third, government has an important training and employment role to play. Older Americans can be successfully served by existing federal employment and training programs *if attention is paid to their special needs and characteristics.* However, the funding of these programs should be substantially increased to allow more eligible and interested older persons to participate.

Fourth, it is undeniable that age discrimination exists in the labor market and that vigorous enforcement of the Age Discrimination in Employment Act by the Equal Employment Opportunity Commission is essential. This age discrimination in the labor market, as well as the availability of retirement-income, partly explains why older persons are less likely than younger adults to seek training.

Fifth, the government should promote the adoption of innovative employer-sponsored practices and programs for older workers. Elimination of practices that inadvertently limit the employment and earnings prospects of older workers should be encouraged. Firms should consider using part-time work arrangements adapted to the needs of retirement-age workers who no longer wish to work full time.

Sixth, compensation-related penalties for workers who wish to continue working beyond age 65 should be eliminated. Serious consideration should be given to increasing as soon as possible the delayed retirement credit from 3 percent to 8 percent before the year 2007, the date currently provided in the 1983 Social Security amendments, and to preventing the actuarial reduction of previously accrued private pension benefits for working past age 65.

Finally, employment must be given priority in the development of overall economic policy. The often hidden but substantial long-term costs to the economy and to older persons resulting from induced retirement caused by high unemployment should be recognized by federal policymakers.

References

American Association of Retired Persons. "All About AARP, Its Programs, Its Services." Supplement to *Modern Maturity* (April-May 1987).

Bolick, Clint. "The Age Discrimination in Employment Act: Equal Opportunity or Reverse Discrimination." *Policy Analysis* 82. Washington: Cato Institute, 1987.

Congressional Budget Office. *Options for Continued Employment of Older Workers: Work and Retirement.* Washington: U.S. Government Printing Office, 1982.

_____. *Tax Policy for Pensions and Other Retirement Savings.* Washington: U.S. Government Printing Office, 1987.

Daily Labor Report. "EEOC Rescinds Rule Allowing Employers to Stop Pension Payments for Older Workers." Washington: Bureau of National Affairs, Inc., March 19, 1987.

Employment and Training Reporter. "EEOC Approves Waivers Under Age Law, Continues Apprenticeship Exemption." Washington: Manpower Information, Inc., August 5, 1987.

Fay, Raymond C. "The ADEA: The Employee's Perspective." In *Older Americans in the Workforce: Challenges and Solutions.* Washington: Bureau of National Affairs, Inc., 1987.

Gollub, James O. "Increasing Employment Opportunities for Older Workers: Emerging State and Local Initiatives." In *The Problem Isn't Age: Work and Older Americans,* ed. Steven H. Sandell. New York: Praeger Publishers, 1987.

Gollub, James O., Thomas Chmura, Douglas Hentson, Shirley Hentzell, John Melville, and Steven Waldhorn. *Older Worker Employment Comes of Age: Practice and Potential.* Washington: National Commission for Employment Policy, 1985.

Johnson, Terry R., Katherine P. Dickinson, and Richard W. West. "Older Workers, Job Displacement, and the Employment Service." In *The Problem Isn't Age: Work and Older Americans,* ed. Steven H. Sandell. New York: Praeger Publishers, 1987.

Jondrow, Jim, Frank Brechling, and Alan Marcus. "Older Workers in the Market for Part-Time Employment." In *The Problem Isn't Age: Work and Older Americans,* ed. Steven H. Sandell. New York: Praeger Publishers, 1987.

Lester, Brenda. *A Practitioner's Guide for Training Older Workers.* Washington: National Commission for Employment Policy, 1984.

Meier, Elizabeth L. "Early Retirement Incentive Programs: Trends and Implications." Washington: American Association of Retired Persons, 1986.

National Commission for Employment Policy. *Older Workers: Prospects, Problems and Policies.* Washington: The Commission, 1985.

_____. *The Job Training Partnership Act.* Washington: The Commission, 1987.

National Council on Employment Policy. "Policy Statement on the Labor Market Problems of Older Workers." Washington: The Council, 1987.

Paul, Carolyn. "Work Alternatives for Older Americans: A Management Perspective." In *The Problem Isn't Age: Work and Older Americans,* ed. Steven H. Sandell. New York: Praeger Publishers, 1987.

Root, Lawrence S., and Laura H. Zarrugh. "Private-Sector Employment Practices for Older Workers." In *The Problem Isn't Age: Work and Older Americans,* ed. Steven H. Sandell. New York: Praeger Publishers, 1987.

Rupp, Kalman, Edward Bryant, John Brown, Caricia Fisher, Helene Hennings, Robin McEntire, and Dave Wright. "The Senior Community Service Employment Program: Participant Selection, Program Experience, and Outcomes." Rockville, MD: Westat, Inc., 1986.

Rupp, Kalman, Edward Bryant, Richard Mantovani, and Michael Rhoads. "Government Employment and Training Programs and Older Americans." In *The Problem Isn't Age: Work and Older Americans,* ed. Steven H. Sandell. New York: Praeger Publishers, 1987.

Sandell, Steven H. "Employment Policy and Older Americans: A Framework and Analysis." In *Current Perspectives on Aging and the Life Cycle: Theory and Practice,* ed. Zena Smith Blau. Greenwich, CT: JAI Press, 1985.

_____. "The Problem Isn't Age: Conclusions and Implications." In *The Problem Isn't Age: Work and Older Americans,* ed. Steven H. Sandell. New York: Praeger Publishers, 1987.

Sandell, Steven H., and Kalman Rupp. "Who Is Served in JTPA Programs? Patterns of Participation and Intergroup Equity." Washington: National Commission for Employment Policy, 1988.

Sandell, Steven H., and David Shapiro. "Economic Conditions, Job Loss and Induced Retirement." Unpublished mimeo, 1987.

Social Security Administration. "Social Security Programs in the United States, 1987." *Social Security Bulletin* 50 (April 1987), pp. 5–66.

U.S. Department of Labor. *Final Report to Congress on Age Discrimination in Employment Act Studies.* Washington: U.S. Government Printing Office, 1982.

U.S. Department of Labor, Pension and Welfare Benefits Administration, Office of Policy and Research. *Employer-Sponsored Retiree Health Insurance.* Washington: U.S. Government Printing Office, 1986.

U.S. Senate, Special Committee on Aging. *Equal Employment Opportunity Commission Enforcement of the Age Discrimination in Employment Act: 1979 to 1982.* An Information Paper, 96-2940. Washington: U.S. Government Printing Office, 1982.

Walker, David M., Deputy Assistant Secretary, Pension and Welfare Benefits Administration, U.S. Department of Labor. "Statement Before the Subcommittee on Labor-Management Relations of the Committee on Education and Labor, U.S. House of Representatives," April 21, 1987.